Making Multiracials

WITHDRAWN

Making Multiracials

State, Family, and Market
in the Redrawing of the Color Line

Kimberly McClain DaCosta

Stanford University Press
Stanford, California
2007

Stanford University Press

Stanford, California

©2007 by the Board of Trustees of the Leland Stanford Junior University. All rights reserved.

Printed in the United States of America on acid-free, archival-quality paper

Library of Congress Cataloging-in-Publication Data

DaCosta, Kimberly McClain.

 Making multiracials : state, family and market in the redrawing of the color line / Kimberly McClain DaCosta.

  p. cm.

 Includes bibliographical references and index.

 ISBN-13: 978-0-8047-5545-0 (cloth : alk. paper)

 ISBN-13: 978-0-8047-5546-7 (pbk. : alk. paper)

 1. Racially mixed people. 2. Racially mixed people—Race identity—United States. 3. Interracial marriage. 4. Minorities—United States—Social conditions. 5. Racism. I. Title.

HT1523.D33 2007

305.800973—dc22

                                                        2006022627

Typeset by Thompson Type in 10/14 Minion

In memory of my grandmothers

Mary Ellen Rafferty and
Mary Emma McClain

Contents

Tables, Figures, and Photos

Tables

Figures

Photos

Acknowledgments

WRITING A BOOK IS A LOT LIKE bearing a child—it becomes a reality only after a long gestation and lots of pain. To endure the process, one needs the help of others. As the mother of three children, the people who helped me "birth" this book are the same people who have helped me care for my children. While I traveled, researched, read, taught, wrote (and occasionally gave birth), I relied upon the help of many caregivers who are quite directly responsible for allowing this book to be born, and so I thank them first: Michelé Harris, Cindy Steele, Jim Stockinger, Yvette Dayce, Barbara Hirsch, Dolores Jackson, Joe Casella, Dorian Lucas, Patty Paige, Jordana Soares, Val and Valerie Abuano, Meaza Yohannes, June Julian, Dawn Ajilore, Janine Burman Nicolau, and Andreza Faria.

While a student at Berkeley, I met many people who shared my intellectual interests and who became friends in the process of exploring them, especially Becky King O'Riain, Kaaryn Gustafson, Cindy Nakashima, Cathy Tashiro, and Caroline Streeter. Caroline saw me through the births of two of my children and the death of my father, for which I will always be grateful. Anne Beard was a constant sounding board as we both labored to become academics while raising children—a process that has proven to be *far* more difficult than either of us imagined it would be. Allison Pugh, Dan Dohan, Scott Washington, and Maren Klawiter gave me helpful advice. Eric Klinenberg has been many things to me: a wonderful reader, enthusiastic cheerleader, and a good friend.

I have benefited tremendously from the support of two writing groups. Carrie Costello, Miki Kashtan, and Karolyn Tyson were writing, thinking, and all around dealing-with-grad-school companions. In the years we met,

I learned not only about writing, but also about living—enduring illness, death, and debilitating grief and moving forward nonetheless. When I came to Harvard, I was fortunate to find another writing group. Kathy Coll, Laura Miller, and Cameron MacDonald made it possible for me to bring this project to completion.

My deep gratitude goes to the men and women who agreed to be interviewed for this study. Obviously, without their willingness to share their stories, this book would not have been possible.

I have been generously supported by several institutions including the Ford Foundation, The National Science Foundation, and the University of California, Berkeley. The Robert Wood Johnson Scholars in Health Policy program at Yale provided a place to work and a great community of scholars to work with, especially Abigail Saguy, Gary McKissick, Eric Oliver, Taeku Lee, Evan Lieberman, Vince Hutchings, Mark Suchman, and Brad Herring. At the Radcliffe Institute for Advanced Study I received generous support from Jenny Mansbridge, Judy Vichniac, and Lindy Hess.

I have been blessed with more than my fair share of great mentors. I thank Mary Waters, my undergraduate advisor, who first encouraged me to pursue a doctorate. While I am sure she does not realize this, I know I would not have chosen this route without her encouragement. Mary showed me that often it is the small act of kindness, rather than the grand gesture, that can have the greatest impact on a student's life. Barrie Thorne always saw the kernel of insight buried within my too wordy sentences. Martín Sanchez-Jankowski gave me much-needed fatherly advice and perspective on academic and social life. Arlie Hochschild, Michael Rogin, and Stephen Small gave expert guidance in the early stages of the project.

I cannot thank Loïc Wacquant, enough. He has been a wonderful mentor to me. His boundless enthusiasm, passion for sociology, and good heart inspire me. Without his guidance this book would have been a much poorer work.

I am grateful to all of my colleagues, past and present, in the Department of African and African American Studies who make it such an exciting place to work. In particular, I'd like to thank Jennifer Hochschild, Larry Bobo, Naomi Pabst, and Bill Wilson. Tommie Shelby and Gwendolyn DuBois Shaw gave me intellectual inspiration and, even more valuable to me, their friendship. Jamaica Kincaid provided me shelter, good food, and laughter when I needed it most. I entered Harvard during a tumultuous time for the university and my department in particular. Despite the upheaval, Henry Louis Gates, Jr.

managed to make it a welcoming place to be. I am grateful for his advice and his kindness.

I have benefited greatly from numerous other colleagues and students who have commented on drafts of the work or discussed these issues with me, especially Paul Spickard, Kim Williams, Lorrayne Ward, Nathalie Miller, Brandon Terry, and Michael Jeffries. The anonymous reviewers of the manuscript provided useful criticism and invaluable advice. Kate Wahl, my editor at Stanford University Press, has done a wonderful job shepherding this book to press. Susan Lambe began this project as my research assistant and has in the process become my friend. Her eye for detail, organizational skills, and intelligence were indispensable in completing this project.

Those most deeply responsible for this project are my family members. My parents, Mary and Jim, both suffered and prospered for what they did in 1962. My mother has always possessed in abundance that most important of motherly skills—the ability to let her children know they matter. I thank my brothers and sisters, Jimmy, Ellen, Beth, Kara, and Matt, my first companions, from whom I learned to negotiate the sometimes painful, often funny, always interesting experience of growing up black and Irish in metropolitan Boston in the 1970s and 1980s.

I am grateful to my husband, Rich, who has suffered with me and because of me throughout this process, yet supported me nonetheless. I thank my kids, Gabrielle, Damian, and Darin. Often people have said to me that having kids must make it easier to get work done since their needs require me to be extra efficient. Any mother who has had to get up at three in the morning to change a diaper and rock a child for an hour with a deadline the next day knows just how laughable that notion is. But in one sense it is true. My children truly are the joys of my life. They give me perspective and motivate me. I hope that through my example I expand the realm of what they believe is possible for themselves.

Finally, I dedicate this book to my grandmothers, Mary Ellen Rafferty and Mary Emma McClain. Though they lived within a few miles of each other, they never met, caught as they were within the racialized boundaries of their time and place. In some small way, I hope that what I have written helps explain, if not bridge, the distance that they could not.

Making Multiracials

1 Introduction

IN 1993 THE U.S. HOUSE SUBCOMMITTEE on Census, Statistics, and Postal Personnel held hearings to discuss the racial and ethnic categories to be used in the 2000 census. Committee members were concerned with whether the racial and ethnic classifications established in 1977[1] were still adequate for counting America's population. At these hearings, many groups challenged the ways the state classified them. The National Council of La Raza, for example, proposed including Hispanic/Latino as a racial designation while Native Hawaiians proposed being counted as Native Americans. Yet the most explosive challenge came from a putatively new contender in America's ongoing racial debate: the multiracial community.

In 1993 the federal racial classification system reflected a uniquely American understanding of race in which individuals were allowed to choose one and only one race. The only choice available to those who did not feel the available categories described them was "other," a catch-all category that critics said conveyed little meaning. Multiracial representatives argued for a mode of categorization that acknowledged multiple ancestry—either a simple "multiracial" check box or the possibility of checking all applicable racial categories. Unlike groups requesting a shuffling of their placement within the existing racial framework, self-identified multiracials claimed to be a formerly unrecognized group challenging the framework itself.

From the vantage point of 2007, it is perhaps difficult to recapture the novelty of multiracial activists' claims. When representatives of the Association of Multiethnic Americans made their claims for official enumeration of mixed race people in 1993, "multiracial" as a basis of collective identification did not exist outside of a few local community groups. Before those hearings there was virtually no broad public awareness of multiracial collective organizing, even among the people multiracial organizers claimed to represent. With a few notable exceptions,[2] scholars were unaware of or uninterested in such organizing, perhaps best exemplified in F. James Davis's contention (as late as 1991) that the so-called one-drop rule (the practice of defining as black persons with *any* known African ancestry, no matter how little) would remain unchallenged for the foreseeable future. Much has changed since then. Despite Davis's prediction, the one-drop rule has been challenged. Largely due to the efforts of multiracial activists, in 1997 the U.S. Census Bureau changed its racial enumeration policy to allow individuals to "mark one or more" racial categories.[3] With that decision, the federal government (hereafter referred to as the state) resumed counting mixed race populations in Census 2000 (U.S. Census Bureau 2002), something it had not done in nearly eighty years.[4]

When in 1997 golfer Tiger Woods told Oprah Winfrey and her television audience of the name he came up with to convey all aspects of his racial identity ("cablinasian" for Caucasian, Black, Indian and Asian), it seemed an idiosyncratic and highly individualized identity. By 2003, a Sunday *New York Times* article declared the arrival of "Generation E. A." (ethnically ambiguous). Whole generations, not just Tiger it would seem, were claiming to be—and being recognized as—mixed race.

Dominant attitudes about racial mixing have shifted as well. Not until 2004 was it widely revealed that Strom Thurmond, the staunch segregationist senator from South Carolina, had fathered a daughter, Essie Mae Washington-Williams, with his family's teenage black maid. Ms. Washington-Williams's paternity was kept secret for over seventy-eight years until she revealed it shortly after her father's death. Both father and daughter understood that revealing their relationship would end his political career. In contrast, for Barack Obama—currently the only U.S. senator of African descent—racial mixedness is showcased in the crafting of his public persona, not hidden or downplayed. In his address at the 2004 Democratic National Convention, Obama made explicit reference to his biraciality (he is the son of a black Kenyan economist and white mother from Kansas). He has since been touted as a viable future presidential candidate and his biraciality depicted as a key reason why he will heal political division.[5]

In other words, over the last decade multiracialism has emerged as a topic of public discussion, and "multiracial" has become a recognizable social category and mode of identification. In the 1990s, organizations for interracial families and mixed race people were loosely organized, only partially aware of each other, and relatively short-lived. While many remain short-lived, collective organizing by people identifying as multiracial has continued, has become more interconnected, and has entered new institutional domains. What was once largely ignored (how the children of interracial unions identify racially), treated as taboo (interracial sex and intimacy), or thought not to exist (multiracial community) is now receiving considerable attention and becoming part of the cultural mainstream. This book tells the story of how that shift began and how it is proceeding.

When I began my research the census issue intrigued me. Like many social scientists, I was interested in the implications of changing state classification for monitoring racial inequality and enforcing civil rights legislation. Kim Williams (2006) has uncovered the political calculations that led to the change in census classification. Other analysts have focused on the challenges of interpreting the new race data (Farley 2002; Harris 2002), particularly for making comparisons with that collected under the previous race question (Tucker et al. 2002) and the challenges the change poses for civil rights law enforcement (Perlmann and Waters 2002). While I was interested in these questions, what intrigued me much more was that mixed race people were organizing in the first place. As a child raised in an interracial family in metropolitan Boston of the 1970s and 1980s, the only other "mixed" people I knew were my five siblings. Moreover, we identified ourselves and were categorized by others as "black." The emergence of organizations for mixed race people and political activism around issues of mixed race seemed unthinkable to me back then.

While clearly the most visible dimension of an emerging movement around multiracialism, and the event that garnered that movement the most attention, the census issue itself could not explain why mixed race people and families were organizing collectively. Indeed, the census issue emerged several years after organizations for mixed race people formed. At the time of the 1993 hearings, at least sixty such social support organizations existed. Most of these had formed at least five years prior.[6]

While interracial groups have existed in the past, beginning in the late nineteenth century and at various times since,[7] this wave of multiracial organizations was different because of the sheer volume formed simultaneously yet in relative isolation. More importantly, groups that formed independently of one another developed into a network of groups in close communication.

While earlier organizations were focused primarily on black/white intermarriage and families, newer organizations were emerging, such as Hapa Issues Forum, that focused on the experiences of Asian multiracials. Still others, like Swirl and Mavin Foundation, sought to develop a "pan" multiracial focus inclusive of all kinds of mixed race experiences.

The expansion of multiracial organizations and political action were important catalysts for the creation of cultural projects as well. Magazines, newsletters, university courses, and Web sites centered on the experiences of mixed race people have emerged, as has a growing body of scholarship, literature, and film with multiracial themes. These organizational, political, and cultural projects reflect a general upsurge in "multiracial" identity as a mode of individual identification, but also as a locus of collective identification.

By 1997 when Office of Management and Budget (OMB) officials were deciding the future of census classification, it was clear that mixed race people were organized and aware of each other. That awareness has only increased since then, due in large part to the attention given the fight over census categories. How that awareness has developed is less clear. How, I wanted to know, had a category of people largely invisible to and isolated from one another, with virtually no institutions or symbolic recognition of them as a group, come together? Why had this movement developed when it did? And what was it about "being mixed" that constituted a compelling basis for such activism? In what ways did such an experience cohere across a variety of ethnoracial "mixtures"? Did these new coalitions of mixed race people signal something new about ethnic and racial group formation?

The resurgence of public discussion around racial hybridity is especially notable when we remember that for most of the twentieth century, the U.S. system of racial classification had been particularly rigid, based on a notion of descent, and with few exceptions, admitting of no racial boundary crossing or the possibility of changing one's race. This was not always and everywhere the case in the United States, to be sure. In the antebellum period, particularly in the lower South, hybrid populations were at times officially counted and had social significance. With slavery's demise, other means of controlling African Americans and maintaining white dominance, like Black Codes and eventually the panoply of segregationist policies that would come to be known as Jim Crow, took its place.

By the end of the nineteenth century, in an atmosphere of fear and hysteria over the specter of racial equality, recognition of hybridity was increasingly less tolerated. Landmark cases establishing restrictions on interracial marriage were decided in the post-Reconstruction period along with the *Plessy v. Ferguson* case that established a legal precedent legitimizing the one-drop rule. The creation of antimiscegenation laws would see their greatest increase in the upcoming decades. Subject to increasingly harsh restrictions imposed under Jim Crow, mulattoes, once careful to assert their difference from "unmixed" blacks, began to form common cause with them, mingling politically, socially, and intimately. By the mid-1920s, the problem of what to do with hybrid populations was largely resolved. The state treated anyone with a known black ancestor as black, a characterization that mulattoes came to accept and even embrace.

The problem of "mixedness" all but disappeared from public debate in the twentieth century through the institutionalization of the one-drop rule and its eventual social acceptance. In the late 1970s when Joel Williamson was writing his history of racial hybridity in the United States, he framed the scope of his project as an answer to this question: "Why is it that American mulattoes of all shades have been brusquely relegated to a single Negro caste along with blacks and, further, have come to eagerly embrace that identity?" (Williamson 1995, 2). At the beginning of the twenty-first century, students of race and ethnicity need to ask a different question. Why is it that American "multiracials" have begun to assert an identity as neither black nor white (nor Asian or Indian), but both or all, and why have they sought official recognition of that identity? The current struggle over multiracial identity owes its genesis to the outcomes of these previous struggles over racial identity and is in part the product of the institutionalization of the one-drop rule and the contradictions to which it gave rise.

In the early stages of this movement, activists seeking federal classification, and some scholars, referred to multiracials as if they were a group constituted as such—conscious of itself, unified, but one that had not received social recognition (Omi and Espiritu 2000; Association of Multiethnic Americans 1997). Multiracials were, they argued, just like other minority groups and had a right to be recognized by the state. Their opponents treated them as if they were not a group at all—merely a statistical population, completely individualized and unaware of each other, and thus not worthy of social classification (J. M. Spencer 1997).

The assumption that mixed race people were merely a statistical population made little sense given the growing number of organizations for them and their remarkable success in garnering public attention. Yet it was unclear in just what ways they *were* a "group." To uncritically accept multiracial activists' claims to group status seemed to ignore the fact that for most of the twentieth century they were not organized or recognized as such. Moreover, such a claim failed to recognize that the battle over official classification was an important means *through which* multiracials were making themselves as a group—by getting the government to recognize the group, and in so doing, to help create its existence. So rather than assume that "multiracials" exist as such (or that they do not), I ask why "mixed" persons are now activating these particular ancestries in this way and why they have become salient bases of public and private identification.

I am very much persuaded by the critiques brought by Bourdieu and others on the tendency of social scientists to reify social groups even as we invoke the mantra that they are socially constructed (Bourdieu 1996; Brubaker 2004; Wacquant 1997). Rogers Brubaker, one of the most persistent critics of this tendency, argues that social scientists need to rethink the ways we view such "groups":

> Ethnicity, race and nation should be conceptualized not as substances or things or entities or organisms or collective individuals—as the imagery of discrete, concrete, tangible, bounded and enduring "groups" encourages us to do—but rather in relational, processual, dynamic, eventful, and disaggregated terms. This means thinking of ethnicity not in terms of substantial groups or entities but in terms of practical categories, situated actions, cultural idioms, cognitive schemas, discursive frames, organizational routines, institutional forms, political projects, and contingent events. It means thinking of ethnicization, racialization, and nationalization as political, social, cultural and psychological processes. And it means taking as a basic analytical category not the "group" as an entity, but groupness as a contextually fluctuating conceptual variable.[8]

The development of "multiracials" as a social category in the United States provides a perfect opportunity to see how such group-making projects proceed. (For an extended discussion situating multiracial mobilization in social theory, see Appendix C).

This approach to studying ethnicity "without groups," however, poses a small linguistic problem, namely how to refer to a group-in-the-making without appearing to presume its existence. The adoption of *multiracial* by activists is itself a group-building device, a new term activists selected to distance their rendering of mixed identity from previous terms for racial mixedness like *mulatto* that they deemed derogatory. The creation of the term *multiracial* is also part of an attempt to persuade others that the group exists in the way activists describe. Throughout this book I use the term *multiracial* interchangeably with others like *persons of mixed descent* and *mixed race*. This is in part to signal a distance between my analysis and the language that movement participants use to advance their cause. I use multiple terms to refer to racial mixedness rather than a single one to avoid giving the impression that multiracials are a group in any fixed sense. My intent is to describe a process of group formation rather than assume its result. Moreover, I use these terms to refer to both persons of mixed descent and to parents of mixed race children, both of whom are key in this group-making process.

The emergence of an organized movement of self-identified mixed race people seems at first glance a relatively easy thing to explain: there are simply more mixed people now, children of the "biracial baby boom" begun in the 1960s, who are now coming to adulthood and seek to have their identities recognized. Between 1960 and 1990, for example, the number of intermarried couples increased tenfold, from about 150,000 to 1.5 million while the number of children from these unions quadrupled from about 500,000 to 2 million (Waters 2000). The mere social fact of mixedness across racialized boundaries cannot, of course, explain this development. People of mixed descent have existed in American society since its inception and, indeed, most African Americans have knowledge of some non-"African" ancestors.

Neither can demographic increases in intermarriage and mixed offspring explain why being "mixed" constitutes a problem worth organizing around nor why a campaign for an official designation for multiracials emerged. Moreover, demographic changes cannot explain why mixed race people began organizing as *multiracial*. The "two or more races" population is comprised of people of a variety of ethnoracial "mixtures" (see Figure 1.1). There is no group "history" or culture that all mixed race people share. Nevertheless, participants in multiracial organizations and expressions of multiracial identity coalesce around a notion of "mixedness" rather than racial sameness.

The development of a movement around multiracial identification is somewhat at odds with what the literature on intermarriage and ethnic group boundaries might predict. According to that literature, intermarriage between members of two given ethnic groups tends to increase when the degree of social distance (for example, occupational and educational differences,

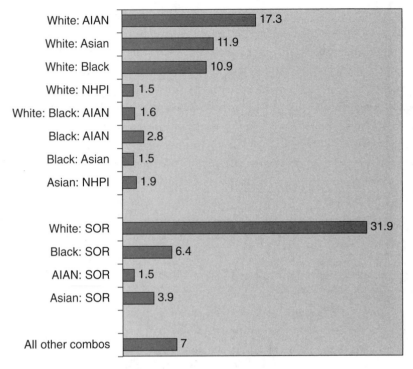

AIAN = American Indian Alaskan Native
NHPI = Native Hawaiian or Pacific Islander
SOR = Some Other Race
Source: Data from U.S. Census Bureau, Census 2000 Summary Tape File 4

Figure 1.1 Two or More Races Population by Largest Combinations: 2000

residential segregation) between them declines. Rising rates of intermarriage between groups indicate the acceptance of each other as social equals. Once established, intermarriage tends to further erode salient boundaries between groups (Alba 1990; Barron 1951; Drake and Cayton 1945; Gordon 1964; Park 1950). When that happens, ethnicity becomes largely a symbolic identification, chosen rather than ascribed, and relatively inconsequential in one's daily life (Alba 1990; Gans 1979; Ignatiev 1995; Waters 1990).

The findings on the trajectory of intermarriage's impact on group boundaries are based on the experiences of white ethnics, the descendants of European immigrant groups who have intermarried extensively. For nonwhites in the United States, intermarriage with whites has been severely restricted by law and social custom, and *racial* categorizations have proven to be neither symbolic, costless, nor voluntary (Blauner 1972; Omi and Winant 1994; Takaki 1993).[9] As intermarriage between whites and nonwhites has increased, however, some analysts have begun to wonder whether or not "racial options" are in the making. Asians and Latinos in the United States have fairly high rates of outmarriage (compared to African Americans). According to Bean and Stevens (2003), almost 30 percent of Asians (27.2 percent) and Latinos (28.4 percent) outmarry while only 10.2 percent of blacks do. Intermarriage rates with whites for Asians, Latinos, and American Indians are comparable to those of Southern and Eastern European immigrants in the early twentieth century who, through intermarriage with American-born whites, expanded the definition of who is white. Latino and Asian intermarriage appears to be following a similar trajectory. With each generation in the United States, and as their income and education levels rise, Latinos and Asians are more likely to marry whites (Bean and Stevens 2003; Sanjek 1994) as shown in Table 1.1.

Patterns of multiracial identification mirror those observed for intermarriage. According to Census 2000 figures, multiracial identification is more common among Asians and Latinos than among African Americans (see Figure 1.2). Of all those who reported being black, 4.8 percent indicated multiple racial identifications compared to 13.9 percent of Asians. Latino mixed race identification, though not represented in this figure, is approximated in the

Table 1.1 Interracial Marriage by Racial Group and Race of Partner

	White	Black	Asian	Latino	Other
Total marriages	n=155,534	n=11,593	n=7,313	n=28,993	n=2,342
	%	%	%	%	%
Same race	94.2	89.9	72.6	71.6	25.8
Intermarried	5.8	10.2	27.2	28.4	74.2
Race of partner					
White	—	69.1	86.8	90	88.4
Black	11	—	4.8	5.3	3.2
Asian	20.7	7.2	—	3	1.3
Latino	55.2	20.7	7.6	—	7.2
Other	13.1	3	0.8	1.7	—

SOURCE: Data from Frank Bean and Gillian Stevens, *America's Newcomers and the Dynamics of Diversity*

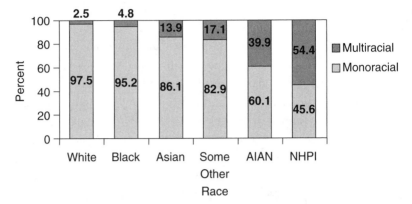

Source: Data from U.S. Census Bureau

Figure 1.2 Multiracial and Monoracial Reporting by Race

"some other race" category (17.1 percent), which researchers have shown is overwhelmingly chosen by Latinos (Anderson and Fienberg 1999; U.S. Census 2001).

Given these rates of interracial marriage and multiracial identification, some analysts suggest that for some Asian Americans and Latinos race is becoming an increasingly optional and symbolic feature of their lives (Harris and Sim 2002; Xie and Goyette 1997) and to the extent that is true, some even speculate that they are "becoming white" (Lee and Bean 2004; Zhou 2004). Relatively low rates of both intermarriage and multiracial identification for African Americans suggest something very different. Some analysts fear they presage the emergence of a black/nonblack divide in which African Americans remain disadvantaged relative to other groups (Lee and Bean 2004; Patterson 1998; Sanjek 1994).

Despite substantial differences in rates of outmarriage between racial groups in the United States, rates of intermarriage have risen for all racial groups over the last thirty-five years and are expected to continue to rise. Multiracial identification for all groups is predicted to rise as well. These facts prompted Lee and Bean (2004, 235) to conclude that "Increases in intermarriage and the growth of the multiracial population reflect a blending of races and the fading of color lines." That multiracials are elaborating a collective multiracial identity, however, complicates such narratives. While rising rates of multiracial identification and intermarriage may indeed indicate the blending and fading of some group boundaries, the collective organization and identification of "multiracials" suggests that other group boundaries are *building up* as well.

The experiences of mixed race people suggest that in thinking about the impact of increasing intermarriage on racialized boundaries we should not assume that the social conditions that lead to increasing intermarriage (such as greater educational parity, declining occupational segregation, and changing public attitudes) somehow translate into social acceptance for the offspring of intermarried couples.[10] Just because intermarried "parents" are merging, it does not follow that their children will "blend into" or act as "bridges between" their respective racial groups. Indeed, multiracials of Asian ethnicities—a demographic for which analysts suggest race is most likely to be symbolic, optional, and costless—were among the most organized in the 1990s and remain quite active in creating organizations for multiracial people and advocating for their public recognition. Rather than blending into whiteness, they are asserting a racialized identity.

Explaining the Making of Multiracials

So why have mixed race people begun to organize collectively, and what does the development of "multiracial" as a social category and identification mean? In the social science literature on mixed race people, the accent has been on individual identification, especially how mixed race people develop a sense of racial identity (Kich 1992; Root 1992, 1996; Taylor-Gibbs and Hines 1992), typologies of mixed race identity expressions (Renn 2004; Rockquemore and Brunsma 2002) and the influence of social interactions in shaping how mixed race individuals develop racial identity (Daniel 1992; Nakashima 1992; Renn 2004; Wallace 2001; Williams 1996). That individualized expressions of multiracial identity have proliferated in the last decade is clear—numerous memoirs and essays exploring personal experiences of being mixed have appeared, for example, and individuals can and do now choose tailor-made racial identifications on the census (Gaskins 1999; McBride 1997; O'Hearn 1998; Rekdal 2002; Walker 2002; G. Williams 1996). But there has been very little emphasis on how individuals' interest in identifying as mixed race is related to *collective* projects of multiracial identification.[11]

In this book, I focus on the cultural, institutional, and political factors that motivate mixed race people in the United States to organize collectively and that have contributed to making multiracials into a recognizable category and social community. Telling the story of how multiracials were "made" requires a discussion of the census classification debate of the 1990s during which self-described spokespersons for "the multiracial community" sought to create, quite literally, a new social category. The political struggle over classification was an important means through which the public became aware that at least some mixed race people were organized and thought of themselves similarly.

While the census issue is key, the making of multiracials is taking place in other institutional realms as well. Of most obvious relevance is the family. Indeed, changes in the racial composition of American families and the conflicts that arise when such changes occur fueled the classification effort. Many of the organizations associated with the classification issue dealt with the concerns of interracial families. Most, like I-Pride in Berkeley, California, were founded by interracial married couples. So the people involved in the classification debate were not only self-identified mixed race people, but also their metaphorical parents—so-called "monoracial" members of interracial families. Understanding the motivations of those organizing, it seemed to me, required understanding the social position of those families. Recently, the marketplace has emerged as a major means through which multiracials are being made. Marketers were quick to focus on the new race data on multiple race populations from Census 2000 (U.S. Census Bureau 2002) and have begun to use images of multiracials in their advertising. In the past, when marketers have recognized and catered to market segments, such as African Americans and Latinos, they have contributed to reinforcing those divisions (Cohen 2003; Davila 2001). Given the scope and reach of advertisements, it is reasonable to assume that their efforts with respect to multiracials will be consequential as well.

In order to understand how "multiracials" are being made into a recognizable category and social community, I knew I would have to engage with the various people who participate in organizations for multiracial people. My analysis draws on in-depth interviews with participants in groups formed for intermarried couples and their families, as well as those formed by multiracial adults. I also conducted fieldwork in a range of settings: organization-sponsored events, public hearings, fundraisers, college campus classrooms, and mixed race conferences. The majority of the interviews were conducted from 1997 to 1999, with a smaller sample conducted in 2003 to 2005. Some interviewees were the leaders and founders of such groups; others were more casual participants. These are the individuals whose actions legitimate and bring to public consciousness the notion of multiraciality—those persons who advocated for state enumeration of multiracial identity as well as being involved in local family-based and identity groups (see Appendix A for a list of respondents).

I focused my search for interviewees on several organizations: Some were originally formed to address concerns of intermarried couples, including Multiracial Americans of Southern California (or MASC, based in Los Angeles), I-Pride (Berkeley, California), Biracial Family Network (Chicago), and Interracial Family Circle (Washington, DC). These first four organizations are the longest-lived organizations dealing with multiracial issues. The Association of Multiethnic Americans (AMEA) is an umbrella organization comprised of those and other groups. Hapa Issues Forum (HIF, Berkeley) was formed in the early 1990s. When I conducted my initial interviews in 1997 to 1999, HIF was the only sustained group focused on mixed persons of Asian descent. I also interviewed members of campus organizations as well as Swirl and Mavin, two groups that emerged in the late 1990s and have been most successful in attracting young adult mixed race people on a national basis (see Appendix B for descriptions of organizations).

My questions centered on several substantive areas, including their involvement in multiracial organizations, family life (relations with immediate and extended family members), attitudes toward racial classification, and concepts of multiracial community. I wanted to understand what motivated them to get involved in an organization for mixed race people or interracial families—to turn personal dilemmas into ones addressed collectively and how they describe, communicate, and create shared meanings of the "mixed" experience.

Official Classification and Beyond

It is difficult to overestimate the significance of the campaign for multiracial classification in the making of multiracials. In large part due to the efforts of groups like AMEA, multiracials as such are now statistically visible. In Chapter 2, I describe the broad set of social conditions that facilitated the growth of multiracial organizing and led to the challenge to state classification in the 1990s. The question of how to treat mixed race people arises in the context of a race-divided society, one in which the black/white division is central and in which blackness is uniquely defined through hypodescent and the one-drop rule. This question, while not a new one in American society, has been resolved in different ways in different periods. While in previous eras racial hybridity was socially and officially recognized in the United States, the social deconstruction of mixed descent persons begins in earnest after abolition through the imposition of legal statutes and segregationist policies that make no distinction between mulattoes and blacks, and is cemented through their spatial confinement in ghettos through the mid-twentieth century. By the mid-1960s, the legislative gains of the civil rights movement and an increasing emphasis on racial authenticity would provide a basis from which the question of racial hybridity would emerge two decades later.

The success of past attempts to prevent and make invisible racial hybridity has direct bearing on the resurgence of the hybridity question at the end of the twentieth century. Multiracials' focus on official classification derives from the emphasis placed on racial classification in American society at large. Since the 1960s, efforts to collect such data in virtually all institutions of social life proliferated while ethnic-specific social programs expanded. In such a climate the imperative of "knowing" one's racial membership was heightened. Mixed race individuals felt called upon to "choose" among ethnoracial affiliations, and for many this imperative to choose one racial affiliation felt artificial. In contrast to previous periods in U.S. history, this cohort of multiracial people had largely been raised with intimate connections to both sides of their families and cultural heritage in a context where interracial marriage was legal. Raised in such a context, multiracial adults came to consider the state's policy of "check one only" racial category as forcing them to choose between their parents and communities. Experiences like these, in which mixed race people report feeling out of place according to dominant American notions of race, led them to create their own organizations in an effort to diminish their own sense of isolation and stigmatization.

Activists in favor of multiracial classification were able to take advantage of the opportunity to publicly comment on potential changes to census classifications when it arose because these social networks of multiracial people and families already existed. They understood what social scientists have long documented—the crucial role the state plays in getting people to see and believe in a group's existence (Bourdieu 1996; Brubaker 2004; Nagel 1996). Presenting themselves as representatives of "the multiracial community," they succeeded in getting the state to change its policy on racial classification to allow and count multiple responses to the race question that began with the 2000 census.

But why did receiving state classification of multiracials seem like an important goal to accomplish for those who advocated it? During the classification debates of the 1990s, when questions of motivation arose, commentators fell back on accusations that mixed race people sought to identify as multiracial primarily to escape a despised status in America's racial hierarchy

(Holmes Norton 1997). This charge was most often leveled at people of partial African ancestry in part because there is a precedent for exclusion and separation by African Americans with white ancestry. Some commentators cast multiracials as naïve actors who sought to assert "personal" identity in a "public" and therefore inappropriate arena (Jones 1997; J. M. Spencer 1997). These assertions were made with little in the way of systematic engagement with those organizing and seemed, frankly, to merely rehash stereotypes of the mixed race person as confused race traitor.

In Chapter 3, I focus in detail on four of the people who were most active in working to change the official classification scheme. Their stories make clear that questions about their racial identity are about much more than wanting to escape being black or Asian. Indeed, their racial identity is about more than "race." Questions of racial identity and belonging encompass a variety of conflicts over class, sexuality, education, and family history that are understood and expressed through race, precisely because we live in an age where race is central to how Americans organize themselves socially and personally. These respondents' recognition of their dilemmas as dilemmas and their desire and ability to do something about them are triggered by their educational experience. Despite the variety of ways they have come to activism, each combines a critical set of social properties that allowed them to take advantage of the broader political and social opportunities present during the 1990s.

Making an Issue of Interracial Kinship

While the census classification issue provided a crucial opportunity for the creation of "multiracials" as a social category, and state institutionalized racial categories shape my respondents' self-understandings, it would be misleading to present the multiracial movement as one primarily oriented and unified around the issue of classification. Indeed, most of the people I interviewed in multiracial organizations were relatively uninvolved in the concrete activities surrounding state classification. Of greater concern to them was providing social support to interracial families and mixed race people and generating public awareness and acceptance of their families. For most of them, some form of official acknowledgment of their mixed racial background was important only to the extent that it seemed to acknowledge their families.

Although most of my respondents were not very involved in the classification debates, they were still interested in how they were officially classified. My respondents did not understand racial classifications simply as neutral descriptors. Rather, they often interpreted them as symbols of their relationships to parents, families, and ancestors. Many proponents of a multiracial category understood the former "check one only" policy of racial classification as a forced choice between their mother and their father. For some, racial categories are expressive of and experienced as essential aspects of one's being, rather than mere administrative categories.

Many of the people involved in multiracial organizations view their activism as an expression of family loyalty and imbue it with great emotional weight. Their involvement in multiracial organizations was designed to make visible relationships that are often hidden to others—those between parents and children who appear racially different. My respondents' stories about their struggles for acceptance and recognition within their families and communities were deeply felt, often poignant, and sometimes painful. Their stories of the role that racial difference played within their families and how they felt about it offer clues to decipher the social and cultural logic that produces such behavior and feelings.

If the multiracial movement is as much about family as race, why is this so? In recent years scholars have turned their attention to the topic of "interracial intimacy" and the legal and historical conditions that shaped and largely discouraged intimate contact between people defined as racially different (DaCosta 2003; Hodes 1997; Kennedy 2003; Moran 2001; Romano 2003). This history is deeply connected to the work of those involved in multiracial organizations. In Chapter 4, I explore how cultural constructions of kinship shape the social experience of race and vice versa. Understanding these connections helps explain why multiracials began to organize collectively.

Sociological work on ethnicity had long linked issues of ethnic identification and group formation to the family. "These matters seem so obvious," writes Richard Alba, "that it is taken for granted among scholars that the family provides the original nurture for ethnicity" (1990, 164). The role that kinship plays in the multiracial movement, however, is somewhat different than that which it has played in other ethnic group-making projects in the United States, particularly those of white ethnics. "Ethnicity," notes Steve Cornell (1996), "is kinship writ large" in the sense that one's relationship to fellow ethnics is often thought of as akin to an extended family relationship. Expressions of an ethnic identity are often used to symbolize relations with family members and ethnic celebrations participated in as a means to preserve the family (Gans 1989 in Nagel 1996). In such cases, ethnicity serves a supporting role to family. For multiracials, however, claims to group status are meant not merely to support individual families and to celebrate a family's heritage. Rather, they are intended to legitimize the very idea of interracial families.

Forging Multiracial Community

Since the release of Census 2000 race data (U.S. Census Bureau 2002), references to "the multiracial community" alongside other racially designated communities are increasingly common. But in what sense can a multiracial community be said to exist? The category "multiracial" encompasses people of a broad range of racial and ethnic ancestry combinations. This is much like the categories "Latino" and "Asian American" in which diverse immigrant populations are lumped into overarching categories on the basis of language similarity (for example, Spanish) or the logic of racial sameness (for example, Asian). The coming together of a diverse group of multiracials is predicated on the logic of *multi*raciality, within which language, tradition, *and* racial identification are variable. Despite this diversity "multiracial" has emerged as a basis of collective identification. In Chapter 5, I explore the ways that multiracials understand their commonalities with other mixed race people (despite ethnic and racial differences) as well as the ways that such differences separate them.

If the census debates of the 1990s provided the key *opportunity* for the making of multiracials, and the desire to belong in family and ethnic communities the *motivation*, the *means* through which multiracials are being made are numerous. I think of these means as a set of concrete activities that create a sense of shared community among multiracials or which make that community appear to exist. Some of these activities are organized by mixed race people, others not. Some involve the physical coming together of people through, for instance, monthly dinners, book clubs, and film nights. Other activities are virtual, as with Internet vehicles like Mixed Media Watch (a site that monitors the portrayal of mixed race people in the media) or magazines like *Mavin* that cater to "mixed heritage" people. These activities are best understood as cultural constructions. They generate a shared vocabulary among participants and define a common purpose. At the same time, they help define the boundaries of multiracial collective identifications.

Yet perhaps more than any other, the tool most effective in the forging of multiracials as such is the marketplace. Marketers became interested in this newly visible demographic shortly before the release of Census 2000 race data (U.S. Census Bureau, 2002). They are beginning to use this data to target multiracial consumers and capture what they regard as a new market. At the same time, marketers draw on and reinterpret culturally resonant narratives of the meaning of racial mixedness for the purpose of selling things to a general market.

While professional marketers are using multiracialism to sell products, mixed race people have become interested in using the market as a tool to advance their own interests. These entrepreneurs are creating products with the explicit purpose of "building community" among multiracials. In Chapter 6, I explore the myriad ways in which the market and multiracials intersect. While still in an early stage of development, the marketing of, to, and by mixed race people is likely to strengthen social perceptions that multiracials exist as such and help craft an image of what they are like.

Finally, in Chapter 7, I examine the implications of the making of multiracials as social category and basis of collective identification. An examination of the experiences of mixed descent people allows us to refine the interpretations of intermarriage and multiracial identification that dominate in the sociological literature. The assertion that multiracials will not coalesce into a group in any meaningful way derives from an interpretive frame in which the offspring of people of different racial designations are treated as symbols—stand-ins for a set of relations between presumably more primary groups. Within such a frame, the emphasis is on what went before (the social and economic conditions facilitating intermarriage) with a ready-made concept of what will come in the future (more intermarriage and the erosion of group boundaries). Instead of assuming that intermarriage leads to a cultural merger between groups and the social acceptance of mixed race children, such an examination shows us in what ways this is and is not the case. In showing the composition of groups for mixed race people and interracial families, the thoughts, emotions, and actions of their members; the context out of which they developed; and how the market, by way of advertising, has begun to encroach upon and shape multiracialism, we can more clearly see the process through which a new category of persons—multiracials—is being made.

A Note on Language

With the constructivist turn in the academy, scholars of race have largely discarded the idea that race is a property of the body and instead have sought to explain the idea of race and racial groups as emergent, contingent, and malleable products of history. To signal this shift and to undermine the popular assumption that races exist as real entities, some scholars have taken to putting the term "race" in quotation marks. In earlier drafts of this book I did as well, to signal that I consider race an object to be constructed and explained, rather than a conceptual tool capable of explaining social phenomena. In the end, however, I have discarded the quotation marks except in instances where the words are indeed quotations, such as when respondents or authors used terms commonly used in other historical periods but not usually used today (for example, "mulatto," "colored," or "Oriental").

At first I made this change for stylistic reasons since nearly every sentence would have required quotation marks which, I felt, became distracting. Yet there are deeper epistemological reasons for doing so as well, which some scholars have noted (Jacobson 1999). The practice of putting quotation marks around "race" has not been accompanied by a practice of putting quotation marks around words like "ethnic," "black," or "Asian," implying, whether consciously or not, that these social distinctions are more real and unproblematic than racial ones. These social classifications, however, denote groups that are themselves products of history and are meaningfully constituted. It is a fundamental sociological precept that all social categories are socially constructed. To be consistent, one ought to put quotation marks around all social categories, like "daughter," "woman," "poor," and so forth. Instead, I choose to note at the outset the socially constructed nature of all ethnoracial signifiers, including "multiracial" ones, and forego this stylistic marker.

These epistemological issues get even more complicated when considering terms denoting multiraciality. Many scholars argue that terms like *multiracial, interracial,* and *mixed race* threaten to reify biologistic understandings of race. Moreover, they point out that such terms are imprecise, for "who is multiracial" depends largely upon how race is defined. Persons labeled "black," for example, may trace their ancestors to Europe as well as Africa and beyond, calling into question the legitimacy of demarcating some people as "multiracial" and others as "black" on the basis of ancestry. With these warnings in mind, I have opted to use several terms, including *multiracial, mixed,* and *persons of mixed descent* when referring to the people who are the subjects of this research. That racial distinctions are ideological and slippery makes no less true the fact that we recognize them. Indeed, the multiracial movement is testament to the ways rigid racial distinctions have shaped the experiences of those who have "crossed the color line" or whose existence blurs those boundaries. In using terms like multiracial then, I do not claim that such a group exists by virtue of a presumed distinct biological inheritance or even social experience. Instead, I am attempting to describe and account for how such distinctions are made meaningful, reproduced, and sometimes challenged.

2 The Making of a Category

Struggles over ethnic or regional identity . . . are a particular case of the different struggles over classifications, struggles over the monopoly of the power to make people see and believe, to get them to know and recognize, to impose the legitimate definition of the divisions of the social world and, thereby, to make and unmake groups.[1]

—Pierre Bourdieu

ON A RAINY APRIL AFTERNOON IN 2005, a multicolored RV rolled onto the campus of Tufts University in Medford, Massachusetts. The vehicle, emblazoned with colorful slogans like "Mixed race people are challenging the way our society looks at race and diversity" and "Get into the Mix!" announced the arrival of the Generation Mix National Awareness Tour—a project in which five mixed race young adults drove across the country, making stops in sixteen cities to "raise awareness of America's multiracial baby boom" and "promote a national dialogue about the mixed race experience." The tour was sponsored by the Mavin Foundation, at the time the most visible organization in the United States advocating on behalf of people who identify as mixed race. As crew members set up informational tables in the campus student center ("Children and Families," "Health," "Community") I spoke with Jamie, a twenty-three-year-old Chinese/white man from Berkeley, California. I asked Jamie how important it was to him that the U.S. census now allowed and counted multiple race responses.

It's very big. It's giving us numbers that we can point to. It's gratifying in the sense that we know just how big the community or the population is. Both for ourselves, so that we can sit back and be like, wow, there's a lot of us, and we really aren't alone. And not just like these pockets of like a couple people here, couple people there. It's like people everywhere. And then it's something that's more legitimating for those people who care strictly about numbers, who aren't going to listen to just your personal experience. They want something to back it up. So, 6.8 million, 2.4%, that's something we can point to for those discussions. So it's a political step forward.

Of all the data collected in the 2000 census, the results of questions on racial identification were perhaps the most eagerly anticipated. This race data would be the first collected using the new guidelines on racial classifications, agreed upon in 1997, that allowed people to "mark one or more" racial category (hereafter MOOM). The U.S. Census Bureau's "Two or More Races Population" brief (2001) showed that of approximately 281 million U.S. residents, 6.8 million, or 2.4 percent, reported more than one race. For Jamie, those numbers are symbolically and politically important—they serve as proof to mixed race individuals that they are part of a collective and they legitimize (for the skeptical) multiracial claims to group status.

To Jamie and many others, census statistics are evidence of the existence of multiracials as a group and the MOOM decision a reasonable response to changing demographics and social realities. To others, the MOOM decision makes more vulnerable the nation's system of racial categorization and policy, perhaps threatening it entirely (Harrison 2002; K. Williams 2006). Whether one reacts to the official enumeration of multiple race responses by the federal government with optimism, caution, or alarm, the fact that such a change took place is a remarkable development. Consider that prior to Census 2000, not since 1920 had the state collected census data on multiple race populations. Moreover, during those eighty years virtually no attempts were made to get the state to do so. For most of the twentieth century, in other words, claiming a "mixed" racial identity and having it recognized by the state was out of the question. By the 1990s, however, self-identified mixed race people began asking the government to identify them racially. When one considers that for most of American history racial classifications served no other purpose than to identify those to exclude, exploit, and oppress, the movement for multiracial classification presents an intriguing historical irony. What changed to make the official classification of multiracial identity very much *the* question in the 1990s?

This chapter explores the institutional, organizational, and cultural factors that led to the challenge to official classification of mixed race people in the United States. I consider how "multiracials" emerged as a self-conscious interest group, how they came to resuscitate the issue of racial categorization and identification as a topic of public discussion, and why this happened when it did. My approach here looks specifically at the conditions motivating mul-

Jamie Tibbetts of Generation Mix National Awareness Tour.

Kimberly McClain DaCosta

tiracials to act. In that sense it is different from the approach taken by others who have examined the classification issue. Political scientist Kim Williams (2006) examines in detail the political opportunity structure that allowed a set of resource-poor multiracial organizations to successfully challenge prevailing modes of racial classification and how this change is likely to affect American politics. She is less concerned with the broader cultural context in which activists formed their grievances. The same is true of Melissa Nobles' *Shades of Citizenship* (2000) and Rainier Spencer's *Spurious Issues* (1999). In *The New Race Question* anthology (Perlmann and Waters, 2002), the authors examine the political impact and technical aspects of counting multirace responses in light of race-based social policy, but the people responsible for initiating the new race question are almost entirely absent. Clearly, the adoption of a multiple race option in the U.S. census arises not only because of the efforts of multiracial activists. Other interest groups and institutions like the state, statisticians, academics, civil rights organizations, and politicians all played a role in the process (see Anderson and Fienberg [1999] for details). My purpose is not to show that process in its entirety but to demonstrate how one such contender waged its struggle.

The movement for multiracial classification is about more than an administrative category. It is also a means to the end of garnering public recognition for those who would claim it and destigmatizing interracial sex, families, and hybrid racial identities. In that sense, this movement's origins lie in the social policies and practices that made mixed descent persons disappear as a social category in the twentieth century (antimiscegenation laws, the one-drop rule, and other segregationist policies) and that helped to stigmatize racial hybridity. This movement is also an unintended consequence of the civil rights revolution of the mid-twentieth century and the widespread institutionalization of racial categories that it engendered. It arises in a social and cultural context in which racial identification is considered an important part of self-identity and norms about racial authenticity and loyalty are strong. These conditions created a dilemma for some mixed race people whose experiences growing up in interracial families made conforming to those norms difficult.

Counting the Racially Mixed

In the United States, decisions about how to classify racial hybrids, like the system of racial classification itself, have largely been made with reference to people of African descent. For most of U.S. history, racially mixed persons have been categorized according to the principle of hypodescent—assigned to the racial group of the lower status parent.[2] Moreover, any degree of African ancestry, no matter how small, qualified one for the categorization. This was not always the case. In the antebellum period, particularly in the lower South, as Joel Williamson succintly states, "[M]ulattoness did count, real distinctions were made, and the one-drop rule did not always prevail" (1995, 2). Even so, Williamson's work shows that one-drop ideology emerges during slavery along with a growing hostility toward miscegenation as the threat of insurrection and abolition loomed. While there have been exceptions to this rule for some types of boundary crossings (to which I refer later), the one-drop rule has been the dominant principle for allocating persons to racial categories, and since about the 1920s, it has been largely accepted, even embraced, by those it was designed to oppress, namely African Americans.

Though racial hybridity has been a part of American society since its inception, the U.S. Census Bureau did not officially record it until 1850. That year the mulatto category made its first appearance on the census. It would remain on all subsequent censuses (with the exception of 1900) until 1920. The categories "octoroon" and "quadroon" appeared on the 1890 census when enumerators were instructed to estimate by visual inspection the relative proportions of white to black ancestry a person had. The results were considered so unreliable, however, that the Bureau dropped the categories before the next census (Anderson 1988).

Distinguishing mulattoes from blacks was considered important during Reconstruction because it was presumed that mulattoes were best suited to assume the leadership positions that would open up in a reconstructed South. With the demise of Reconstruction and the concomitant rise of Jim Crow segregation, those distinctions became less relevant. Under Jim Crow, what mattered to the state was not how much white ancestry an individual had, but whether one had any black ancestry at all. For the purposes of identifying who was subject to racial exclusion, any degree of known African "blood" (even one drop) made one a black person.

The one-drop principle of racial classification received state sanction through the *Plessy v. Ferguson* decision in 1896. That U.S. Supreme Court decision infamously upheld the constitutionality of racial segregation in public facilities. But it also affirmed the state's right to racially categorize people according to one-drop ideology. Homer Plessy, seven-eighths white (an "octoroon") by ancestry and with a white-looking appearance, made that fact known while seated in a whites-only railroad car. According to Randall Kennedy (2003), Plessy sought to challenge not only racial segregation but also the legitimacy of the state's presumption that it could assign individuals to racial categories without regard to their wishes. The Court ruled against Plessy, deeming him to be colored despite his mixed, mostly European, ancestry. The census would continue to distinguish between blacks and mulattoes for another two censuses. By the 1930 census, the mulatto category was dropped as census officials turned their attention to more pressing matters, namely the tracking of swelling European immigrant populations. With the demise of the mulatto category, official racial categories and the principles upheld in the *Plessy* case were now in sync (Davis 1991; Nobles 2000). In the struggle over U.S. racial classifications, the black/white division was and continues to be epicentral. The one-drop rule was developed specifically to manage blacks in the aftermath of slavery and to preserve the prerogatives of whites. Relative to the scrutiny it paid black/white sexual and social intermixing, the state has been comparatively unconcerned with recording and controlling the degree of racial mixing between other groups. Moreover, the one-drop principle of racial classification was not applied to persons of non-African descent with any consistency (Davis 1991). Nevertheless, the state has often involved itself in the classification of such persons. Much as it has with blacks, the state has used the recognition of mixed race people as a tool in the management of relations with Asians, Indians, and Latinos. For example, as part of its campaign to "civilize" American Indians at the end of the nineteenth century, the government embarked on a policy of land redistribution wherein individuals, rather than the tribe itself, would hold property rights. While full-blood Indians were restricted in how they could use their land, no such restrictions were imposed upon mixed bloods. Because of their white ancestry, Congress presumed mixed bloods better suited to handle their affairs (Moran 2001; Spickard 1989).

State-sanctioned differential treatment of the racially mixed was in evidence during the World War II internment of Japanese Americans as well: government officials exempted some intermarried and mixed race Japanese Americans from imprisonment. The rationale? Japanese Americans who had intermarried or were of mixed descent probably felt loyalty to the United States because of their social connections with whites. Putting them in camps with full-blood Japanese Americans might erode such loyalty (Spickard 1989).

The strategic interpretation of racial classification by state institutions is evident again in the treatment of Latinos, particularly Mexican Americans. When formerly Mexican territories were annexed to the United States in the Treaty of Guadalupe-Hidalgo, residents of those territories were to have full rights of citizenship, equal to those of whites. Despite being white by law, social acceptance of people of Mexican descent as white has been regularly challenged by whites, largely because Indian ancestry and brown skin are at odds with American notions of whiteness (Moran 2001).

The ambiguity of Mexican's racial status has made it a flexible tool in adjudicating racial disputes. Sometimes, that ambiguous racial status allowed people to escape the harshest consequences of transgressing racial boundaries. For example, the numerous marriages between Mexican origin women and Punjabi men in 1920s California technically violated the state's antimiscegenation laws. These couples were seldom prosecuted because Mexican origin women were considered white in name only. The violation of antimiscegenation laws did not upset the prevailing community norm of who was really white and thus in need of the putative protection the law provided (Leonard 1992; Moran 2001).

Yet the ambiguous racial status of those of Mexican origin could also work against their interests. In segregated 1920s Texas, a black man and a Mexican woman attempted to send their children to the local white school on the grounds that the children were of Mexican ancestry and therefore white. Rather than admit the children, school officials had the couple prosecuted for violating antimiscegenation laws. In an effort to save her husband from prison, the wife testified that she too was part black. Local school officials seized on this admission, effectively redefining all Mexicans as black and establishing a school for black and Mexican children.

The social classification of mixed descent persons is variable by group and social context. In general, mixed race persons of African descent have generally been accepted as black but not as white. In contrast, Davis argues that racially mixed persons of Asian or Mexican (Indian) ancestry "have been treated as assimilating Americans after the first generation" of mixing with whites (1991, 118).

The Social Organization of Racial Hybridity Among African Americans

By the time the census ceased distinguishing between mulattoes and blacks in its race counts, the social deconstruction of mixed race persons that began after abolition was largely accomplished. By the 1920s, with segregation becoming more entrenched as blacks migrated to southern cities (and later, en masse to northern ones), the one-drop rule had gained social and legal acceptance by most whites *and* black Americans (Davis 1991; Williamson 1995). The class structure that had emerged among African Americans at the turn of the twentieth century was in transition. That structure, according to Frazier, "was based upon social distinctions such as education and conventional behavior, rather than upon occupation and income" (1957, 20). Those on the upper rungs of this hierarchy—the mulatto elite—owed their position in part to their mixed ancestry. That ancestry and the material and social privileges it brought derived from slavery, in which light-skinned slaves, primarily the offspring of white men and slave women, were granted relative privilege vis-à-vis their darker counterparts.[3] While mulattoes were no longer officially designated, racial hybridity would continue to matter in the social life of African Americans. Educated and more class privileged mulattoes distinguished themselves from the black masses by creating social clubs like the Bon Ton society of Washington, D.C., or the Boule in Philadelphia, that chose members primarily on the basis of both social class, but also by skin color (preferring, of course, higher class status and lighter skin). Members are said to have developed criteria for measuring light skin color, such as "paper bag" tests (no darker than a paper bag) or the visibility of blue veins (Daniel 2002; Drake and Cayton 1993 [1945]; L. Graham 1999; Wu 2002).

For a while this elite would attempt to resist being lumped with blacks, but in a post-*Plessy* world in which Jim Crow segregation was taking hold, mulattoes understood they had little choice but to accept and even embrace their categorization with "unmixed" blacks. These social organizations, while maintaining a class and color boundary, were also inextricably a part of Negro community. Members understood themselves as nurturing a "talented tenth" engaged in a project of group uplift for all African Americans.

In the first few decades of the twentieth century, color and ancestry would become less directly important in securing material privilege. By World War I, increasing black migration and urbanization facilitated the attainment of education by a broader segment of the black population, not just the descendants of free people of color. Gradually, attributes such as education and occupation, and later income, became the primary determinants of membership in the black elite. Color and ancestry became like status symbols, helpful, even necessary in some quarters if one were to gain access to the Negro elite, but not sufficient alone to secure such a status.

Light color and mixed ancestry had diminishing power to signal a privileged status in part because they were no longer scarce commodities. By World War I, intermarriage between mulattoes and "unmixed" blacks was so extensive that social scientists estimated most Negroes had some non-African ancestry (Reuter 1918). Herskovits (1928) would argue that due to such extensive mixing, sharp differences in physical appearance among Negroes—the proportion who were very light or very dark—were diminishing, and they were becoming a new physical type—neither black nor white, but brown.

In the interwar years, distinctions of color and ancestry—though less determinative and indicative of social status—would remain relevant among African Americans, though largely within the confined social spaces that persons of African descent now inhabited. St. Clair Drake and Horace Cayton (1993 [1945]) described in detail the relevance that mixed ancestry and intermarriage had in Chicago's Bronzeville neighborhood. "Colorism"—prejudice and discrimination on the basis of color—largely in the direction of a preference for lighter, more European-looking features—continued. In segregated Chicago, whites and blacks who intermarried were confined to black social spaces. According to Drake and Cayton, for the whites who engaged in it, intermarriage was "sociological suicide" in that, much like their children, they took on the lower social status of their spouse (Drake and Cayton 1993 [1945],

142). For black partners, intermarriage was generally not a springboard to greater social mobility among whites or blacks. Though intermarried couples were tolerated in black communities, African Americans also discouraged the practice. Drake and Cayton characterize this taboo against intermarriage among African Americans as a strategy to prevent group members (particularly men of higher socioeconomic status) from leaving the group and taking their resources with them.[4]

Indeed, in matters of racial equality, intermarriage was the rare issue over which blacks and whites largely agreed. They differed sharply in their attitudes toward economic opportunity, and to a somewhat lesser degree, residential segregation. Yet blacks and whites were in agreement that social equality did *not* include "(1) intermarriage, (2) membership in white cliques, churches and social clubs, and (3) visiting and entertaining across the color line" (Drake and Cayton 1993 [1945], 126). By World War II and continuing through the 1960s, African Americans, though increasingly race conscious, would remain indifferent to intermarriage restrictions, despite the fact that as late as 1962, "white Chicago still forces most Negroes to marry Negroes, to have Negroes as their intimate friends, and to participate in all-colored churches and associations."[5]

Restrictions on marriage decisions are ground zero in the maintenance of social inequality. For Drake and Cayton, African American indifference to these restrictions amounted to a "conspiracy of silence" that represented an accommodation to segregation—a decision to love their fate rather than struggle against it.[6] Moreover, African Americans fully accepted the one-drop rule. Though it had been designed to facilitate their exclusion, they would come to see it as a source of group cohesion. It would be another thirty years before that rule was challenged.

Seeking State Categorization

The appearance in 1993 by multiracial activists at federal hearings assessing the U.S. government's racial classification schema represented a significant shift in adjudication over racial categories. Prior to these hearings, the most significant decisions made over racial classification, like the *Plessy* decision or the U.S. Census Bureau's decision to drop the mulatto category, were initiated by government institutions. This time around a group of parents of multiracial children and multiracial adults approached the state and *asked* to be racially categorized. They made the claim that since the state collected racial data, it had an obligation to "accurately" count an individual's race, which to them meant that the state would have to in some way count *multi*raciality. In this they were like many others who have come to see the state's racial categories as opportunities to declare personal identity (Cornell 1996; Nagel 1995; Waters 1990). What was different about multiracial activists' claims was the contention that ethnoracial self-identification was a person's right. They employed the codes of liberal individualism, which constructs persons as choice-making selves who ought to be treated with dignity and respect.

The "Right" to Racial Classification

The contention that racial classification is a right is a relatively recent understanding of racial classification. Prior to the 1970s, racial classification had largely been considered an objective characteristic of persons that the state merely labeled. As such, racial classification per se did not need to be claimed as a right. Racial struggles generally centered on the rights accruing to one classified in a particular way, or one's categorization within a given set of categories. Multiracial activists claimed that the individual, rather than the state, should decide how one is racially classified. They pointed out that despite a census policy of racial self-enumeration in place since 1970, the limits placed on the number of categories one could choose effectively took away a multiracial person's ability to self-designate race. Moreover, they argued that the interests of other parties (be they the state, institutions such as schools, or other officially recognized ethnoracial groups) were secondary to those of the individual checking the box. Finally, activists situated the right to classification as one pertaining not merely to the individuals that the classifications were meant to identify, but to those individuals' *parents*. Racial classification, according to activists, was an important means by which parents could lay claim to their children and through which children might signal their affiliation with and relation to their parents.

Multiracial activists' arguments cast racial classification in very individualistic terms. In calling for the option of checking multiple racial categories, they treated the state's racial classifications as a menu of options that could and should be customized to fit each unique individual, rather than a set of mutually exclusive categories into which individuals must fit themselves. In order to advance this individualistic agenda, however, they had to argue on behalf of a group. Multiracial activists argued that the right to such a classification was essential to safeguard mixed descent persons' equal protection under the law. In doing so, they began to talk about multiracial people as a distinct class, equivalent to any other ethnic group protected by civil rights legislation. Carlos Fernandez (1994), legal advisor to and past president of the AMEA, tried to make the case that the Revonda Bowens incident in Alabama in 1994 could be a test case for gaining recognition of multiracial/ethnic people "as a distinct class by an agency of government." In that incident, Bowens was told by her high school principal, Hulond Humphries, that she and other mixed race people like her were "mistakes" as he attempted to ban interracial couples from the prom. The case settled out of court.

The specific policy on racial classification against which multiracials argued was over fifteen years old. In 1974, the Federal Interagency Committee on Education created an Ad Hoc Committee on Racial and Ethnic Definitions whose task was to standardize the racial categories used by federal agencies. In the absence of such a standard, state agencies were collecting racial statistics using disparate categories, making comparisons across agencies difficult. The Committee's work resulted in the adoption of Statistical Policy Directive 15 by the OMB in 1977. This classification schema is commonly referred to simply as Directive 15. The 1977 version of Directive 15 included the racial categories white, black, American Indian, Asian/Pacific Islander, and Other. "Hispanic" was treated as an ethnic category.

The reactions of other contenders in the debate to the claims of multiracial activists were almost uniformly negative and challenged multiracials' claims to group status. While these civil rights organizations focused on the possible harm such a change in the system of racial classification would have on the monitoring of compliance with civil rights legislation and the likelihood that such a change would diminish the population size of established ethnoracial groups, they justified their opposition by challenging the assertion that multiracials shared sufficient commonalities as a group to warrant such protected status. The National Coalition for an Accurate Count of Asians and Pacific Islanders, for example, questioned "the salience of biraciality or multiraciality in relationship to the specific provisions and intended benefits" of civil rights programs since: "What can be stated about common experiences shared by biracial or multiracial persons? . . . biracial or multiracial persons have the burden to document what distinct experiences or disadvantagement, in contrast to persons of protected single race backgrounds, that have because of their biraciality or multiraciality before the decision to establish a multiracial or biracial category would be appropriate." [7]

The basis of the disagreement between opponents and proponents of multiracial classification lies in the way each camp interpreted the meaning and purpose of state racial classification. Opponents of multiracial classification were essentially arguing that decisions about changes to Directive 15 should be guided by the purposes for which the Directive was originally created—as a means through which to track the effects of racial domination. For them, the question of *how* to classify persons was settled. What mattered to them was how the data gleaned from the given classifications was employed. Multiracials, they argued, could not demonstrate that they had been unfairly treated because of their multiracial status and thus did not warrant the recognition *as a group* that state classification confers. To multiracial activists, on the other hand, the question of classification was far from settled, and mattered to them because they understood classification as symbolic of their personal identity, which they believed they had the right to choose for themselves.

Creating a New Constituency

Despite these competing interests, multiracial activists gained a substantial measure of success in changing the way that race was enumerated. While the stand-alone multiracial category that some activists wanted was not approved, individuals are now instructed that they may mark multiple responses to the race question on federal government forms.[8] That they achieved this success is particularly interesting when one realizes how few multiracial activists were involved in the negotiations at the state and federal levels. The most active lobbying groups, Project RACE and AMEA, were represented at these official events by only a handful of individuals. Yet they presented themselves as representatives of an already-existing community that was unified in its support for multiracial classification. Project RACE claimed to be a "national organization"[9] while AMEA stressed its role as an umbrella organization representing numerous local multiracial organizations.

The swiftness with which multiracial coalitions were able to respond to the call to revise the racial and ethnic standards suggests there was a preexisting level of collective consciousness and organization among multiracial people that had been largely invisible to the broader public. And indeed this is true. Both AMEA and Project RACE drew personnel and resources from existing multiracial organizations. I-Pride, Biracial Family Network, and MASC, for example, are signatories on AMEA's charter.

While it is true that AMEA and Project RACE draw support from various organizations, the impression put forth by activists that they represent the community of multiracials differs somewhat from the reality. The most visible representative of Project RACE was its founder, Susan Graham. Since membership lists of the organization are not made readily available, it is difficult to assess the extent of its support or the social position of its members. When I spoke with Susan Graham during the classification debate and in my discussions with others who worked with her, it appears that Project RACE is largely Susan Graham and those few associates. AMEA's organizational structure more closely reflects a representative body. Its leadership, for example, is elected by the membership of its signatory organizations. Even still, it is difficult to say that AMEA represents "multiracials" as such. While long-standing networks have developed among various "groups," and those groups have contributed resources to the lobbying effort put forth by AMEA, these ties exist for only a fraction of the universe of multiracial organizations. Although no official tally exists, based on advertisements published in multiracial organization newsletters and media accounts, more than sixty local community organizations have formed in all parts of the country since 1980—many more when one counts campus organizations. Of those, thirteen were signatories of AMEA's charter during the census debates of the 1990s. So while multiracial organizations were forming in all parts of the country, and many were at least nominally involved in the classification debate, most were not. Moreover, these connections between "groups" are more accurately described as connections between *individuals,* typically the nominal leaders of the organizations, whereas the rank and file of these organizations are relatively uninvolved and/ or uninterested in the debate over official classification.

One local organizational leader recalled being "pressed into service" at the last minute for the 1996 Multiracial Solidarity March, with virtually no advance knowledge of either the event or the issues at stake. That event, organized by Charles Byrd, self-styled multiracial leader from Queens, New York, and operator of the Web site Interracial Voice, was intended to persuade the government to include a multiracial category on the 2000 census through a showing of the putative popular support such a measure enjoyed. Byrd billed the march (which took place on the Mall in Washington, D.C.) as something akin to the 1963 March on Washington in both scope and aim, but it was neither. Reflecting on the small number of participants, journalist Clarence Page (1996) dubbed this "march" a "hundred person picnic."

The question of what community multiracial spokespersons represent is even more complicated when we note that many of the multiracial organizations that formed in the last twenty years no longer exist. I conducted a phone survey in 1997 of the multiracial organizations advertised in the now-defunct

Interrace magazine. Of the nearly 60 organizations listed, fewer than half were still in existence in 1997. Many organizations that were around in the early 1990s are no longer meeting regularly, if at all. Several of the past coordinators of these groups said their groups fizzled out because the participants' children "outgrew" the group. Others pointed to the difficulties of coordinating busy schedules. The temporary nature of many organizations suggests that the "multiracial community" as such is only loosely organized.

The point here is not that the goals of multiracial activists are entirely divorced from any constituency. Rather it is to point out that gaining *state* recognition of social identities *requires* that activists make their claims on behalf of a putative group—to *create* a constituency. Activists' references to a "multiracial community" were (in part) rhetorical devices self-consciously employed to bolster claims that they represented a constituency. As Ramona Douglass, past president of AMEA put it, "we made it seem like we were a massive force to be dealt with." This illustrates a fundamental feature of struggles over social classifications. It is not unusual for activists to claim to represent a "community" of shared interests that in reality does not exist as such, wherein the presumed members of the community are relatively uncommitted to the goals that motivate spokespersons of that "community." Activists must make "the community" *appear* to exist in order to bring it into existence.

While key to multiracial activists effectiveness was their ability to present themselves as representative of a community, they also had to present that community as unified over the issue of classification, even though there were significant differences in philosophy within the coalition of activists organized around classification. Susan Graham of Project RACE was deeply committed to getting a separate multiracial category on the census, while AMEA eventually backed a category that allowed for specific ancestry responses. Although in June 1997, just before the OMB was to make its final decision, Project RACE had agreed to support the multiple check-off option in conjunction with AMEA, that coalition broke down shortly after, with Project RACE ultimately supporting a stand-alone multiracial category. In the end, OMB adopted a version (MOOM) that more closely resembled the one backed by AMEA.

Key to AMEA's effectiveness was its ability to forge coalitions with strategically placed individuals and organizations. First, it drew on the symbolic capital of academics, several of whom either sat on its board or provided it with advice. Moreover, the messages in some of the writings by these academics, most of whom identify as mixed race or are themselves intermarried, are indistinguishable from those of activists. The "Bill of Rights for Racially Mixed People" written by psychologist Maria Root illustrates the extent of this parity.[10] Academics lend legitimacy to the notion of organizing along the principle of multiraciality. Their work (creating courses on multiraciality, writing anthologies and memoirs) serves a powerful legitimating function because prestigious and seemingly neutral institutions like universities and publishing houses support it. Moreover, the simultaneity of these messages alongside populist appeals makes the phenomenon of multiracial collective organization appear more coherent and widespread than it is in fact.

Perhaps more important than the support AMEA garnered from academics is the coalition it formed with persons of partial Asian descent, represented by HIF. Prior to 1997, HIF had not been active in the classification debate. As Greg Mayeda, one of its founders, noted, "The classification issue seemed less urgent than building relations with the Japanese American community." As the Interagency Committee's deadline for making recommendations to OMB approached (July 1997), however, Ramona Douglass of AMEA made a concerted effort to bring HIF into the debates over racial classification and succeeded in getting representatives of HIF to join the lobbying effort. The presence of HIF was important primarily because it lent strength to the contention that multiracial activists' support was broadly based. In particular, the support of Asian multiracials eased the suspicion of some that those in favor of multiracial classification were really interested in being a little less black. In another attempt to counter such accusations, multiracial activists stressed that the multiracial community contained within it persons who were "double minorities"—not part white—who, therefore, could not be accused of trying to gain white privilege.

Greg Mayeda recalls that HIF board members initially supported a multiracial box, though largely before they had thoroughly considered the issues. Soon after becoming involved, however, HIF moved to a position supporting any alternative that allowed multiracials to "respond to multiple boxes" without "diminishing the count of anybody else." Mayeda believes that because AMEA and HIF decided to lobby for a multiple check-off option rather than a stand-alone multiracial category they were able to "build a coalition" with the National Association for the Advancement of Colored People (NAACP):

> The thing that sort of broke it open for us to build a coalition was when I told him that our position had always been multiple check-offs, that we weren't going to support just a multiracial box, that we wanted a choice. We didn't

see multiracial classification as hiding from anything. We wanted the ability to fully embrace all aspects of our culture. So he plain old just didn't know that. We had never spoken in a manner that he would have heard it. They were just hearing who was speaking the loudest because at the time Susan Graham (of Project RACE) was running around, you know, with every paper in America—"Oh, it's so horrible, and we want this multiracial box." She wanted the multiracial box "for her children and the children of America." But she was affiliated with Newt Gingrich which was a disaster, and I think [she disregarded] the political reality that some people were trying to get a multiracial category so as to undermine the counting of ethnic minorities in this country.

It is difficult to validate Mayeda's characterization of the NAACP's relation to HIF or AMEA as a coalition. Harold MacDougall went along with the multiple check off option when it seemed its passage was a foregone conclusion (K. Williams 2006). Neither the NAACP nor other civil rights organizations were interested in encouraging their constituents to check multiple boxes. During the administration of the census in 2000, for example, the Congressional Black Caucus mounted a "check the black box" campaign on radio and television encouraging African Americans not to mark multiple boxes. Reminding listeners that African Americans were once counted as three fifths of a person, media personalities like Tom Joyner and Tavis Smiley suggested that checking multiple boxes could amount to the same thing (Nelson 2000).

Making the Acceptable Problematic

While relatively few people, representing relatively few organizations, were actively involved in the classification debate, these organizations were quite important in facilitating the reemergence of questions of mixed racial identity. Multiracial activists were able to testify at public hearings because they were already organized in local groups that developed in the 1980s for social and supportive purposes. Those organizations, such as MASC in Los Angeles, I-Pride in Berkeley, California, and Biracial Family Network in Chicago, served as networks where grievances incubated and which led to the more public and political expressions of identity. Carlos Fernandez, one of the original members of both I-Pride and AMEA, described such a transition. While in I-Pride, he noted "(W)e were spending a lot of time talking about cosmic questions and it began to get a little tiresome so we decided we've got to have national organization so we can really do something about this instead of wasting our time talking about it. And that's how AMEA got started." Most of the membership of these organizations was uninvolved in the campaign to change racial classifications. What they *were* concerned with was destigmatizing the idea of a multiracial identity and multiracial families. "Talking about cosmic questions" is part of coming to understand what experiences and troubles one shares with others and leads to the politicizing of those concerns. It is through the organizations, formed for reasons other than changing official classification, that the challenge to state classifications emerges.

Multiracial organizations bring similarly situated persons into close, sustained contact with each other, providing a forum in which to begin to understand their commonalities. This is particularly salient because it allows us to understand why it is that an issue that has formerly been considered personal and private became the focus of group mobilization. Many adult multiracials have grown up not knowing personally other mixed persons, which breeds the perception that they are alone in their circumstances. Under conditions of social isolation, people are more likely to commit what social movement scholars call the fundamental attribution error—to explain their situation as a function of individual deficiencies rather than features of a system. Moreover, during the 1980s and 1990s, these organizations began to communicate with each other, through newsletters, Web sites, magazines, and conferences.

The OMB's solicitation for public comment on revising Directive 15 provided a political opportunity for AMEA and Project RACE to challenge how racial data was collected and to present themselves as an already-existing community. Because the format of the hearings allows interested parties to prepare testimony and deliver it publicly, AMEA and Project RACE produced detailed testimony in which they questioned the legitimacy of the current system of racial classification.

The political opportunity to testify in a national forum allowed both groups to convey their messages to a much wider audience than they could have reached on their own. The public exposure given these hearings led to new opportunities for multiracial groups to frame their issues and disseminate their messages. In the 1990s, activists like Carlos Fernandez, Susan Graham, and Ramona Douglass appeared on several local and national broadcasts because of their exposure at the hearings, thus introducing their issues to a much larger audience.

Collective organization around the principle of multiraciality created new understandings of what it means to be mixed and facilitated the political mobilization of activists. That mobilization in pursuit of multiracial classification in turn strengthens the impetus for *further* organization around the principle of multiraciality. In 1994, in the thick of the classification lobbying effort, Carlos Fernandez of AMEA offered this to attendees of MASC's annual conference:[11]

> We don't really have a sense of [who we are] as a community yet. We can't really talk about a multiracial multiethnic community yet. That sense of community is not there. *That's precisely why we have our organizations.* It's because there is not a place for us . . . This community did not exist in the past to respond specifically to our issues. Now we do exist, in whatever form we are, however flimsy and fragile, we do exist. We have our *concept,* we have our name, and we have our *groups. And we need to build that.* And in fact the theme coming out of our meeting in Pittsburgh just last year was that *building a sense of community* is our next task. We're on the map. Our first five years were to establish the issue, publicize the issue, create it in a sense . . . But now the task is to develop a sense of community, an idea that we have something in common. [You] may not necessarily as a black/white couple have something in common with someone who's Asian/Latino but you do have that—your interracialness—in common [emphasis added].

Perhaps more so than he intended, Fernandez's comment illustrates the process of group making. Building organizations and developing shared understandings of their situation encourages multiracial activists to *construct* a community.

The public nature of struggles over social classification makes possible the irony that even if census officials had opted not to enumerate multiraciality, the very process of adjudicating state classification aids in the construction of multiracials as a group. The process of state classification requires that claims be made on behalf of a group, and therefore encourages the construction of group organization and identification to reach such recognition. Moreover, the process gives a public presence to identifications once considered personal, such that it gets *others* to know and recognize such an identity. "Categorical identities," Craig Calhoun argues, "can be invoked and given public definition by individuals or groups even when they are not embodied in concrete networks of direct interpersonal relationships. Indeed, they are quintessentially objects of such public address"(Calhoun 1994, 26).

The "multiracial community" on behalf of whom activists claim to speak does not capture the universe of mixed descent persons organized according to a sense of shared identity, but neither is it completely unorganized or lacking a common set of unifying experiences. In mobilizing around multiracial classification, activists named what they believed those unifying experiences to be, providing for those persons who are unconnected to multiracial organizations a vocabulary with which to describe themselves, with a new sense that such an identity has a community to support it.

Enabling Conditions

The ongoing construction of a notion of multiracial community was facilitated by the classification debate. Knowing the strategies and organizational resources multiracial activists used to challenge state racial classifications in the 1990s shows the immediate causes of the most public example of the reemergence of mixedness as a civic issue.[12] Yet knowing how these activists mobilized limited resources tells us little about why they deemed racial classification a significant issue and why framing the issue in terms of rights and personal identity made sense to them. After all, since the civil rights and Black Power movements (as well as "Yellow," "Red," and "Brown" movements) of the mid-twentieth century, ethnoracial organizations and activists have successfully politicized issues of exclusion, invisibility, poverty, and discrimination, yet the issue of racial classification criteria, and most especially the one-drop rule, remained unpoliticized. Moreover, knowing that groups like I-Pride and AMEA challenged state classification begs the question why such organizations were forming in the first place.

There have been several interlocking reasons why these people came to redefine their experiences in a way that made public recognition of a multiracial identity in the form of official classification seem obvious to them. First, changes in racial policy brought ever more frequent encounters with the task of describing one's racial classification and strengthened the social importance of ethnoracial identification and affiliation. Second, multiracial activists responded to changes in the ideological consensus on the meaning of racial identity. Finally, the social location of multiracial activists—particularly their education and family profiles—made them especially susceptible to the questioning of dominant methods of racial categorization, and encouraged the creation of multiracial organizational networks of which multiracial activists then took advantage. The cause lies not in the fact of classification itself. If it did then this challenge might have emerged earlier. Rather, it is the new *experiences* around classification, which stem from changes in broader demographic, political, and social contexts that facilitate the reemergence of this issue.

Changes in State Racial Policy

For most of its history, state racial classification has arguably served no other purpose than to define persons in categories so as determine who to exclude and exploit from the full benefits of citizenship and who to entitle. In the 1960s, however, with the passage of civil rights legislation[13] such as the Civil Rights Act of 1964, the Voting Rights Act of 1965, and the Housing Act of 1968, racial classification became an increasingly important tool for redressing the effects of racial domination. Although the intent of the landmark legislation of the 1960s may have been to achieve a "color blind" standard, race consciousness became central in its implementation. Because legislative victories on these issues did not translate into actual achievements of equal access to public accommodations, schools, and employment, state officials instituted administrative systems to monitor compliance with the law. While affirmative action in education and employment was guided by the principle of equal opportunity, the efficacy of such programs was measured by the numbers of persons from underrepresented groups they served, and how those numbers compared to the overall size of each group. As such, the size of ethnic groups took on new significance (H. D. Graham 1990; Skrentny 1996). Moreover, the addition of ethnic groups to the list of protected categories and the public attention given to whether or not institutions were in compliance with federal standards gave previously private groupings a new public identity.

These programs provided a renewed purpose for collecting data on racial groups (for the purposes of redressing discrimination against racial minorities) and an increased reliance on such statistics for compliance purposes. It is precisely the government's need for "accurate" data on racial and ethnic groups that led to the hearings to revise Directive 15, providing an opportunity for multiracial activists to present their grievances—grievances that were themselves generated out of the state's insistence on categorizing people by race. Race-based policy to redress discrimination has brought with it a need to know one's race. It is this need that has galvanized many mixed race activists, encompassed in the dilemma of "which box to check" that has served as a rallying point for multiracial people: "Each and every time we confront one of these forms, we are faced yet again with the awkward, irrational and for many of us the offensive task of selecting a race or ethnicity which does not truthfully identify us and has the further result of failing to count our community" (AMEA testimony, July 1994). The proliferation of efforts to collect racial data coincided with a new practice of recording racial data. Since 1970, the U.S. census has allowed respondents to self-enumerate their race. Before this time, a census taker upon visual inspection enumerated an individual's race. Self-enumeration of race on the census gave control over categorization to the individual, albeit within the limits of the categories offered. The practice of self-enumeration lent support to the idea that the person being classified has the right to choose her classification. Moreover, it provided the conditions whereby an individual was obliged to wrestle with the choice of categories on her own, rather than have an outside agent determine that choice for her. In so doing, it fostered the sense that the purpose of state racial categories was to record the individual's self-identity, something that only the individual could determine.

The precedent for self-enumeration made those situations in which respondents had a racial category assigned to them by someone else appear arbitrary and anachronistic. This is important because in administrative settings such as schools and medical facilities, someone other than the person being classified often records race. Multiracial activists explicitly objected to this practice, which they dubbed "eyeballing" because it violated the ethos that individuals should determine their own identity.

The ever more frequent encounters with racial classification and the structure of "the box" such that a decision must be made about which racial category to check are important reasons why state racial policy matters so much for multiracial mobilization. But these beg the question why the categories themselves are considered meaningful. The decision of which box to check only becomes a dilemma in circumstances where one has knowledge of and feels that there are equally valid alternatives, one or more of which will necessarily be left out if only one box is checked. But the conditions under which one comes to see these options as equally relevant are related to the social context in which individuals find themselves.

Particularly important here is the family context of mixed descent persons. Unlike in previous generations where children born of cross-category unions were often conceived in coercive conditions, today such children are most often born in the context of legal marriage. Many of these children share a household with both parents. Moreover, many respondents grew up having regular and intimate personal contact with relatives from both sides of their extended families, distinguishing their experience from previous generations and from "generationally mixed" persons.[14] Both activists and rank-and-file members of organizations described the fact that they are born of differently classified parents as unique and significant in shaping their experiences and their actions around multiraciality (an issue I describe in detail in the next chapter). So significant are questions of kinship that they are the foundation on which multiracial organizations—whose formation preceded the challenge to state classification—rest. Interracial couples formed most of the local community organizations that later became involved, if only partially, in the issue of official classification.

The Rise of Identity Politics

Throughout the struggle over state classification, multiracial activists likened their struggle to the civil rights movement of the mid-twentieth century, whose values of interracialism they admired and believed they were advancing. Yet while the civil rights revolution serves as inspiration for these activists, the more proximate ideologies shaping their concerns are those that made explicit claims about the importance of racial consciousness and cultural authenticity.

During the 1960s, the integrationist paradigm of the civil rights movement gave way to an era in which consciousness and celebration of ethnic difference dominated. At this same time, a national black identity, as opposed to regional identities based on a North/South dichotomy, was emerging among African Americans, shaped by and fueling black protest in the 1960s (Marx 1998). In the mid- to late 1960s, Black Power, a modern variant of black nationalism, emerged, putting questions of racial identity and solidarity at center stage. Black Power activists, disillusioned with the failure of the civil rights movement to achieve economic equality for blacks and skeptical that whites could truly commit to ending racial oppression, articulated a vision of black political, social, and economic advancement that emphasized self-sufficiency and required black unity, racial consciousness, and black pride. Integrationist policies, nationalists contended, rather than a means to achieving racial equality, would more likely result in the assimilation of the few blacks who gained access to white institutions and their abandonment of the black masses. Separation from whites, not integration with them, would be necessary for blacks to achieve social equality.

Perhaps not surprisingly, Black Power advocates were highly critical of intermarriage. Well-known nationalist figures like Malcolm X, Stokeley Carmichael, and Eldridge Cleaver explicitly criticized blacks who would intermarry with whites, concerned that in doing so they were turning their backs on the community, reinforcing beliefs that whites were more attractive and desirable than blacks, and hindering black advancement. For Black Power advocates who one married was not simply a personal choice, but a political one as well. So too was how one identified racially. Just as intermarriage was interpreted as a sign of divided loyalties by Black Power advocates, asserting that one was "mixed" (much like asserting one was "Negro" or "colored") was seen as antithetical to the kind of cultural pride and self-determination they were engaged in defining (Carmichael and Hamilton 1967; Jewell 1985).

Concerns about intermarriage and racial identity evinced in black nationalist rhetoric reflected a more general concern with racial authenticity that emerged in the post-civil rights period. These battles over what constituted blackness emerge with earnest in a period when the conditions governing black lives were in flux, given that legal segregation was no longer and substantial numbers of blacks were beginning to gain access to mainstream educational and economic institutions. In such a climate, cultural markers of identity took on greater political and symbolic significance (Romano 2003).[16]

Concerns with racial authenticity were not the sole province of African Americans, of course. By the 1970s, Asian Americans, American Indians, and Latinos were forming panethnic coalitions to address their exclusion. These coalitions emphasized their common experiences borne of the tendency of others to "lump" together persons from distinct cultural and national groups in one racialized group without regard to class, language, and historical differences among such ethnic groups.[17] Much like Black Power advocates did, groups like La Raza and American Indian Movement (AIM) promoted a heightened group consciousness among coethnics and encouraged them to declare their group loyalties, not only through declarations of racial identity, but through signs like language and dress that signalled knowledge of one's culture and history (Espiritu 1992; Nagel 1995; Oboler 1995). Racial identity, in other words, came to be understood as indicative of one's political beliefs and group loyalty. The emphasis on racial solidarity in a time of great social change fostered the development of essentialist views among groups of color over how to authentically "be" a member of the group. Ironically, the reframing of the meaning of racial identity and its importance for group cohesion and collective advancement among groups of color helped create the conditions that lead to the fragmentation of monoracial identities. Just as essentialized and highly politicized understandings of racial identity were taking hold in the 1960s through the 1980s, the cohort of mixed descent persons challenging state classifications was growing up. Moreover, many of those involved in multiracial organizations were being raised in contexts that made it difficult for them to display their cultural credentials at a time in their lives when it mattered most, namely when they entered the highly politicized and racially polarized environment of the college campus.

The sense of racial *in*authenticity that many multiracials express feeling (or are aware that others attribute to them) in monoracial settings[18] arises not necessarily because they disagree with the political goals of such groups. Rather, they feel inauthentic because demonstrating ethnic loyalty usually requires one to demonstrate one's ethnic "credentials"—a variety of dispositional characteristics (for example, accent, language proficiency, dress, hairstyle), physical attributes (for example, skin color, hair texture), class (particularly personal experience with poverty), and other criteria (such as being the victim of discrimination) that serve as emblems of authenticity.[19] Raised with limited contact with the communities to which they are presumed to belong (by virtue of their physical appearance or ancestry), many mixed descent persons do not possess the appropriate dispositions and cultural knowledge to secure their authenticity. Their sense of being inauthentic, then, comes not by virtue of having mixed ancestry, but because key aspects of their biographies do not fit with the conventional definitions of racial membership.

Multiracial activists constructed their positions in opposition to exclusionary membership criteria. By the 1980s, multiracial activists began to challenge the logic of the one-drop rule that they believe Black Power endorsed and that had become largely accepted in nonwhite communities. Although the one-drop rule was developed with specific reference to blacks, has not been applied to other groups with any consistency, and multiracials of non-African ancestry have been accepted as whites, it is still an important factor shaping nonblack respondents' understandings of their situation. The logic of hypodescent underlies the belief, currently fashionable in many ethnoracial communities, that individuals can and should have only one racial identity or affiliation. Respondents of Asian ancestry often located their grievances in Asian American notions of race that locked them out of authentic membership in Asian American communities because of their mixed status.

Most often respondents cited experiences with persons of color, not whites, as important for shaping their grievances over how multiracial people and identity are perceived. So while the broader ideological force against which multiracial activists struggle is the logic of hypodescent, the more proximate ideological antecedents of multiracial activism have to do with the stringent criteria for ethnic membership often employed by members of racialized groups. [20]

But even as politics waged by ethnoracial groups helped spur challenges to the claims of such movements, these movements provided a model along which demands for multiracial identity would be couched almost 25 years later. On the one hand, multiracial activists use the logic of the importance of taking pride and declaring one's racial identity that Black power activists put forth so compellingly, arguing that the psychological health of multiracial people ("self-esteem") is at stake (e.g., S. R. Graham 1996; Root 1992, 1996). At the same time, multiracial activists justify their positions using the values of self-determination that Black Power activists struggled to legitimize. Arguing that they are entitled to determine their own identity for themselves, they argue for "choice" in racial identity rather than determination by the logic of hypodescent. Rejecting the idea that a monoracial identity could "accurately" reflect their racial identity, multiracial activists do *not* reject the idea of racial authenticity itself. Rather, they argue that one-drop ideology forced them into racial categories that cannot describe their authentic inner self.

The emergence of multiracial activism was facilitated by a combination of factors. Since the 1960s civil rights revolution, new policies of racial *self-enumeration* by institutions collecting racial data, the proliferation of efforts to collect such data in virtually all institutions of social life, the expansion of ethnic-specific social programs, and the increasing institutionalization of ethnic organizations had heightened the imperative of "knowing" one's racial membership, creating new experiences wherein multiracial individuals were constantly called upon to "choose" among ethnoracial affiliations. At the same time, multiracial individuals were living in contexts that made this imperative to choose one racial affiliation feel artificial. In contrast to previous periods in U.S. history, this cohort of multiracial people had largely been raised with intimate connections to both sides of their families and cultural heritage. Raised in such a context, multiracial adults came to consider the state's policy of "check one only" racial category as forcing them to choose between their *parents* and *communities*. These experiences led multiracials to create their own organizations in an effort to diminish their own sense of isolation and stigmatization.

Activists in favor of multiracial classification drew upon already-existing social networks of multiracial people and families. A few committed and well-placed members of these organizations took up the challenge to racial classifications—the most visible symbolic manifestation of those grievances—taking advantage of the opportunity to publicly comment on changes to Directive 15. Presenting themselves as representatives of "the multiracial community," they succeeded in getting the state to change its policy on racial classification to allow and count multiple responses to the race question beginning with the 2000 census.

Bodies in Search of Identities

In making the case that their multiracial identities ought to be recognized by the state, multiracial activists needed to present their demands on behalf of a putative group. That so few people were actually lobbying for such a change lends credence to Melissa Nobles' assertion that the category "multiracial" was "in search of bodies" (Nobles 2000). Since the MOOM decision and Census 2000, that category has "found" nearly seven million people—a figure that is expected to grow. The availability of an option to check multiple race responses has invigorated interest in mixed race as a cultural category as evidenced by business interest in and media coverage of multiracials (a point I return to in subsequent chapters). Young people of mixed descent, like Jamie from the Generation Mix Tour, are drawing inspiration and confidence from those numbers.

The perspective that categorization can bring about that which it appears to only describe is essential for studying racial formations. But it is important to keep in mind the rather obvious point that categories do not make themselves. Without the pressure of multiracial activists, MOOM would not have happened. So while the identity "multiracial" may indeed have been in search of bodies, we should also ask why some bodies at least were in search of such an identity. Why did some multiracials come to believe that a monoracial identity could not convey their identities "truthfully"? Why did multiracial activists seek to make their public identities consistent with their private feelings about identity? And how did *racial* identity come to be seen as crucial in conveying self-identity? In the next chapter, I address these questions by focusing on four of the people most active in mobilizing multiracials in the 1990s.

3

Becoming a Multiracial Entrepreneur: Four Stories

SO JUST WHO WAS RESPONSIBLE FOR MAKING MULTIRACIALITY a topic of public debate in the 1990s? In this chapter you will meet four "multiracial entrepreneurs"—a sample of the people most active in bringing issues of multiraciality to public awareness. Each was recognized by both insiders and outsiders as a "leader" of organized multiracials at the time. These individuals serve as spokespersons for a putative multiracial group. I focus here on how and why these activists transformed what was once considered a private dilemma into a public issue.

Multiracial entrepreneurs are, by definition, neither "representative" of persons of mixed descent generally, or even of those involved in the multiracial movement in particular. In being as active as they have been, they are already unique and set apart from the people they claim to represent. These people are far more active than most of the rank-and-file members of organizations that I interviewed. They devote nearly twice as much time to group activities than other respondents.[1]

Therein lies their significance. No matter the broader structural and ideological roots of social change, such changes propel and are propelled by people. Often such change spreads outward from an initial core of innovators, like the southern black college students of the Student Nonviolent Coordinating Committee (SNCC) who initiated the lunch counter sit-in movement (Carson 1995 [1981]) or Freedom Summer volunteers, who went on to participate in subsequent movements in later years (McAdam 1982). Multiracial entrepreneurs are such innovators. Entrepreneurs engage in enterprising acts. They organize, operate, and assume the risk of undertaking a new venture. In this case, their venture is not primarily economic but *symbolic*. Through the concrete actions in which they engage—lobbying congress for state enumeration of individual of multiple ancestry, providing forums for multiracials to come together, writing about multiracial experiences—they do the work of *group making*.

While the degree of involvement these four respondents have in multiracial issues is atypical of the persons of mixed descent they claim to represent the dilemmas they express and the ways they talk about them are less so. Their stories express in an intensified way a common set of existential and social dilemmas, while their actions highlight multiracials' social position and the dilemmas they face. As such, they are especially useful for showing the logic behind and the concrete action comprising this work of group making.

The answer to the question orienting this chapter (why multiracial entrepreneurs make a public issue out of multiracial identity?) may seem obvious to even a casual observer of the recent collective activities undertaken by persons of mixed descent. Multiracials are organizing, some argue, because they are not recognized by the state. Because the state does not have a procedure for enumerating multiple ancestry,[2] they are, according to activists, journalists, and some scholars "discriminated against," "denied equal protection," and treated as second-class citizens[3] and so have organized to address these problems.

Yet such explanations leave hidden the most interesting aspects of the question. They limit the problem to its most visible dimensions—the absence of state recognition—which presumes that a "multiracial" group actually exists, and that receiving state recognition of that group is what animates their activity. But as we saw in Chapter 2, activists lobbying for census classification spoke on behalf of a group that does not exist as such. Moreover, while multiracial entrepreneurs may seek public recognition of multiracial identity, this begs the question of whence the desire for such an identity springs. Is it "racial" recognition they seek, and if so, what is the meaning of such recognition to them? Finally, such explanations leave unexplored why *these* individuals, and not others, have been the ones to engage in this struggle. Rather than relying only on the most visible dimensions of multiracial activism (for example, multiracial classification) as explanation for why multiracial entrepreneurs engaged in this struggle, I am interested in understanding how these individuals became competent actors with both the desire and ability to engage in this struggle to make "multiracial" a socially recognized identity.

First, I examine in more detail the practical logic—dilemmas, decisions, constraints, contingencies, and sensibilities—motivating these actors and shaping the action in which they engage. Next, I look at the social properties of these multiracial entrepreneurs—the particular competencies and skills that make them likely candidates to become multiracial entrepreneurs and the social context through which they acquired them. In the next section, I present the trajectories of four multiracial entrepreneurs in depth. This allows me to present more of the details of their stories, how they explain their path to becoming organizers to themselves and to others, and what they understand to be the struggles with which they grapple, in more context than would be possible if I were discussing the entire sample. Respondents were not chosen for the dramatic value of their stories, but because they illustrate four types of "crossings" of the private to public threshold. As we shall see, the different paths they have taken to becoming multiracial entrepreneurs owe much to their different positions in social space.

Informants often talked about their activities in personal terms, in which they cast their activities as forms of emotional healing for themselves. The personalized ways in which they talk about their work make it tempting to conclude that these are merely interesting, idiosyncratic stories of personal dramas. I read them differently. My intention is not to psychoanalyze respondents, but to "socioanalyze"[4] their activities and understandings—to draw links between what appears to be personal and broader social structure. Throughout the stories, I emphasize the social conditions that produce these private, psychologized conflicts that in turn generate and motivate activism and group identity construction. Doing so will help answer why these particular individuals (and not the millions of potential others who might have) became multiracial entrepreneurs and the final question of this chapter, why they have chosen this *public* route to address their grievances rather than more private paths.

I argue that the existential crises ("who am I?") of persons of mixed descent encompass a variety of conflicts over class, sexuality, education, and family history. These dilemmas are understood and expressed through race, precisely because we live in an age where race is central to how Americans organize themselves socially and personally. Both the recognition by these entrepreneurs of their dilemmas *as* dilemmas, and their desire and ability to do something about them, are triggered by their educational experience. In particular, their entry into college highlights a "mismatch" between how they learned to understand race in their families and neighborhoods and how race is understood in the more politicized environment of the campus. The credentials and skills they acquire through their education, however, allow them to address those dilemmas in other arenas—most especially in lobbying the state for multiracial classification.

Story 1. Rage and Reconciliation: Lareina Williams

For the past thirteen years, Lareina Williams[5] has juggled the demands of her sales job with the various activities required of someone leading a grassroots organization. When not traveling from city to city selling computer hardware, Lareina sojourns between the West Coast and Washington D.C., testifying at congressional hearings in favor of multiracial classification and lobbying anyone who will listen (especially representatives of traditional civil rights groups) to support her cause.

A woman of seemingly boundless energy, Lareina exudes confidence whether she is running community meetings, appearing on television, or speaking to students. The people she admires are, in her words, "straight talkers" much like she is—vibrant, take charge, articulate.

When meeting with Lareina at her home, I get the sense that this is the first time in ages that she has been in any one place for very long, not to mention had the time to sit and talk to an interested researcher for more than four hours. Her rented apartment is sparsely decorated and its relatively unadorned walls expose the suburban-tract cookie-cutter bones so typical of apartment complexes in this city. The house is dark and cold, except for the kitchen where Lareina is preparing brunch for our get-together—an egg dish heavy with cream, cheddar cheese, and bacon. As she prepares our meal, we chat about the latest developments in the deliberations over how to tabulate responses to the race question now that the OMB has adopted the "check one or more" format. Our conversation, however, quickly turns to more personal matters. Lareina is in an agitated state, upset over a falling out with an associate. Her anxiety is reflected in the repeated, almost driven way she eats slices of cheese as she alternately layers them in the pan.

Lareina is of African, Portuguese, and American Indian descent with softly curled hair, light mocha-colored skin, and dark brown eyes. Lareina's looks are hard to place racially. While many could probably deduce that Lareina is of African descent, she could just as easily be taken for a darker European or Latina in the right context.

Neighborhood Context

Lareina grew up in a racially diverse city outside of Manhattan in the 1960s—a time of social upheaval that would challenge and indeed overturn the most obvious racial restrictions that had shaped the lives and identities of earlier generations of African Americans. In her neighborhood, whites, black Americans, and West Indian immigrants lived in close proximity, and in her daily interactions she was as likely to encounter whites as blacks. Despite this diversity, or perhaps because of it, Lareina was not embedded in a black community, in institutions like the church, school, neighborhood, and family where blacks predominated. The significance of place and time for shaping her experiences is highlighted if we imagine Lareina in a different setting. Had Lareina grown up in the Jim Crow South, for example, chances are that she would have been fully enmeshed in a segregated black community in which maintaining networks of extended kin and neighbors was crucial for material and psychic survival.[6] Despite being of black, Indian, and European descent, Lareina's racial designation would have been made obvious by where and with whom she could live, love, worship, and learn. She would have been clearly designated "colored."

Lareina says she has always described herself as multiracial despite being challenged by peers and authority figures for not describing herself as "black," even in situations where claiming a multiracial identity marked her as an outsider. She rejected being labeled "black" and felt different from other black kids in school in two ways. First, Lareina's appearance marked her as different. Her long hair provoked jealousy and anger from black girls, who accused her of thinking she was "better" than them.[7] Add to this the fact that for the most part Lareina did not use Black English, further emphasizing her difference from her classmates, and making her vulnerable to accusations that she was acting "white." Second, Lareina was spatially separated from most black children in school, most of whom were tracked into nonhonors classes, while she was an honors student.

Q. [Was] having long hair [an issue]?

A. Oh, yeah. I was later told by some of the black girls, you know, when we got to just talking outside school, "We really thought you were a snoot." They never got close enough because I was in the honors class and they weren't. They weren't mean to me but it was just like, "we just didn't know where you were coming from, who you thought you were . . ." There was resentment that I ran in circles with honors kids. I was in the Honor Society.

These experiences contributed to making Lareina feel isolated from her black peers and ambivalent about assuming a black identity. In particular, Lareina associated a particular construction of blackness (as jealous, vengeful, and not achievement oriented) with black *Americans*. Lareina told me she gravitated more toward West Indian classmates who, it seemed to her, held values and orientations more like her own and were "much more centered, much more self-assured."[8]

Lareina presented her identity to me in very matter-of-fact terms, describing the multiracial designation as simply an accurate description of who she is and one that she has always used to describe herself. Yet this description of multiracial identity as relatively unproblematic—a logical, almost natural classification—obscures the reality that Lareina worked hard to achieve and maintain such an identity. In college, for example, Lareina continued to describe herself as multiracial even as the dominant ethos of campus life among students of color was to assert pride and allegiance to one's ethnic heritage. In such a climate, Lareina's description of herself as part white seemed naive at best, traitorous at worst, and earned her the attribution of "lesbian" by her black (mostly male) peers—a way of marking her as an outcast. Far from being unproblematic, Lareina's assertion of a multiracial identity and the various dispositional traits that marked her as different from other blacks stigmatized and isolated her.

While Lareina continuously described her choice to identify herself as multiracial as generated out of a sense of pride in all her cultures, this characterization obscured the deeper feelings of ambivalence about both her relationship to black people and culture and her status as a mixed person. This ambivalence stems from and is reflected in the dynamics of her particular family.

Family Dynamics

Lareina's parents were married in the late 1940s, making them one of the few intermarried couples around. While city-level data are not available, national data show that around 1950 intermarriages were quite rare, representing less than .5 percent of all marriages.[9] Mr. and Mrs. Williams settled in a northern city where intermarriage was never officially illegal.[10] Still, intermarried couples faced various forms of extralegal discrimination. Drake and Cayton, in their landmark study of black life in Chicago (1993 [1945]), describe the hardships facing such couples, including social isolation from black and white families and communities, difficulty keeping a job and finding a place to live, violence, and aspersions cast on the sexual propriety and social status of the partners involved. Living in a city that tolerated but did not embrace intermarried couples, Lareina's parents were obligated to deal with such problems on their own. At the time, there were no organizations in their area for social support of couples like them.

In many ways, John and Lourdes Williams's marriage was typical of other marriages of the period. She was a homemaker while he worked at various skilled and semi-skilled occupations, as a janitor, at a deli, and as a printing pressman. They were also typical in some ways of the few intermarried couples. Following the common gender and race patterns of intermarriage, John was categorized as black (although his mother was Native American), and Lourdes was white. Yet John Williams was atypical of many of the men of his generation in that he was unusually well-educated, receiving a college degree when few men of any color did so. Moreover, his father also had received a college education, while his mother worked as a teacher.

Lareina spoke with pride about her family's educational heritage and the importance of her father's interest in ideas to her own educational success (she received a master's degree in engineering). Yet she also spoke of the darker consequences of living with a father who had limited opportunities to use his skills. Her father, Lareina tells me, resented being treated as a *black* man rather than just as a man. His rage toward his subordinate status, she believes, was often unleashed on her in the form of an overbearing, rigid demand that she conform to rules. She often challenged them and suffered physical and psychological abuse for doing so. Such rage was also vented on Lourdes, who would often retaliate by calling John a "nigger" when they fought. To further complicate the situation, Lareina's mother suffered from mental illness and was often incapacitated and unable to care for her. To cope, Lareina often ran away and eventually began to spend summers with a black family.

Lareina's story highlights the importance of the relationship between family and racial identity, particularly for individuals of multiple ancestry. Lareina was, in her words, "farmed out" by her parents "to people who truly welcomed me," something she enjoyed. Chief among them were her maternal grandparents whom she says "adored" her. Her grandparents "represented her Portuguese heritage" with which she associated positive qualities such as excitement and unconditional love. Lareina saw little of her father's family, who lived far away. Her impressions of them were formed from brief, intermittent encounters—like meeting a drunken uncle and hearing stories of family fights—that were largely negative. Looking back, Lareina assesses her impression of her black relatives as "fucked up." Moreover, her impressions of her black and white families shaped the meaning of racial identity for her:

Now, I am not into connecting with pain and I'm just now uncovering, probably the reason I pushed [away] a lot of the African American aspects of my culture, all that translated to was rage and hate. Now, I could deal with it in books. I could deal with it at a distance, but I didn't want that in my face on a daily basis. So I connected to the things that made me feel better. When I was in my [white] grandmother's house and she was cooking fish and I could eat in the bed—there was no rules about eating in the bed—that was a good feeling. When I could live away from home and go to my friend's house—and that was a black family, I could have buttermilk biscuits and greens and all these other foods that were not being cooked at my household and they tasted good and I could relate to that.

A distinction must be made between racial identity as membership in an abstract community "out there" and one anchored in relationships "close to home." Lareina felt little connection to that abstracted notion of "black community," just as she was well aware that she was not "white." Her intimate connections with white family members made being Portuguese feel like something she wanted to be. The strife she associated with her black family made being black something she did not want to be. It is only because of a very close connection with a black family whom Lareina describes as being "just like family," and her exposure to black history through books ("I got to appreciate blackness through James Baldwin, through Martin Luther King, through reading about Gandhi. People of color became alive to me from history, not from day-to-day dealings") that she developed a countervailing, more positive impression of the meaning of being black.

Path to Activism

No longer a child, Lareina still struggles with some of the ambivalence about family and racial identity formed in her youth. At times she has wished for a more definite identity, longing for a less racially ambiguous appearance, "so the questions will stop from within and without," and stronger connections with her family to feel less ambiguous and more connected to others in both a personal and communal sense.

Lareina's home conveys in visual form a similar longing for connection and a sense of self. Much like an adolescent's, her bed is overflowing with stuffed animals, while her bedroom walls are adorned with various certificates of accomplishment. Crowding the vanity space in her bathroom is a shrine of sorts, filled with religious icons drawn from various cultural traditions. Having given up the Catholic membership of her childhood because official church doctrine conflicts with her beliefs on women and sexuality, Lareina has replaced it with a more eclectic, new-agey spiritualism drawing from the ethnic traditions of her own ancestry. Around the mirror hang, among other things, a dream catcher, Black Madonna, and angels—icons through which she tries to forge and express a synthesis of her own cultural heritage and personal beliefs.

Lareina's activism is a direct result of this desire to experience a more definite sense of identity. She joined a support group for mixed descent persons, she told me, to challenge the prevailing image of multiracials as necessarily pathological. Lareina expressed righteous indignation at current practices of "eyeballing" children in schools to determine their race or challenging those who assert a multiracial identity. While she talks about her path to activism in the readily accessible language of race, however, her activism emerges out of a broader desire for emotional healing. Because understandings of the self are intimately connected with race in the United States, such that to exist socially one must possess a racial identity, it is not surprising that struggles over racial identity (which are struggles over social existence) are often fueled by quests for self-understanding.

The close connection between American selfhood and race is mirrored in the difficulty Lareina has in separating her emotional difficulties from being multiracial. Other activists, she claims, also carry around pent up frustration that she suggests is related to being mixed. "There's a lot of rage in our community," she believes, yet she then wonders if this rage is "racially connected or is it dysfunction that you find in any family no matter what?"

This quest for identity, and the intense feelings of rage and humiliation that surround it, fuel her tireless activity on behalf of "the multiracial movement." Getting together with other people who identified with multiple racialized identities provided a forum wherein one dimension of insecurity (rejection on the basis of claiming a multiracial identity) could likely be neutralized, such that the possibility of it becoming a "safe" place where she could work on some of the other dilemmas she faced might be realized. Of her first meeting with other multiracials, Lareina said:

> [W]hat would it be to have biracial adults our own age, in the forties or whatever, get together without the parents, their input, and discuss what we feel. What would that be like? So I called some of the women and people that I knew that were biracial adults that had never really gotten together with

each other. And you would have thought we were declaring we were gay. I mean to be honest with you, it was like coming out of the closet. People who had pretty much identified as black in the past because they saw no opening or safety in declaring it anywhere else, especially if they grew up in a black community and that was pretty much a very cultural experience, this was the first time that people were able to say what it was like to, although know that they were quite black according to black people, there was something else going on and there wasn't quite a fit, that something was missing and there was a yearning, a longing to be able to express themselves like they were that night, oh, (unintelligible) and they were grateful there was nobody there as an observer.

The analogy to being gay suggests the risk of rejection as well as high emotional investment she had put into finding this place to be "at home." Lareina explicitly links her involvement in a multiracial support group to emotional healing, encapsulated in the metaphor of "home": "Finally after over ten years of analysis, seven years as an active member of a multiracial support group, I've come to realize that finding my way back home was as simple, though painful, a journey as discerning and affirming my own reflection in my own eyes. Home will always be where I choose to be, not where I've been."

Armed with an interpretation of her situation as a problem created for her by others, and emotionally charged with righteous indignation and indeed rage, Lareina became active in multiracial issues publicly. Lareina has stated that, as if compelled by magic, she had "no choice" but to "champion the cause" of interracial families and multiracial people. In a word, Lareina understands herself to have been "called" in the prophetic sense that Weber[11] described. Unlike the prophet, however, it is through being active with other people of mixed descent that Lareina personally reveals herself and discovers her own charisma. While ostensibly about race, the motivations and goal of her activities are about reconstructing her*self*—revaluing and reaffirming her sense of the goodness within.

> [I]f you try to make it a color issue none of it makes sense. If you make a racial issue none of it is consistent. Some people may say that people respond to your color, but what people are committed to is their culture. I mean outsiders may respond to your color but what you are about, what your passions are about, what really calls to you as you get up in the morning and feel good or bad is your relationship to your culture, not to this (points to arm). The

sense of belonging certainly isn't about this. It's about what you share in terms of tradition, what you share in terms of history, what you share in terms of feeling connected.

The details of Lareina's biography suggest how key social mechanisms (for example, dynamics of class and skin color stratification in the black community, social stigma, isolation) shape people's experiences, identities, and actions. Lareina's objective characteristics (highly educated, Catholic, in an interracial family) marked her as different from both blacks and whites, even as a few important intimate relationships afforded her a way of connecting with "black" and "white" culture writ large. Out of both these experiential distances and proximities to both individuals and groups, she gives meaning to and justifies her multiracial identity. Her path to activism is shaped by the need to continually negotiate that identity.

Story 2. The Journey Home: Xavier Upton

In 1949, Xavier Upton was born into an African American family in the segregated South, the son of two highly educated, middle class "Negroes." His father's occupation as a doctor and his mother's as a schoolteacher placed Xavier's family at the top of the class structure for blacks (both then and now).[12] In keeping with the prevailing pattern at the time, Xavier's parents, like many of the black elite, were "light-skinned,"[13] as is Xavier, who often referred to himself as "tan," in contradistinction to the darker-skinned children with whom he went to school.

Xavier represents to many that person so often vilified in public debates about multiraciality—the proverbial light-skinned person who doesn't want to be black. As the son of two African American parents who identifies himself as "multiracial," Xavier is unusual among my informants and from the vast majority of people involved in multiracial organizations. Yet his story is notable precisely because of its atypicality. His unique position and the perspective it affords him, sheds light on a different set of multiracial dilemmas than discussed by Lareina.

Several social properties distinguish Xavier from other informants. He is a "black" man according to conventional definitions, yet he identifies himself as multiracial. Raised in the segregated South, his family met all the educational and social credentials for membership in the black elite. Not only did his father achieve a medical degree, his grandfather was also a college graduate. On his mother's side he is the third generation to go to college, and Xavier holds a doctoral degree.[14] While such credentials might have made it easier for him than for other multiracial entrepreneurs to become ensconced in an ethnic community (the small and insular world of the black elite), Xavier was isolated from it in large part because he did not accept the idea that he was a "Negro." At the same time, though structurally bound to a black community by the laws of segregation, he shared, in his words, "little cultural affinity" with lower-class blacks, and perhaps even less with whites. Moreover, being gay made each of these negotiations that much more complicated. Finally, while he identifies as multiracial, these social properties have shaped his experiences in ways that are significantly different from those typical of the majority of multiracials organizing today. These factors taken together position Xavier not simply "between two worlds," to employ a hackneyed multiracial mantra, but between several—those of self-identified multiracials, middle class and poor blacks, whites, and gay/straight.

We met in a hotel room in San Francisco where Xavier was attending a conference, an appropriate place to meet, it struck me later. As places where people live when they are away from (leaving or heading toward) home, the hotel symbolized a theme Xavier continually referred to—that of not fitting in, being without a home. Dressed in a crisp white button-down shirt and neatly pressed black trousers, Xavier looked the same as he had the last time we saw each other three years prior. Almost fifty, his full head of woolly dark hair and smooth unlined face suggest he is much younger. Outstretched on the bed with shoes off, Xavier's white ankle peeked out from beneath his pant leg in sharp contrast to the black socks he wore. His light complexion bespeaks his European ancestry, while the texture of his hair readily signals his African heritage.

Xavier is a consummate storyteller, inserting captivating details and dramatic contrasts where appropriate to emphasize a point, changing his facial expressions and voice to mimic the characters in his stories. He speaks crisply, fully enunciating his carefully chosen words, yet he peppers his speech with black slang, often with a Southern twang, when he wants to emphasize a point. Xavier's ability to "code-switch"—to shift between the linguistic styles associated with blacks and whites—hints at his familiarity with and immersion in black cultural life. This is just one characteristic that distinguished him from other multiracial entrepreneurs, who by and large did not "perform" the cultural styles of nonwhites.

"It was a War": Negotiating Blackness, Mixedness, and Class

Xavier represents a double violation of U.S. racial logic. By asserting a multiracial identity despite having two black parents, he violates a tacit collective agreement that anyone with a black ancestor "is" black. At the same time, he also violates a less well-developed agreement about who is "multiracial," that is, a person with two differently classified (biological) *parents*. While many people who claim multiple racial identities are accused of seeking to escape a stigmatized status, they are less vulnerable to such attacks than is Xavier. These "immediately mixed" (what Xavier dubs "first-generation") multiracials can call upon their ties to a nonblack *parent*, trading on the perception that their relationship to nonblack "cultures" is closer (in genealogical and social distance) than that of a "multigenerationally" mixed person, as a way to legitimate their identity claims. Xavier's claim to be multiracial is downgraded in the face of such logic.

Xavier says he has always identified as multiracial even at a time when public expression of multiraciality was nonexistent. Growing up, he was quite aware of his light skin, and the difference it marked from others in his segregated neighborhood. Yet when he would ask about his family's ancestry, he was met with dismissive references to a variety of European ethnicities, as well as Indian, all neatly encapsulated in an explanation that when all was said and done, they were Negroes. As he tells it, his insistence on calling himself "tan" as opposed to Negro, and questioning their "denial" of what they "really" were, lead his parents to seek psychological help for him:

> They wanted to shut me down, and this is where they had me in places where they try to deal with children who have cognitive dissonance problems. There's something wrong with him. Oh, my God, our child—so I had to kind of hide to protect myself from the family. Because they didn't want to deal with this and here I am running around saying I'm tan and they were very color conscious about being tan as opposed to black—but I'm not saying it about being better. I'm just saying that's what I am. (In a very matter-of-fact tone) "No, no, you're not. You're a Negro."

Despite repeatedly being rebuffed when he asserted that he was different from other blacks, Xavier told me he continued to insist that he was multiracial. Xavier presented his story as a struggle in which as the heroic protagonist he battled against a hostile world out to get him. While he stated at the outset of our interview that he tends to "overdramatize" things, the emotional weight underlying the stories he told me of his struggles with social acceptance and racial identity was palpable. When I asked him to give me an example of a time when he insisted on a multiracial identity and their reaction, Xavier replied:

> What I would say depending on the context was that I was mixed or ways of talking about mixed that would convey that I was not just this one thing. And inevitably there was—I'm trying to think of a really good example—there's so many and why can't I think of one that would crystallize this? (answering his rhetorical question) Because it was a constant war. It was a war—in fact, there was—at home I was very careful—I was curious about genealogy. I wanted to know more about who our family and what our background—and they would go, "Well, you're living in the past." That's the way they would respond to it. There was this real tacit—they did not consider themselves to be mixed. My family saw that as—and we had relatives who were passing as white. But those who were—they were light-skinned Negroes and that, of course, implies that there was quote unquote very clearly immediate mixture but that was not what the identity was based on. So I knew to be very careful. I did not talk about "*we* are mixed"—*I* am mixed. They weren't.

A sense of being under siege pervades Xavier's descriptions of much of his life. He continued to assert a multiracial identity through college, during which time he began to style himself as an Arab and hang out with Arab students. He describes himself at that time as a "mulatto militant," going so far as to reply, when students in college classes would ask for a "black perspective" on an issue, "I don't know. Why don't you ask one." Such recalcitrance did not endear him to black students on campus, this being 1968 and the height of the black consciousness movement. Xavier describes feeling guilty about "not being able to respond appropriately" to other blacks calling him "brother." He described a general discomfort with black people, especially darker, poorer blacks, but also with light-skinned, middle class blacks as well. At times, his discomfort seems more like fear, motivated out of the rejection he expects to find from blacks. In 1968, on the day Martin Luther King, Jr. was assassinated (coincidentally this was Xavier's birthday), he taped a story he had written:

> It was called "Dawn Brother" and it's about this man who's a multiracial man who was caught up in a revolution, a race revolution that's taking over the country and he's about ready to go before a firing squad. And he's in this prison

and there's all these maggots and the darkness of the cells and whatever and when he's standing before the firing squad, which is an all black firing squad, he can see the whites of their eyes and they're getting ready to kill him, but they've given him a chance to say a last few words, he says something like— talks about the notion of being marginal, of being in between two worlds, and that the metaphor of the dawn is who he is. And he says, "This is a half breed whom you're killing, but indeed he is your brother." Then they just *waste* him. Of course, it's very melodramatic. I'm saying that if anybody had told me then at the height of the black consciousness movement what I was saying, "Yeah, I'm mixed but I'm your brother," and people were not buying it, if you had told me that just wait, twenty years from now, in 1988 you will see why you were doing—life will make sense to you—I would have said that's a cruel joke. You know that's not possible.

Given the many rejections and slights he had suffered, why did Xavier insist on asserting he was multiracial? Why was he searching for "his people" outside the black community? Why did he not feel "at home" among African Americans, even the generally light-skinned, decidedly middle-class blacks with whom he had contact in youth social clubs like Jack and Jill?[15] Although he did not explicitly make this connection, Xavier's discussion of how he had dealt with his racial identity seemed to be a parallel conversation about the dilemmas he faced as a gay man. Xavier's reference to being institutionalized by his parents because of a presumed psychological problem over a racial identity echoes the threat of institutionalization often held over the heads of gay children. The stories of rejection, loneliness, and fear of discovery could also apply to someone wanting to assert, yet feeling pressured to hide, a stigmatized (gay) identity. Xavier did not broach the subject of his sexuality until more than an hour into our discussion, and then only in the more shaded terms of gender identity. When his grade school became integrated, his "cultural identity" became more complicated, he says, because he began to hang around white kids who were in his advanced tracked classes:

So my social world got very weird. The people who made me feel comfortable and welcome and then didn't pick on me because I didn't—see, I grew up in the hood, even though I lived at the top of the hood in terms of the class structure, I grew up around some really rough folks. So my code of masculinity was called into question because I was a sissy and so not only was my gender identity held hostage, I wasn't—"I think you're half girl." So here I am half girl.

Despite the difficulties he faced in asserting a multiracial identity while growing up in the 1950s and 1960s in the South, asserting a gay identity posed even greater risks. Talking about multiple racial identity, although stigmatized, could at least be verbalized. The language of race provided an accessible language with which to convey difference and to explain his felt sense of difference to himself. Xavier's dilemmas around masculinity, sexuality, and race were temporarily alleviated by socializing with white students.

My gravitation towards white quote-unquote community culturally created some problems for me because I knew I was not a white person and yet I knew that my lineage contained that and yet I had no illusions about them seeing me other than as the little darky—not even a demi-darky but a darky. So how do I explain to someone that my affinity here is not because of a racial obsession with whiteness but I want to go somewhere where I'm not made uncomfortable. I also know that if they make me uncomfortable it's not about me being multiracial or not, it's that I'm the colored boy there and I know the line they draw, but they don't pick on me. But the black community didn't pick on me because a lot of the people that I grew up with were lighter than I was, so I was never much the victim of color discrimination from dark-skinned African Americans because I was not around them. Like I said it was beige and bourgie. But they were like Negroes that were beige and bourgie and I had very little cultural affinity with—it would be European American. So it was an unpleasant world because there was nowhere—a place comfortable. I was not a member of the community racially. The communities I was being defined as racially part of, I didn't feel completely part of racially and culturally I had very little affinity with. So I was in the music world. Musicians in New York, those were the kinds of people that I had for friends, people who didn't fit in with any group. Whoever the folks were that didn't fit in I was friends with but I never felt a sense of being anywhere. I've never felt that I had a people of any kind.

Xavier tells a story of a journey toward finding "his people" (an expression he uses often) and continually having the rug pulled out from under him if he revealed too much about himself (either about his family background or sexuality). As such, he adopted a kind of survivalist approach to social life, doing what he had to do to get by. At one point, Xavier says, he would secretly select friends to study with on the basis of skin color, which signaled mixedness to him and possible understanding.

Becoming Somebody

Trying to manage how others saw him took its toll, however. As he puts it, "I was nobody." Tired of the work required juggling his identity, in his early twenties Xavier simply became someone else. He changed his name to sound more Portuguese, going so far as to alter his birth certificate. For the next nine years he presented himself as the son of a Brazilian mother and an American father.

[T]he freedom that I found and the ambiguity that I had, because I had this new name, nobody knew what I was. I was very ambiguous and it was so liberating because I could be anything I wanted to be. If anyone asked me anything I said my mother's Brazilian and my father's American. Sometimes they would see African ancestry and sometimes they wouldn't. But if they asked I always told them and I would always break (it) down. The only way I could embrace my African ancestors and still be who I was was to be from somewhere else. It had to be generational. It was like one parent's this and one of them is this and one of them is foreign and that African ancestry didn't come to the U.S. Somehow or another, I did not become an African American by virtue of that. Foreign nationality and the biraciality, first generation. And I lived that way for years. And my family, they really thought I was off center. (switches to a distraught expression) "This is terrible. My God, what's he going to do?" I was very pleased. This was all calculated. It was a way of controlling the space where I could give myself enough flexibility to create what I wanted to be so I could control what someone treated me as. And yet what happened was that it was not real and when I had to move beyond that—but it gave me the freedom for a period of my life to come to terms with who I was and then, of course, I gave it up and returned.

As Xavier tells it, he was "passing" in two ways: as a foreigner and a "first-generation" multiracial (with two parents of different racial categories). Both social categories gave him more latitude for acceptance as multiracial. As a "foreigner," he was somehow exempt from America's rigid racial rules. Donning a Brazilian mother makes Xavier appear interestingly foreign, rather than disturbingly alien. As a "first generation," he could claim more recent genealogical and social ties to European ancestry through one of his parents, giving him better odds that an assertion of multiracial identity would be accepted as legitimate.

While Xavier implies that his change of identity was the result of a "very calculated" decision that he controlled and which he enjoyed, it was also an attempt to make a virtue out of necessity. Insisting he was multiracial was a useful way to express (by not quite expressing) a sense of not fitting in (and perhaps not wanting to fit in) because of his sexual identity. At the same time, manipulating his identity and challenging the identity others would impose on him is a way to exert control and preserve a sense of autonomy over one's self in the face of denigration. Presenting himself to family and classmates who had previously known his given identity was not merely a "running from" blackness but a challenge to the restrictions and humiliations he suffered as both a black and a gay man.[16]

Path to Activism

After nearly forty years of feeling that his "true" identity as a multiracial was, in his words, "behind the shadows," one of Xavier's students gave him a newspaper article on a local group for multiracial people. Just when he had resigned himself to the fact that he'd never be able to be who he "really was" in the United States, he met the founder of this group. Of his first meeting with this woman, who accepted him as multiracial without questioning him, Xavier says, "It was my moment, my first entry into, shall we say, the journey home." Xavier describes his first time attending a meeting with other self-identified multiracials as:

> [L]ike walking into the land of Oz. There were all these creatures, these mixes—it was strange, I felt like I was in a foreign world where people who, quote unquote, looked like they could be what they were but I had seen them before but the designator was different and all of a sudden these people were saying they were multiracial, mixed race or mixed whatever and it was like normal.[17]

Xavier's crossing of the private-to-public threshold begins with this epiphany. The realization that there were others out there like him—that his dilemmas were not merely personal but shared and that others were working collectively and publicly to address them—is the catalyst that leads him to become a multiracial entrepreneur. Without the existence of a local support group, however, that crossing may never have taken place. His understanding of himself as multiracial rather than just black may have remained a personalized, private dilemma. Since finding others who felt as he did and through the institutional apparatus of the organization, Xavier has spent most of the last ten years actively working to publicize multiracial issues in his work as both writer and teacher.

Story 3. Feeling Like a Fraud: Pedro Santana

Pedro Santana has the look of a professor—not the rigid, bow-tied, *Paper Chase* type, but the slightly rumpled, liberal 1960s' variety. Although slightly too young to have actively participated in the civil rights movement of the 1960s, he is old enough to remember his parents' active involvement. I can only guess that he came of age in the mid- to late 1970s, since he declined to state his age. In fact, Pedro declined to divulge many of the details of his personal life, such as whether he's married and his income. Annoyed upon reading the questions he chafed, "boy you want to know everything!"

True to the rationalist origins of his profession (he's a lawyer), Pedro conveys a sense that feelings are beside the point when it comes to the "objective" goals of the multiracial movement: "Well, one thing I've learned about over many, many years, a lot of it just being an observer, being a child observing all the groups that were around in the sixties and seeing how they operated, without being a participant, up through this whole movement, I've observed that personality conflicts can be rendered irrelevant if one sticks to, again, objectivity as closely as possible."

As someone who has been involved in the organizational and political arenas, writing testimony in support of changes to federal racial categories, serving in leadership positions in local and national organizations, Pedro has had his eye on the same prize for nearly twenty years—to legally challenge Directive 15 (the OMB guidelines on racial classification).

We analyzed the situation objectively, primarily as a legal issue or a constitutional issue, and I discovered that OMB 15 was the key to the whole thing. You could not get a multiracial classification without changing OMB 15. You also couldn't get multiple checkoffs without changing OMB 15. I also connected that with how I understood the history of this issue, that this was connected with the one-drop rule. It looked to me like there was a perfect connection there between the law and this tradition and that hence that was the focus. Objectively that would be the best focus and if people had different ideas on it, that's fine. I mean that's a debate. People need to assess for themselves whether, even though we're purporting that this is an objective analysis, we have to check that with other people because we can never tell if our own feelings are anywhere in this.

Pedro's singularity of focus can come off as gruff. Although he sometimes laughs, he has a serious, intense demeanor that seems tinged with a hint of sadness. Pedro has sacrificed a lot—perhaps too much—for his work. When I asked him how much he had worked at multiracial activities he replied, "A lot. More than I should have. I put myself in an iffy situation, even right now, as far as taking care of personal business. I guess I figured it was extremely important and I didn't hear anybody else saying some of the things I was saying so I'm going to have to do it."

We met in a cafe, outdoors on an unusually warm winter day that allowed us to sit outside while we talked. I had brought with me copies of his writings from various multiracial newsletters, as well as notes from the last time we met six years prior. Pedro chuckled at that, relieved to hear that he had been "consistent" in his position. Being "consistent" is a theme running through Pedro's position on multiracialism—not only in terms of his ideas, but also in how he thinks of himself. Consistency over time suggests clarity of purpose (in contrast to messy and conflicting emotions) and integrity in both a moral and psychological sense:

> There is a stereotype I alluded to before, of the "overcompensating multiracial." That's one aspect. And it can go both ways. It's not just I'll be more of a minority than the minority I'm affiliated with. It can also be "I pass. I'll become white." Yeah, it can happen but that's why I tagged on there peace of mind and integrity because I do not regard a person who is doing that as having peace of mind or being in any way integral. And I think it shows up. I think it's obvious. I think a lot of people, even people who are not multiracial recognize it right away and may even be snickering about it. And people, they put blinders on to that snickering. They don't realize that people see through it. Again, I think the respect comes when people are certain of themselves, even though the respect is not spoken right away, it often comes out as hostility, but it's there.

Pedro's use of psychiatric language is interesting in that it echoes the rhetoric employed to stigmatize people of mixed descent for the last one hundred years. Goffman (1963) refers to this as a general phenomenon employed by spokespeople of stigmatized persons when considering themselves from the standpoint of "normals" who tend to see the stigmatized as psychiatrically deficient. It probably also stems from the fact that Pedro's father was a psychiatrist.

A search for a more authentic sense of integrity motivated him to create a group for multiracials—a search that began during his college years and given first expression during a meeting with other students who lead ethnic civil rights-oriented groups:

> All of us are sitting around—shared some wine and we were just kind of laughing and making stupid jokes. And then pretty soon we started talking about the fact, isn't it interesting that every single one of us is mixed background and yet we're representing these various discrete groups and each one of us went down the line just volunteering what a *mess* we were, what our backgrounds were. And that's how we handled it. We were laughing nervously. And wouldn't it be nice—I remember we said, wouldn't it be nice if we had our own group and that stuck in my mind because many times I'd felt sort of awkward. Here I would be president of the Chicano group and I would always tell people, you know, I'm not really 100 percent. That's okay, isn't it? Oh, yeah, no problem. All right. Then I would go—but I still felt like this was a con job, that it was kind of fraudulent. And I wondered if other kids felt the same way. I noticed that it was just odd, the more active people in the various groups tended to be the more racially ambiguous people, as if there was a hidden identity, insecurity going on that made them try harder. Okay. And then the converse stereotype: the person who was quite clearly black or Asian or whatever, they turned out to be some of the most rabidly right-wing conservative, apathetic people, and they had nothing to do with anything like a black student union. Very odd circumstance.

Pedro juxtaposes as "converse stereotypes" the multiracial person who represents an ethnic organization with the "monoracial" person who does not claim membership in ethnic organizations and seems to deny their affiliation with others of their group. In his analysis, both are perpetrating con jobs with different, yet equally deceptive, goals. The "overcompensating multiracial" is trying to "be" more Mexican than he really is. The "apathetic" black person is trying to "be" less black than he is. Pedro's comment epitomizes the heart of the authenticity dilemma. He suggests there can be a truthfulness to identity, where one's inner (and in this case, more "true") self matches one's outer presentation of self. Pedro implies that one's inner self should reflect one's history, experience, and ancestral heritage.

Despite serving in a leadership position in a Chicano students organization in college, Pedro never fully felt authentic—as if he was playing the part of a "real" Chicano. Pedro had few of the cultural credentials that may have felt more authentic, chief among them his limited ability to speak Spanish. His experience was atypical of his Chicano peers in other ways as well. As a psychiatrist, Pedro's father was part of the most highly educated strata of Mexican society. Moreover, Pedro is the third generation in his father's family to go to college. For Pedro, a college education was both assumed and possible to attain—expectations and possibilities that elude most Chicano men. Pedro grew up in what he describes as a white neighborhood where few if any Mexican Americans or other nonwhites lived. While Pedro was not totally separated from people of color (he lived in an ethnically diverse city and attended schools with students of color), neither was he immersed in the cultural life of a Chicano barrio, the experience that tends to define understandings of "authentic" Chicano identity.

Pedro's disclosure to other Chicano students that he was "not really 100 percent" Chicano, and the question "that's okay isn't it?" seems intended as a protective measure—to let them know before they find out—so as to ward off the unpleasant consequences he anticipates if he is "found out" later. That he and his friends were "laughing nervously" when they talked about all being multiracial suggests that something was at stake in declaring they were multiracial that they were not quite sure they wanted to risk. The major consequence of such an unmasking, Pedro suggests, is a loss of acceptance by the group to which he only tentatively belongs.

Path to Activism

At the college he attended in the 1970s, a time when political and social life on campus was structured by deep ethnoracial division, Pedro was a leader *in spite of,* not because he was multiracial. It is this conditional acceptance that moves him to seek involvement with other individuals of multiple ancestry. Many times he tested the waters to see in what ways he might be able to explore and assert a multiracial identity. Shortly after college, Pedro made his first attempt to organize with other multiracials. He sent letters to many multiracial acquaintances about starting a group but received no responses. He recalls that, "I could hear the embarrassed silence." No one, it seemed to him, wanted to risk associating together on the basis of multiraciality because of the stigma such an identity carried. It would be a few more years before

Pedro would find an already existing group for multiracial families, in which he would quickly take on a leadership role.

Yet upon finding a multiracial group to join, Pedro was still a bit apprehensive; worried that he would have to justify his place in the group because he is not a black/white multiracial. As he tells it, black/white is the paradigmatic "mixed" person in U.S. history and consciousness. He had worried that others assume being black/white was the most difficult position to be in as a mixed person, and that people of other ethnoracial "combinations" would be considered—even by other multiracials—if not less "real," less entitled to "complain" about their dilemmas. He had prepared himself for the arguments he anticipated having to make, reaffirming to himself that, "Hell, I have a stake in this too. I'm not going to shut up," at the same time that he still wondered "Do I have a voice here? Can I have a voice here?" To Pedro's surprise, he faced no such challenge: "They were happy to see me. And I was taken aback. I didn't expect that. I thought I was going to be at war right away. I was ready with all my arguments. So maybe this is kind of defensive if you look at—there may be a defensive way to look at it." Like Xavier, Pedro's dilemmas of authenticity come up not only in relation to "monoracials" (in this case, Chicanos) but also in relation to other people of mixed descent (this time from black/white multiracials).[18]

For Pedro, becoming very involved in multiracial causes and asserting a multiracial identity was a way to manage the ambivalence and stigma associated with being multiracial. Through organizing with like-minded people who were similarly positioned in America's racial regime, he sought to achieve the sense of authenticity and *respect* that was fleeting for him when he acted in an "overcompensating multiracial" role. The search for respect guides Pedro's intense devotion to changing U.S. racial categories, which he has pursued despite personal and financial costs to himself. He sought collective solutions to formerly private dilemmas because he understood early on that private solutions (like therapy, for example) would not suffice. Authenticity would elude him and other multiracials if the state did not confer symbolic legitimacy on multiracial identity in the form of counting it and making it appear to exist.

And then the next thing is, then where do you fit? Because I . . . I could [not] just neutralize this issue. It always comes back to me. I'm not treated as if I'm white. I'm treated ever since I can remember—it's assumed I'm Latino so I knew I wasn't going to get away from that. So it's sort of like, well, how do you deal—how do you address this?

Q. Where does the sense of being a fraud come [from]?

A. It comes from being in situations among Mexicans, not among whites, and realizing—and they're also realizing very strongly—that you ain't Mexican, not like you think you are. And I'm sure the same thing may happen to people from other backgrounds as well. Even an American black who goes to Africa immediately discovers the real world. My God, like all the color drains from me (chuckles). But I think once you realize that, you have to say, wait a minute, *I am legitimate in my identity*. I am not one or the other. I am but I'm also not. And some of it is a matter of dignity or ego. You have to center yourself in that authenticity of where you really are. Otherwise, I don't think you can really function. Also, I don't think you can speak with authority. People won't respect you. We're getting more respect now being recognized as multiracial people. There's a lot of initial, "Oh, you're messing things up. You're making it hard for—outright hostility, you know, they don't like the idea of interracial at all. After a while we've built up some respect.

Like Xavier and Lareina, the social properties that expose Pedro to experiences wherein multiracial identity becomes an existential dilemma are the same ones that allow him to become a multiracial entrepreneur. Pedro's educational inheritance and achievements and spatial isolation from other Chicanos contribute to his cultural isolation from them as well. This education, however, provides him with the skills to relate dilemmas over who he is personally to broader legal issues regarding racial classification, to articulate them to other people of mixed descent, and to address them concretely with his skills as a lawyer.

Story 4. "Hapa" All His life: Steve Tomita

Steve Tomita lives just blocks away from his alma mater. I arrive one December morning, a day after he has completed a business school final exam. I have not seen Steve in several months and have not talked in depth about his activities on multiracial issues since I first interviewed him three years prior. At that time, Steve had just helped form an organization for multiracial Asian Americans. Unlike most college alumni who leave behind associations joined in college, Steve has maintained a leadership position in the group, allowing him to fulfill his dream of making it a national organization, even if at this stage this is more true on paper than in terms of actual organizations and membership.

Steve greets me at the door, apologizing for the state of his apartment, which to me seems quite neat, save for the random pieces of paper scattered near his computer, evidence of the end-of-semester frenzy that marks the seasons of a student's life. Ever the group leader, Steve jibes me again about when I'm going to start supporting his organization by becoming a (paying) member. I laugh and say (yet again), "Just send me the material and I'll look it over."

Evidence of the degree of his involvement in the group is not immediately apparent in his sparsely decorated apartment. I realize later that's only because Steve has a large closet, one that is stuffed to overflowing, it seems, with "hapa"[19] paraphernalia: posters announcing "upcoming" but now long past events; reference materials on multiracial issues; overstock pamphlets, some designed by Steve, describing the mission and aims of the group. As a friendly (and [marketing]) gesture, Steve offers me a T-shirt with the words "Hapa Power" emblazoned on the back.

The T-shirt, like Steve himself, conveys a playful approach to identity, not the seriousness or militancy usually associated with phrases like "Black Power." Easy with a laugh, Steve often wears a wry smile, quick to see the ironic humor in any situation. Other members in the group seem to share this sense of play. An upcoming issue of the hapa newsletter, Steve tells me in our first interview, will include a discussion of what Steve calls "the chameleon factor"—the ability of hapas to blend into their surroundings, or rather, how others often attribute ethnic membership to them based on the setting in which they find themselves and their physical ambiguity. Steve, with his dark hair and eyes and slim, medium-tall build has often been mistaken for Latino and Italian. "One thing we're going to do for the newsletter," he tells me. "It's like the big joke, 'Find the Hapa in the Picture' " (he laughs).

Yet this sense of fun in talking about multiracial identity belies the seriousness with which Steve approaches his work as a multiracial entrepreneur. Now twenty-seven-years-old, Steve has devoted much of his time to the group since it was founded five years earlier. Such dedication to his cause is mirrored in the passionate way he describes his decision to collectively organize other hapas and assert a public multiracial identity. Forming an organization for multiracial Asians, he says, came out of an "inner burning desire" to challenge the negative depiction of hapas put forth in monoethnic, especially Asian, communities. He was moved to act after an Asian American guest speaker in a college history class presented a lecture on the impact of increasing rates of outmarriage in Asian American communities. In the lecture, according to Steve, the speaker suggested that intermarriages are always tainted by the unequal gender and racial hierarchies in which they occur, and as such, the individuals within such marriages could not possibly truly love each other. Upon hearing the lecture, Steve says: "[I had] an inner burning desire and I was just waiting to get out and get on a soap box—I think really because I've been hapa all my life. I don't know what else to compare it to and I never presumed anything was wrong or icky about it or anything."

Judging from the way Steve describes his racial identity before that fateful day in history class, however, one would be hard pressed to have predicted the degree of activity he has since devoted to "hapa" issues. For him, being multiracial was normal, not "icky"—something he had always seen himself as being. Unlike Lareina, Xavier, and Pedro, the normalcy Steve attributed to mixedness came *not* out of a long work of trying to reconcile himself with a stigmatized identity. Up to that pivotal moment in history class, Steve says, he had not really given much thought to how multiracials were perceived: "Before (that class) I had never really thought of it, how mixed race people relate to the rest of society or identity issues or cultural issues. Just up until then it was just naturally me and I'd go without thinking about it."

At other points in the interview, he described himself as not very racially conscious. His parents, he says, never talked about race. Steve's father, a second generation Japanese American, was the first person to marry a non-Japanese person in his family. Married before to a woman of Japanese ancestry who later died, Steve's father has a son from that marriage, who Steve considers a brother "in every way." While he had contact with the Japanese side of his family, spending family and Japanese cultural holidays with them, Steve's paternal grandmother spoke no English so establishing a close relationship with her was, Steve says, difficult.

Much closer to his maternal grandmother, and to his mother who is white, Steve described his greater familiarity with "white culture" as coming "easier" to him, primarily because it's "unavoidable" in U.S. society. It's the side that doesn't come easier to him (Japanese) that he is engaged in an effort to challenge. Steve's mother seems to have shielded him and herself from racial insults. Steve recalls that his mother actively avoided reading about interracial families: "[B]ecause she has like this overall fear that she's going to turn the page and find out some scholar somewhere is going to say the exact thing that she had done, you know, raising me was the most terrible, rotten thing that you could do."

Even though his parents did not explicitly talk about racial issues with him, Steve did develop a sense of what it meant to be Japanese early on: "The things I remember about race, like, one I looked at my father's old photo album and photos from the internment camp and I am the same age as he was, looking at them when he was an intern and why were you there, so I guess that would make an impression In that respect we were talking about race, you know, kind of [in] a simple [way]."

Yet asserting that he is part Japanese, Steve believes, has less to do with identifying with his father than with the collective struggle of other Japanese Americans. While as a boy he may have related to being Japanese through his father's experience, he no longer does. As he has gotten older, Steve has become estranged from his father and learned more about Japanese American history through his education.

I first interviewed Steve when he was twenty-four years old, at which time he described his racial identity as "half-Japanese and half-white," and said he does not identify "fully as either one," something with which he appears to be very comfortable. The difference between the difficulties of Lareina, Xavier, and Pedro, and the relative ease with which Steve seems to have negotiated his multiracial position, stem in part from demography and generation. Unlike Lareina, Xavier, and Pedro, Steve came of age in a place (northern California) and time (the 1980s and early 1990s) in which being in an interracial family and talking about a multiracial identity were very much *less* stigmatized, and almost normalized, particularly for multiracials of Asian/white parentage. Steve grew up around many multiracial kids; he says:

[A]nd it never phased me as weird until, not that it's weird now but I mean I never thought hey there is this interracial couple and there's the other one, you know, it wasn't like that. I had friends that were black and white and Asian and white . . . But you know it went both ways. There were people who had like, you know, a Japanese mom and a white dad and a Japanese dad and a white mom and a black mom and a white dad and a black dad and a white mom—you get what I'm trying to say (laughs).

Even within Steve's family, he says, there are "more and more white people and then little hapa kids" at family reunions, a smaller scale representation of the demographic changes taking place in the Japanese American community at large. Steve was not isolated from other multiracial kids—they were at school, his friends, and part of the family—and thus he did not experience feelings of being significantly different from his peers.

Steve is also younger than the other activists profiled here, crossing the private-to-public threshold at a younger age (twenty-three years old) in a place (a college campus) where there are many persons in like circumstances, he is unconflicted about organizing with other individuals of multiple heritage. He feels no need to test the waters of multiracial acceptance like Pedro did, no need to alter his identity to express multiplicity in identity like Xavier, and his descriptions of being with other hapas reflect none of the dramatic tension encapsulated in the "coming out" parallel Lareina used to speak about first joining a group.

Path to Activism

The relative ease with which Steve approaches his multiracial identity is important for understanding his somewhat quick transition to action. It is when he is confronted with less-than-flattering beliefs about Asian/white intermarried couples, in a setting that lent such views legitimacy (the academy), that the relative ease he had enjoyed before was challenged, and he felt it personally. As he put it, the event in history class was: "[T]he first time that I had really heard it in my face, articulated in such a nasty style, kind of ignorant tone was in that class and I was just ghastly offended, as were a lot of the other people in the class, because it was insulting. I'd never been—no one had ever been that rude to me essentially. It angered me."

Interestingly, Steve was most affronted by the stereotypes about intermarried couples the speaker was putting forth, and he was not reacting to any characterization of the multiracial children of these unions. I asked him if he had been aware of the perception that multiracial Asian Americans in ethnic communities with the highest outmarriage rates had been characterized as representing the cultural and physical "death" of those communities. Steve said he had not heard of such characterizations before, not having been involved in Japanese American clubs as a kid, but learned of them later.

Steve felt disgusted that people "who should know better" (because they have been victims of racial oppression) have chosen to exclude others on equally arbitrary grounds. This concern, which fueled his motivation to challenge Japanese American community rules, parallels a story Steve told me about his father:

[W]e were going to take some camping trip somewhere and my brother—I got to take one of my friends. We were on a vacation or something and I got to take one of my friends and one of my brothers (unintelligible) this guy Cooke who was black. I don't remember exactly how it broke down but the bottom line was my dad wasn't going to let Butch Cooke come because Butch Cooke was black was the bottom line, and I remember being pissed off about that. This was again when I was probably under ten years old and it just seemed completely arbitrary and made no sense that Butch Cooke couldn't come with us because he was black. I mean obviously in retrospect someone who had been subject to the nastiest form of racism that there is, being jailed for it . . . and then turning around and being equally as petty and lashing out.

One gets the sense that he had never had to really assert that he was "multiracial," because he was never explicitly challenged to choose sides or declare allegiances to one group. If bodily gestures could describe one's disposition toward their identity, Steve's multiracial identity would be better represented by a shrug of the shoulders than by a clenched fist. "It's no big deal, really," he seems to say. This laid-back, self-evident approach to his multiracial identity is reflected in how Steve understands his activism around multiracial issues. When Steve and others formed the organization for people of partial Asian ancestry, there already existed another campus group for multiracial students, this one without a specific ethnic focus. Steve did not seek to join this group because, as he put it:

[That group] was primarily like a social group or even sort of more of focusing on being kind of a nurturing or supportive environment. It wasn't action oriented and I didn't really want to spend a whole lot of time sitting around in a circle talking to each other about how horrible it was to be mixed and all the other bad people out in the world. I wanted to go and educate people essentially—[the lecturer in history class's] problem was ignorance and for better or worse, at the time when she was doing her research, you know, how was she to know any different? There was no place for someone to go and look critically at what it means to be mixed race Asian American or hapa or whatever. There was a little bit of that tone in the Japanese American community, too, and I don't know—the whole thing was getting stuck with the responsibility of being the end of the community and the end of the world as you know it.

For Steve, "sitting around in a circle talking to each other about how horrible it was to be mixed" simply did not resonate with his experience being multiracial. To him, the negative stereotypes of mixed descent people that he had only recently been confronted with were in his words "blather," ludicrous, and not worth lamenting. Yet why, one might ask, did Steve get so involved in a group that sought to educate Asian Americans in particular to disabuse them of their wrongheaded beliefs? Goffman (1963) argues that representatives of stigmatized people are often called upon to play an "educational" role for those considered normal, which is predicated on their position as stigmatized persons. This educational role is most often oriented toward convincing "normals" that stigmatized people are "just like them."

After that day in history class, through his involvement with the other hapa students in the class, Steve learned more about the particular mechanisms in place that discriminated against people of partial Asian ancestry in the Japanese American community. He describes this period as his "political awakening," after which he had to become involved "on principle":

> [T]here's like these weird rules in the basketball, Japanese American basketball leagues, youth leagues, that say there has to be so many people with Japanese last names and that's what really got me cookin'. Uh, you know and then there's like the Miss Cherry Blossom Festival and like this one girl in the class was the first hapa girl ever to have won it and they were really surprised that she could speak Japanese, and all that kind of stuff . . . So I mean I didn't really want to be part of those things but it just pissed me off on principle that if I wanted to participate in them that there was people somewhere, there was a system set up that they could make it difficult for me, for no other reason than just because I was mixed.

Unlike Lareina, Xavier, and Pedro, who dealt with existential dilemmas privately for quite some time, Steve did not have such dilemmas (or at least did not divulge them to me) and so did not have to struggle on his own to resolve them. When he became aware of the negative beliefs others held about hapas, he immediately sought collective solutions to this challenge to his identity. The very same social properties that led him to an awareness of the problems of multiracials are the ones that allow him to create public solutions to them. First, he is embedded in a college milieu wherein he has access to others who share his grievances (beginning with the other students in history class) and resources (campus support for the creation of a student group) with which to nurture the development of a fledgling organization. Second, he comes to realize the stigmatized view of hapas at a point in time where other multiracials have already begun to organize collectively, providing a model and lending legitimacy to such an undertaking. Third, his education and "on-the-job" training as a student organizer have given him the skills (knowledge of history of Japanese American political organizations, how to get funding, managing an entrepreneurial organization) that have allowed him to grow his "business" of getting hapas to be seen and recognized by Asian Americans and by the wider culture.

Crossing the Private-to-Public Threshold

These four stories illustrate the existential dilemmas many individuals of mixed race face. Ever present in their stories of personal dilemmas, however, is a social context that shapes that experience. The dilemmas described by multiracial entrepreneurs come not by virtue of "being" of multiple ancestry, for if we were to magically transport our multiracial entrepreneurs to another place (for example, Brazil), their dilemmas cease to be the same, and the construction of mixed identity put forth by them no longer makes sense. Their dilemmas must arise, therefore, out of a particular social context.

Cultural Constructions of Mixedness and Deviance

Multiracials are considered deviant by the standards of American culture.[20] According to Goffman (1963), one becomes labeled as deviant, or feels that he carries a stigma when, in certain contexts and under certain conditions, he violates or is said to have violated a set of social rules—rules that define which actions are right and good and which actions are wrong and bad in a given context. Stigmatized individuals are unable or unwilling to conform to standards deemed normal.

The rigidness of racial division—which insists both that all individuals possess race and have one and only one race—makes those who identify themselves as multiracial outsiders in the prevailing racial scheme of things. In violating these racial rules, their character has been called into question, and they have been labeled "confused," "disloyal," and "weak." Many informants talked about the conditional acceptance they often got from groups of color—an acceptance liable to be revoked if the suspicion that they are not really loyal to the group is confirmed. Asserting that one is multiracial (as opposed to black, Asian, Chicana, and so forth) is often taken as sufficient evidence of such disloyalty and contributes to a stereotype of people of mixed descent as "suspect."[21]

The characterization that they are deviant from dominant racial norms engenders in many people of mixed heritage feelings of ambivalence and inauthenticity, a theme present in much of the newly emergent literature by persons of multiple ancestry (McBride 1997; McReynolds 1997; G. H. Williams 1996). Multiracials express mutually conflicting thoughts and feelings about many aspects of experience, from being "forced to choose" between racial affiliations to being stigmatized for not doing so. The imperative to "choose one," gives rise to questions like, "who am I?" "what am I?" "where do I fit?" The dilemmas these multiracials describe are about confronting the same challenges: to ward off challenges to their sanity and character, and to be seen and recognized as existing, all the while resisting the temptation to give into the deceptive promise offered by white supremacy—that one can escape a stigmatized status through the belief in and connection to whiteness.

Grappling with feelings of ambivalence and encountering cultural messages that one should know what one "is" racially and where one stands politically subjects those who feel ambivalent to accusations (and internal thoughts) that they are less "real" and therefore less legitimate than others.

Lareina, Xavier, and Pedro describe their racial identity in Goffmanesque terms, using theatrical metaphors to convey the sense that they have been "wearing a mask" or "playing a role." But whereas Goffman and other symbolic interactionists understand role playing to be an inevitable dimension of social life, these informants see it as a problem to overcome. For them, playing a role is *inauthentic* and makes them feel fraudulent and deceptive.

Interpretation, Emotion, and Action

Despite the variety of experiences they have had, the stories of Lareina, Xavier, Pedro, and Steve share similar interpretive and emotional qualities. Their stories comprise what Goffman (1963) called a "moral career"—a narrative composed of those crucial turning points by which members of a stigmatized category come to terms with and attempt to transform that stigmatization and themselves.[22] Each *interprets* his or her situation in a particular way: first, coming to understand that the perception and treatment of multiracials is wrong, and that in a crucial way, this violates a value that each holds sacred. Yet they would not act on a perceived violation, unless they felt sufficiently aggrieved about it. In other words, not only do our four multiracial entrepreneurs have an interpretive understanding of their positions, but they *feel* that violation to be meaningful. Each describes feeling humiliation, shame, offense, and in some cases, rage (what Katz [1988] calls the "moral emotions"). Finally, our multiracial entrepreneurs *act* on their understandings and feelings about their existential dilemmas. The activities in which they engage (attending meetings with other people of mixed heritage, writing congressional testimony, rallying others, and so forth) shore up the sense that they are not alone, that the stigma they feel is generated not from their personal failings, but rather from the social rules set up by others. This activity is crucial for maintaining the interpretation and emotional posture that lead them to becoming multiracial entrepreneurs in the first place.

Knowing about the existential dilemmas multiracial entrepreneurs grapple with, the ways multiracials are stigmatized in U.S. culture, and how they interpret and feel about both is important for understanding the desires, dreams, hopes, and hurts motivating these people and their activities. Those pieces of the puzzle, while important, leave us to wonder why these individuals, and not others, have taken up this cause. For while people of mixed descent may be stigmatized in U.S. culture, it is also true that few multiracials interpret, feel, or act on their dilemmas in the same way or to the same extent as these multiracial entrepreneurs have. In the next section I look at the social properties that position these individuals as the likely candidates to interpret these dilemmas as dilemmas, to feel them to be meaningful, and to act upon them collectively.

Historical Conditions of Possibility

As C. Wright Mills (1959) pointed out, our lives represent the "intersection of biography and history." That is, the broad economic, political, and cultural relations of the times in which we live shape who we are and what we do. Moreover, our position within a social context shapes our self-conceptions, perceptions, and experience of the world within which we find ourselves. Bourdieu advances Mills's understanding of the relationship between biography and history with his notion of habitus. Bourdieu conceives of habitus as social structure embodied, manifest in the mental categories one uses, and in the very desires that we experience as "personal" and generated from within. One's sense of position in social space, and agents' categories of perception of the social world represent a "practical mastery" of the world as it is, an "embodied" social structure. These categories of perception are taken for granted as how the world is and, as such, incline agents to accept the social world in which their habitus was formed as it is.

Yet the "fit" between biography and history, as McAdam (1988) points out, is not always seamless—times sometimes change in unanticipated ways, presenting a disjuncture between the lives we were raised to expect and the world that we encounter. With such unanticipated changes, "individuals confront new possibilities for social action and self-conception."

Generation. Lareina, Pedro, and Xavier were born during America's baby boom (1946–64), in a time of unprecedented economic and social optimism. They are part of the first generation around which a distinct youth subculture developed, in which extraordinary national attention was focused on the young. The two combined created what Doug McAdam describes as a "unique sense of generational identity and 'history-making' potency among the young" (1988, 17) and made them "prime candidates" for collective political action.

Lareina and Pedro both mentioned the civil rights movement—either their own personal involvement in it or that of their parents—as formative for their development of a sense of justice and the confidence that collective action could redress their grievances. In this, multiracial entrepreneurs typify the larger sample of multiracials in this study. While most respondents are too young to have themselves participated in civil rights activities of the 1960s, more than half recalled their parents' involvement and cited both their example and the ethos of that time as inspiring their activities. In particular, they cite its humanist pleas and values of interracialism as particularly relevant to what they are doing today.

Yet while all four multiracial entrepreneurs invoke the civil rights movement as the ideological ground on which their actions stand, their politics have also been profoundly shaped by a competing political ideology—that of Black Power. Multiracial politics have been constructed largely in opposition to the group separatism popularized through Black Power and taken up by other "official" ethnic groups. They see the authenticity tests to which they are so often subjected as by-products of separatist ideology, forcing them to declare ethnic allegiance in order to be deemed a worthy member of the group (recall Xavier's refusal to identify himself as black in college, despite pressure from others to do so).

Ethnic honor and social existence. Black Power and the civil rights movement provided new ways of understanding race that inform contemporary multiracial politics. Each brought into the open, through their explicit discussion of racial inequality, a long-standing American ethos that equates social honor with ethnic honor.[23] To exist in American society is to possess an ethnoracial identity—one that is recognized by the state and treated with dignity and equality. Both movements were oriented toward recouping the ethnic honor of African Americans. In particular, Black Power's emphasis on taking pride in, declaring and expressing racial identity, and the interpretation of such actions as indicative of the psychological and social health of black people forms the context within which demands for multiracial identity are couched. Pedro repeatedly described his actions as continuations of the civil rights struggle. Through ethnic recognition, individuals of multiple ancestry would gain respect. And as Lareina and Xavier explained, such respect would confirm the essential humanity of multiracials.

Despite the psychological resonance that the civil rights and Black Power movements have for multiracial entrepreneurs, much of their active organizational work began in an era (the early 1980s) when the urgency and organization that fueled these movements had ebbed. While these multiracials may have long felt that their personal racial identity was different from what they thought they were *supposed* to declare publicly, by the 1980s they sought to make their public and private identities consistent. Much like the "turn toward the self," [24] truth, and authenticity visible in other movements of the era (such as gay liberation and the women's movement), concerns over self-realization have replaced preoccupations with political allegiance to monoracial groups in shaping expressions of identity for people of mixed ancestry. The concern with self-actualization is evident in the stories of Lareina and Xavier (and more obliquely in Pedro's) when they describe their public claiming of a multiracial identity as a "coming out" ("It felt like we were coming out of the closet" and "You would have thought we were gay").

Biographical and Structural Conditions of Possibility

While it may be true that what people do stems from the confluence of "biography and history," it is also true that the impact of changes in historical circumstances is not equally felt by all. Where one sits in social space is crucially important for understanding which, how, and why people think, feel, and act in the ways they do and why others do not.

The college milieu. College life exposed these entrepreneurs to a set of experiences that profoundly reshaped their understandings of multiracial identity. The college campus is a site wherein the dilemmas of multiethnicity are brought to the fore (Renn 2004). The U.S. college is a highly particular social milieu, in which social life among students is highly stratified by race. Moreover, students are repeatedly asked to self-designate their race (on virtually all applications from admission to scholarships to financial aid, in housing decisions, and so forth). On campus young adults live together, often for the first time away from the direct authority of parents, and they are expected to discover for themselves who they "really are." For many students, particularly students of color, this often means "discovering" who they are racially.[25]

For Lareina, Xavier, Pedro, and Steve, this meant discovering that the ways of understanding and negotiating race that they had learned in their families and neighborhoods were not the same as those operating in college. In college these informants are faced with confronting the meaning of asserting a multiracial identity in political terms, rather than the familial terms in which it had been meaningful to them. While Xavier's description of himself as "tan" may have been tolerated by his family, at college he was going to be ostracized for it. The sense of normalcy about mixed identity that Steve had cultivated among family and friends was called into question on campus, while Pedro's involvement in ethnically based student organizations brought feelings of being a fraud front and center.

Their feelings of being "misfits," then, emerge out of a *mismatch* between their habitus and the new field (college life) in which they find themselves. For these multiracial entrepreneurs, entry into college life triggers and/or heightens their racialized existential dilemmas. The sense of inauthenticity that each expressed feeling (or were aware that others attributed to them) arose not necessarily because each disagreed with the political goals of other students of color. Rather, they felt inauthentic because demonstrating ethnic loyalty usually requires one to demonstrate their ethnic "credentials"—a variety of dispositional characteristics (such as accent, language proficiency, dress, hairstyle), physical attributes (such as skin color, hair texture), class (particularly personal experience with poverty), and other criteria (such as being the victim of discrimination) that serve as emblems of authenticity.[26] These multiracial entrepreneurs, raised with limited contact to the communities to which they are presumed to belong (by virtue of their physical appearance or ancestry), do not possess the appropriate dispositions and cultural knowledge to secure their authenticity. Their sense of being inauthentic, then, comes not by virtue of having mixed ancestry, but because key aspects of their biographies do not fit with those of others.

While these kinds of experiences created dilemmas of belonging for Lareina, Xavier, Pedro, and Steve, they also helped shape their understandings of the particular grievances they had with dominant ways of understanding race. Experiences like these proved to be catalysts for their assertions of a very public multiracial identity.[27]

Education and class.   Perhaps more than any other factors, the educational and class backgrounds of these informants suggest why they, and not others, have become multiracial entrepreneurs. While the details of their stories differ, our multiracial entrepreneurs are quite similar to each other in educational terms, yet highly *unusual* from the population at large. First, while none has particularly high economic capital, they were all raised and currently live in middle-class circumstances.[28] Second, each has above-average levels of education (among them two master's degrees, a law degree, and a doctorate). Not only do these informants possess high levels of education, their parents do also. Except for Lareina, all of these activists had at least one parent who attained a college degree. Both Xavier's and Pedro's parents earned graduate degrees. This educational attainment and inheritance distinguishes them from the average U.S. citizen, but especially so from nonwhite Americans.

This educational inheritance contributes to their social distance from other persons of color, one that was highlighted in their educational experiences. Yet it also provides the skills necessary to compete as multiracial entrepreneurs. Higher education in the United States encourages students to think of themselves as autonomous individuals who think *for* themselves and are endowed with the ability to impact the society in which they live. Their specific training (in law, history, business, and engineering) also provides the practical skills to articulate and organize other multiracials. Moreover, each is engaged in occupations (lawyer, professor, sales) that require them to reflect on social issues or in workplace settings wherein racial politics are continually present. (In Lareina's corporate environment and Steve's and Xavier's college campuses, affirmative action is widely debated; Pedro works as a civil rights attorney).

Geography (spatial and social).   Finally, where informants were raised and currently live has shaped their trajectories toward becoming multiracial entrepreneurs. Each currently lives in urbanized centers with ethnically diverse populations. Moreover, these cities are in regions with significant numbers of multiracial people, providing a context where multiraciality is more normalized than in other regions and a population available to be galvanized.

Equally important to their stories is the spatial and social distance from ethnic communities when they were growing up. Each of our multiracial entrepreneurs was raised on the margins of the ethnic communities of their ancestries—not fully immersed in either community socially, culturally, and for all except Xavier, geographically. Family connections did not always bridge those distances. Lareina, while intimately familiar with her Portuguese heritage through her connections to her grandmother, was relatively isolated from her black and Indian family and those traditions. Steve, estranged from his father, was less conversant in Japanese cultural traditions than with "generic" white ones.

At first glance, it seems that a combination of luck, circumstance, and sense of personal calling lead these informants to their positions as multiracial entrepreneurs. Certainly. Yet each possesses particular social properties that make them ideally suited to becoming multiracial entrepreneurs. Their education, occupation, family experiences, geographical location, and generation shape how they see their circumstances, the problems they identify as such, and the means they have to address them. Armed with their particular confluence of cultural capital, and located in areas that provide opportunities for them to meet similarly situated and like-minded people (urbanized, ethnically diverse cities with relatively high multiracial populations), they are poised to address their dilemmas over multiracial identity *collectively*.

Finally, while we know why they are *able* to seek collective solutions to their dilemmas, we are left with the question of why they have sought such collective solutions (a kind of collective therapy) rather than individual solutions to address their dilemmas. The simple answer is that individual solutions just did not work. Lareina, Xavier, and Pedro struggled alone and remained unsatisfied. More importantly, once each had located the source of his or her troubles in the broader system of racial classification and racial logic, individual solutions were beside the point, and collective solutions were the only feasible means to address their grievances. Once the problem came to be defined in terms of social recognition of an ethnic population—a status that only the state has the legitimate power to bestow—multiracial activists knew they needed to work collectively, since changing the state's rules would require the work of more than one individual.

The dilemmas of multiracial entrepreneurs are only partly "racial"—that is, they are as much about existential concerns with self-identity as they are about race. At the same time, these existential dilemmas only appear to be "personal"—unique, idiosyncratic, and originating in the private circumstances of their lives. Instead, the dilemmas these multiracials describe and the particular constellation of emotions they feel about these dilemmas (confusion, rage, loneliness, and so forth) are shaped by (and shape) their objective social position (class, education, occupation) in a racially stratified society. The social context in which they live overdetermines the kinds of questions these multiracials ask of themselves and provides the impetus for them to resolve their private dilemmas through collective means.

4 Making Multiracial Families

IN 2005, THE SECOND ANNUAL LOVING DAY CELEBRATION was held in New York City. The celebration is part of a larger campaign to build support for making June 12—the day in 1967 that the U.S. Supreme Court declared antimiscegenation laws unconstitutional—a national holiday. The Loving Day campaign is the brainchild of Ken Tanabe, a twenty-seven-year-old graphic designer who has produced a series of video public service announcements to raise awareness of the *Loving v. Virginia* case. "Americans learn about landmark civil rights cases such as *Plessy v. Ferguson* and *Brown v. Board of Education*, but many of us have never heard of *Loving v. Virginia*," says Tanabe. "[S]ince interracial relationships are still an issue, Loving Day encourages us to think about our civil rights and how they apply to us today" (Tanabe 2005).

The Loving Day campaign explicitly links issues of civil rights and racial justice to the legal and social acceptance of interracial relationships and families—a theme that runs throughout multiracials' collective organizing. As we saw earlier, the attempt to create a new multiracial label grew in part out of a desire to make visible and legitimize family relationships that are often not assumed by others—relationships between people who appear "racially different."[1] That multiracial politics and collective organizing have to do with families is not surprising when we consider that, for most of U.S. history, the state actively prevented the formation of families across racial lines, and interracial sex and family relationships have been considered taboo. Those who are organizing on the basis of multiracial identification are attempting to legitimize their own interracial families and the very idea of interracial kinship itself. The project of "making multiracials," in other words, is inseparable from the project of making multiracial families.

Loving Day Promotional Campaign.

In this chapter I explore why family issues are central to multiracial organizing. Local community organizations like Biracial Family Network in Chicago, I-Pride in Berkeley, and MASC among others, were formed explicitly to address issues of social isolation and stigma facing interracial families. These groups are largely comprised of parents of mixed race children, a substantial proportion of whom are white women. As a cohort, these parents were relatively uninvolved in the issue of federal racial classification and are more focused on local projects that provide support for themselves and their families. In college-based organizations formed by mixed race students, issues of family are central to their formation as well.

My respondents tried to address dilemmas that racial difference within the family posed with both individual and collective strategies, managing relationships within their own families, and through union with other multiracial families. Whereas policies of racial segregation in public and private realms prevented the creation of families across racial lines, these respondents have organized to actively construct and maintain interracial family bonds. In effect, they attempt to move multiracial families from being a cultural contradiction in terms to a realized social category. They seek to extend the cultural obligation to love one's family members across racial boundaries, and in so doing, they help to make "multiracial families" exist.

The Disappearance of Interracial Families

Lena, a black/white woman, recalls what is was like when her large family was out in public:

> We came to expect that complete strangers would approach us, bending down for a closer look and smiling enthusiastically as they commented on how "beautiful" we all were. It almost felt as if they were trying to figure out which parts of us were white, which black, and which too blended to really tell the difference. To the liberal-types we were their equivalent of poster children for racial harmony. But other times I sensed that some people thought we were freaky.

Assessments of racial difference inform our interpretations of familial relatedness and responsibility. When people stare at multiracial families in public, when they are "horrified" at the prospect of having a racially different son-in-law and grandchildren, and when they "match" families in public according to how they look, they are attempting to reconcile the intimacy displayed between differently "raced" people acting like family with their own racialized conceptions of what families are supposed to look like. While this can be interpreted as relatively benign ("racial harmony") or hostile ("freaky"), Lena's story underscores that in either case, the multiracial family is positioned as an object to be gazed *at*.

Lena's story is a common one among my respondents and points to the peculiar cultural position of interracial families. Such families are highly visible because they violate racial norms of what families are supposed to look like. Their visibility today is due to the fact that attempts to make them *in*visible in the past were so successful. The category "multiracial family" is a recent creation. For most of U.S. history, multiracial families did not exist as such and were actively prevented from forming. The social nonexistence of interracial families was first established during slavery and was maintained through law and social policy thereafter. Rules governing racial classification and antimiscegenation laws forbade sex and marriage, the transfer of property, and public acknowledgment of relations between persons of different racial categories.

In her review of antimiscegenation case law, Rachel Moran (2001) traces how the doctrine of "separate but equal" in the realm of sex, marriage, and family was institutionalized through the court system. Antimisecegenation statutes were important tools through which distinctions between the political equality newly afforded blacks during Reconstruction and *social* equality, which whites were unwilling to grant them, were wrought. In the early years of Reconstruction some bans on racial intermarriage were struck down. The Alabama Supreme Court did so in *Burns v. State* (1872), arguing that marriage was a contract, and blacks had the right to enter all contracts that whites could. Five years later, however, the Alabama Supreme Court overturned the *Burns* decision, arguing that the state had a compelling interest in regulating marriage to promote the general welfare and that miscegenation undermined it. Racial difference was deemed so profound that intermarriage would necessarily undermine family life and therefore social life. Over the next five years, restrictions on interracial marriage and sex were further entrenched, culminating in the U.S. Supreme Court's 1882 decision declaring such restrictions constitutional (*Pace v. Alabama*).[2] In the wake of this decision, "twenty states and territories added or strengthened bans in interracial sex and marriage between 1880 and 1920" (Moran 2001, 80). By 1940, thirty states had antimiscegenation laws (Roberts 1997, 71). The right of states to restrict interracial marriage would remain in place for close to 80 years when in 1967 the U.S. Supreme Court declared such laws unconstitutional in *Loving v. Virginia*.[3]

Bourdieu (1996) has pointed out that what we take for granted as "family" (which is always an arbitrary definition that has been legitimated and imposed as natural) is only possible under certain social conditions. These conditions, such as a shared residence and legal relationship, are in no way universal or even uniformly distributed. As such, the family is "a privilege instituted into a universal norm," from which those who conform enjoy a "symbolic profit of normality." Antimiscegenation case history demonstrates how interracial kinship was made *abnormal*. Throughout most of U.S. history, the major privileges that family membership tends to provide, and which in dominant discourse are definitional of family, such as access to a family name, household, and the accumulation and transmission of cultural, economic, and symbolic capital from one generation to the next—were restricted along racial lines. Antimiscegenation laws codified cultural notions about the undesirability of interracial kinship. In justifying these laws, proponents asserted the unnatural basis of interracial procreation and sexual relations and asserted the inferiority of mixed race offspring (D'Emilio and Freedman 1997 [1988], Nakashima 1992).[4] In legally and socially prohibiting interracial families, the normative "good" family was constructed as monoracial. As a result, interracial families have not enjoyed that symbolic profit of normality because of their racial mixedness.

While for most of U.S. history interracial families have been prevented from forming and interracial sex considered taboo, what then are the conditions that have allowed these families to emerge *as families?* Since the lifting of antimiscegenation laws in 1967, approval of racial intermarriage has increased steadily. A decade before interracial marriage was decriminalized in 1967, in 1958 the Gallup organization reported that 98 percent of whites (the only group polled) disapproved of interracial marriage. In the immediate aftermath of the civil rights movement and *Loving,* however, approval of intermarriage among whites had increased somewhat to 27 percent in 1972. In marked contrast, 76 percent of blacks approved of intermarriage in 1972. Over time, black and white attitudes toward intermarriage have converged, and acceptance of intermarriage overall has increased. In 1997, the year the OMB adopted its policy of enumerating multiple race responses, 67 percent of whites and 83 percent of blacks approved of intermarriage. By 2003, 73 percent of Americans said they approved of intermarriage (Gallup Organization 2004).

There is of course a difference between attitudes and behavior. While three quarters of the population may say they approve of racial intermarriage, very few Americans actually intermarry. Only about 13 percent of U.S. marriages were between differently classified individuals in 2000, up from about 3 percent in 1990 (Lee and Bean 2004). Very low numbers of intermarriages today testify that whom Americans love, care for, and feel responsible to is hardly natural and spontaneous but very much been shaped by racial division. A statistical manipulation illustrates the point. If marriages were randomly distributed with regard to race, we should expect that 45 percent of marriages would be between partners of different racial classifications.[5]

Low levels of intermarriage are partly an unintended effect of sedimented racial inequality and not necessarily racial prejudice. That is, whom one marries is shaped by whom one meets. Whom one meets is often shaped by income, education, and occupation, patterns of which are deeply shaped by race. But clearly, racial prejudice explains some of the reasons why racial intermarriage rates are so low. The stigma attached to interracial couples and multiracial families has not completely dissipated.[6] While three-quarters of Americans claim to approve of intermarriage, one-quarter openly admits to *disapproving* of such marriages. Given that survey takers are prone to provide answers they deem socially acceptable, it is likely that far more Americans disapprove of intermarriage than will admit it (Kuran 1995). Bonilla-Silva and Forman (2000) found that people responding to surveys are more likely to indicate favorable opinions of intermarriage, but when interviewed in-depth, they reveal much more opposition to such marriages, particularly within their own families. Even if we accept these relatively high approval rates at face value, inter-marriages are seen as next best alternatives to same race marriage. According to a survey conducted by the *Washington Post*, the Kaiser Foundation, and Harvard University, in 2001 "nearly half of all whites—more than any other group—still believe it is better for people to marry someone of their own race" (Fears and Deane 2001). A survey conducted by the Organization of Chinese Americans study in 1998 found an even stronger preference for endogamy. When presented the statement "I prefer that my children marry someone in the same ethnic group," 69 percent of Chinese American parents agreed or strongly agreed (Wu 2002, 268).

The overwhelming monoraciality of American families is taken for granted as natural and is seldom framed as a manifestation of racial segregation and a mechanism through which such segregation is reproduced. We tend to regard the fact that there is relatively little intermarriage as a matter of happenstance. American notions of love are guided by an ethos of romantic individualism. We imagine that decisions about whom we are attracted to, marry, and love are driven by the ineffable qualities of our partners (Illouz 1997; Moran 2001). Race is said to have little to do with it.

In the discussions that follow, respondents show just how much considerations of race still matter in family life and how those concerns lead them to organize collectively. In the course of describing why they became involved in multiracial organizations, respondents invariably talked about the dilemmas that the prospect of their monoracial families becoming multiracial ones created. Stories about a variety of issues came out, through which we see the presence and consequences of racialized understandings of family. In general, their concerns fell into four broad categories: (1) telling family members about interracial relationships; (2) relations with extended family, especially parents and grandparents, because of those relationships; (3) racial identification of children and changes experienced in parents' racial identifications; and (4) strangers' reactions to interracial families in public.

Guess Who's Coming to Dinner: "Coming Out" to Parents

Ann Fox, a white Jewish woman in her forties, recalls that during high school when a black classmate showed interest in dating her, her parents "forbade me to go out with him." So in college when she met and became attracted to Monroe, also black, Ann felt it better not to tell her parents about him. Instead, she devised various methods to keep her relationship with Monroe, and the fact that he was black, a secret from her parents. When describing Monroe to her parents, Ann stressed the platonic nature of their relationship. When Monroe sent her letters, she recommended that he use a pseudonym. By the time she knew she was in love with Monroe, the stress of keeping their relationship a secret caused her to become ill:

> I was so stressed out because I hadn't told my parents about the relationship and was very much involved and I was considering moving out after graduation to California and I just didn't know how I was going to tell them. My father had had a couple of heart attacks and I was worried about giving him another heart attack, being disowned, and my mother had been suffering from depression and I was worried about making her worse. I had a lot to worry about so I was driving myself crazy.

Aside from children, for the parents in my sample no other topic raised during my research generated an emotional response comparable to disclosing to relatives that one was romantically involved with someone of another racial category. Questions like "How did your parents react to your relationship?" or "How would you describe your relationship with your extended family?" often elicited detailed descriptions of fear, anxiety, shame, sadness, and anger that surrounded the initial revelation to relatives of one's interracial relationship. Sometimes these emotions seemed to remain for the respondent, while for others, they were presented as feelings from the past, bygone emotions with which the family had since gotten over. For no one, even those respondents who were met with acceptance by their parents, was the event not laden with emotion.

Revealing an interracial relationship to one's parents, grandparents, and siblings was an anxiety-producing experience that introduced a discussion of race into the family, one that for many respondents (particularly white ones) was, if not a taboo topic, an uncomfortable one to discuss. Respondents' stories read like the "coming out" stories of gays and lesbians and encompass similar kinds of struggles around the meaning of family, love, and self. Kath Weston writes that for gays and lesbians, "Coming out to a biological relative put to the test the unconditional love and enduring solidarity commonly understood in the United States to characterize blood ties . . . [C]oming out to biological kin produces a discourse destined to reveal the 'truth' not merely of the self, but of a person's kinship relations" (1991, 44). "Coming out" to one's parents left respondents vulnerable to utter "rejection," although it offered the possibility of complete "acceptance." It was the uncertainty of what they might find once they told family members that created the anxiety.

Of all the relatives who might accept or reject someone for "coming out" as part of an interracial relationship, these respondents seemed most concerned about the reaction of their parents. In keeping with prevailing cultural notions of family, respondents understood parents as "heads" of the family, vested with the power over financial resources as well as the power to determine who was and would remain a member of the family. Concerns over whether or not kin ties could be maintained in the light of their disclosure often depended on their parents' reactions. Indications of acceptance, their stories suggest, included verbal affirmations that this news did not affect their relationship ("You're still my daughter"), and actions like agreeing to meet the boyfriend or girlfriend. Respondents marked complete rejection with "disowning"—the severing of all material and emotional ties.

In actuality, few respondents received either unfettered acceptance or total rejection. More typically, parents' reactions fell somewhere in between these two poles. Moreover, parents often sent mixed messages about their feelings, indicating they were able to accept some aspects of the relationship, but not others.

Thus far I have characterized the issue about which respondents "came out" to their parents as having to do with their interracial romantic relationships. In terms of the questions such relationships raise for the family, however, it is important to distinguish between casual relationships and those that appeared to be headed toward marriage. Both the respondents and their parents distinguished between each type in their assessments of which ones potentially challenged the family's understanding of itself. More often than not, in anticipation of resistance from family, respondents only bothered to disclose their relationships to parents when they had begun to contemplate marriage. It was only when Ann Fox knew she wanted to marry Monroe that she was willing to risk her relationship with her parents and finally divulge her secret.

The symbolic and legal importance of marriage to signal and concretize status as a family was very real for respondents and their families. The prospect of marriage had the power to test familial love and solidarity in a way that a "casual" relationship could not. While perhaps less potent litmus tests, casual relationships *were* sometimes taken as harbingers of things to come.

For some parents, knowing their child was "dating" interracially rang alarm bells of the potential for this relationship to lead to something more permanent. The preemptive strike taken by Ann's parents when a black high school boy showed interest in her—in the form of forbidding her to date him—is one example.

Even the disclosure of marriage plans still did not stop some parents from trying to dissuade their children from outmarrying. Most of those who opposed their children's marriages stated so in no uncertain terms, blowing up in anger or refusing to speak with their children for a period of time. Other parents had more ambivalent reactions. When Kathleen Wong, an Irish Catholic woman raised in the Bronx of the 1950s, told her parents she planned to marry Robert, a Filipino-Chinese graduate student, according to Kathleen her mother said: "Kathleen, I'm going to tell you not to marry," she said, "but if you don't marry him, either one of two things is wrong. Either you don't love him enough or I didn't raise you right."

The wedding ceremony—that very public ritual of marriage—and who attends, was described by many as a measure of family members' acceptance of the relationship. Some respondents' parents refused to attend their weddings. Others were denied the opportunity, either because the couple eloped or, more rarely, because they opted not to invite relatives who were unsupportive. Whether or not one's parents attended the ceremony was not necessarily indicative of their acceptance, however. For example, while Peggy Walters' parents attended her wedding, they did so begrudgingly, "resigned to" the fact that she intended to go through with it. Peggy says her parents said "Well, now that you're an adult we can't stop you from doing this," even if they did not like it. Karen Britton's parents, on the other hand, refused to attend the ceremony but did lend the couple money to buy a house.

Parental Concerns

So what are the parental concerns when a child seeks to marry interracially? The stories respondents told about why their parents reacted as they did reveal some of the hidden links between cultural notions of race and family. I should note that these stories of how parents reacted and felt about respondents' relationships are explanations constructed by the respondents *about* their parents' behavior.

Concerns with status and position. When Eileen Sullivan, an Irish woman from a small East Coast town, told her mother she had eloped with her boyfriend, Mrs. Sullivan was surprised. When Eileen revealed to her mother that her new husband was black, her mother was, according to Eileen, "horrified." According to Eileen, Mrs. Sullivan's overriding concern was for "her reputation and her position in the community." When Eileen gave birth to her first child, Mrs. Sullivan was very interested in its skin color. Eileen believes that her mother experienced having "black" (as Mrs. Sullivan described them) grandchildren and a black son-in-law was something "happening *to* her." Eileen's characterization of her mother's reaction suggests that she believed the addition of black people into the family would alter her social identity in unwanted, negative ways. Moreover, she experienced this development in her life as some kind of a punishment. Her words are tinged with the notion of symbolic taint—a fear of pollution that accompanies contact deemed too intimate between persons of different status categories.

Fear for child's safety. According to respondents, parents often described their resistance to their child's intermarriage as borne of concern for their child's well-being. Ann Fox's parents invoked their own suffering as German Jews during the Holocaust as reason why their daughter should not marry Monroe. "Why tempt the wrath of others who disapprove, perhaps violently, with her choice?" they seemed to say. African American respondents described a similar kind of rationale given by their parents to discourage their intermarriages, usually warning that white people would inevitably betray them.

Greg Douglas, an African American man in his early forties, and his wife Rachel who is white (Jewish) decided to marry around the time when Greg's father was dying. Greg implied that his father's imminent death was partly the reason he so readily gave his blessing for the marriage, though not without first warning Greg about the difficulties. He said, "You're already outspoken. You always have been. Now you're going to be with a white woman and be outspoken." He said, "You ought to learn to temper yourself so you can get through this."

Pat Simpson, a black woman married to a white man, says her mother-in-law was completely welcoming to her. While as president of a local multiracial organization, Pat says she has heard "a lot of horror stories" about parents' reactions to outmarriage, she says, "I think a lot of them are just mother-in-law stories manifesting into racial stories . . . you know socioeconomic differences, it's not always racial." Even so, Pat says her husband has "some redneck heritage," by which she meant that there are relatives, her father-in-law included, who refuse to see either her or her children.

Loss of a child.   Upon learning she planned to marry Robert, Kathleen Wong's parents told her they were having a "funeral" for her.

What did your mother mean by a funeral?
  I think what she meant was that they were scared out of their mind, that I shouldn't be doing this. My mother said to me, when I went there, she said, "Kathleen, he's a lovely guy but the world is not ready for you and I just don't think you should do this." But I think my parents were definitely very, very scared. You know, isn't that a scary thing, someone in the early seventies, for a kid to marry another race? No one in my family married anyone that was even Protestant. No one married an Italian. It was strictly O'Reilly, O'Sullivan.

While Kathleen's parents did not have a ceremonial funeral, to them Kathleen's marrying "outside the race" made them feel as if she were dead—symbolically, if not actually, lost to them. Funerals symbolically mark the passing of a loved one from one world to the next and represent a physical leaving of the family. In this case, Kathleen's parents understood her outmarriage as a passing from their Irish Catholic world to an unknown and inaccessible "other" world.

What of the children?   Perhaps the most commonly stated reason for why parents did not want their children to outmarry was out of "concern for the children." Respondents said their parents feared the children would be socially challenged—"rejected," "confused," "torn." When interracial couples have children issues of multiraciality (the combining of so-called "races") emerge with urgency. When interracial couples have children, they cement their status as "family," as they transgress the taboo of "miscegenation." Even those who claim to tolerate interracial relationships may utter statements like "what of the children?" In doing so they invoke childhood innocence ("what did *they* do to deserve this?") in an effort to discourage. Underneath this concern, however, is the implicit belief that children who *are* born should be "monoracial."[7] It is not surprising that children are the lightning rod around which competing concerns about race and family gravitate, since children are often used to justify people's opinions on contentious issues (abortion, gay marriage, gun control, and so forth). Invoking children allows people to transform their feelings of anxiety, fear, and disgust into protective feelings for kids.

  This stated concern for the (grand)children, however, is closely allied with concerns for both themselves and their adult children. In a particularly blunt example, a white father said to his daughter upon hearing she was pregnant by her black partner, "You'll never be known for being anything other than the mother of a black child." This man's words encapsulate several important links between cultural constructions of family and race. First, his use of one-drop logic is evident in that he clearly thinks that whiteness is trumped by blackness in a zero-sum game of racial assignment. Not only are her children black, but in bearing black children, his *daughter's* whiteness is, if not trumped, less certain. She becomes tainted in the process. Moreover, this father seems to transfer some anxiety about how this will affect his own status onto his daughter; his statement contains a warning ("look what you've gone and done!"). Any woman who claims the title mother assumes she will be identified in some ways as the mother of a child. For the father, that this child "is" black makes what would otherwise be a rather ordinary fact worth noting. Moreover, the characterization of the child first in racial terms, and as black (as opposed to say, "mixed"), is a distancing move from himself.

Grandchildren. When actual as opposed to imagined grandchildren arrive, however, the concerns of parents generally shifted from warnings about the dire consequences of having a "mixed" baby to how they would integrate the baby into the family. As many people in intermarriages reported, the presence or absence of children often shapes the tone of family relations and the types of concerns expressed. For the majority of respondents in my sample, extended family members such as parents and siblings were more accepting of intermarriages once children were born, although this sometimes took a while to develop. Ann Fox's father, for example, showed little interest in his daughter's first pregnancy, being polite and distant when he addressed the subject at all. To get him to at least address the issue, Ann told him: "'You know what, Dad, this kid has got your blood in it. This is going to be your grandchild, too.' I don't know what else I said but he softened after that and that was good."

Like many parents, Ann used an appeal to "flesh and blood" as the commonsense reason for why her father should love or at least show interest in his future grandchild. While for Ann this seemed only "natural" for them to do so, for her father, this relationship and the decision to have children was, if not unnatural, definitely unwise.

The birth of children was often treated as a point of no return for all those involved in interracial families. In keeping with the cultural model of family that treats children as "completers" of the family unit (much like the creamer and sugar bowls of a tea set), when interracial couples have children, they cement their status as family. Emma Russell noted how children lend an element of "seriousness" (as in permanence) to an interracial relationship that others may not have granted it before. She says: "It's odd, for some people they think that you really are serious about your relationship once you have kids. Oh, I guess he's not going anywhere. You got kids now and it's a biological connection to us and I guess we better deal with this, whereas when you're dating and before you have kids they don't think it's as serious."

While concerns about the children are often invoked by those who dislike or fear the idea of people marrying across racial boundaries, many respondents reported that once they had children, extended family members moved toward mending old estrangements. While those hoping to discourage intermarriage often invoked the "innocence" of children as a rationale for not inflicting a presumably difficult life of confusion and hostility, this concern for the children was often cited as the reason family members made an effort to get along.

> [W]hen we had the first baby it changed the whole thing. [My mother] came out and she spent a week with us when the baby was born and took care of everything. We go back at least once a year and we stay with them. You know, the whole family stays with my family when we go back and my mother and father have changed a hundred percent, because a boy—now they have a connection with grandkids.

Families are comprised of many kinds of relations, codified in language by the names we give to designate family members. The terms "aunt," "husband," and "grandfather" are used not only to denote biological relationships, but social ones as well, carrying with them expected forms of communication and interaction. Family members are supposed to have feelings of responsibility, generosity, and caring toward them. Our cultural "obligation to love" other family members appears not cultural to us at all, but rather very natural. We do not think of ourselves as loving our children because our culture "tells us to," but rather because we want to and feel as if we are naturally compelled to do so. For the members of the interracial families described here, recognition of the ethos that one is obligated to love one's relatives was in tension with the social costs of demonstrating that loving disposition.

The birth of grandchildren sometimes served to temper parents' opposition to their children's marriages. This was more often likely to happen when grandparents were able to put aside the idea that racial difference negated or lessened family connections. Ben and Roxanne Cohen made that transition easier for his parents when Roxanne, an African American woman converted to Judaism, a move that "relieved" his parents, he said, because it meant that their children would now be Jews according to Jewish law (since membership is granted through the mother). When grandparents were unable or unwilling to accept family connections across racial boundaries, such reconciliation did not take place. Grandchildren sometimes served to counter the image that intermarriages were likely to be fleeting unions, thus prompting grandparents to reestablish connections with their children.

Concerns of People in Intermarriages

Reevaluation of Relationships

The "coming out" to parents was often an emotional ordeal for respondents, one that often occasioned a reevaluation of those relationships. For those whose parents reacted with anger, hurt, or a sense of betrayal, such re-evaluations were particularly important. Several respondents described having to reassess who their parents "really were" in ways that were distasteful.

All of these interviewees constructed explanations for why their parents reacted as they did, usually focusing on some aspect of their social position to "explain" and make reasonable their behavior. Yet the tone of these explanations suggest they were intended less as justifications of their parents' behavior and more as ways respondents could *feel* okay about their parents. They represent what Arlie Hochschild calls "emotion work"—attempts made to feel in the culturally appropriate way about family members.

Most respondents cited their parents' "generation" to make sense of their behavior. Kathleen Wong took pains to come to terms with her parents' reaction to her wedding, stressing they did so out of fear (not bigotry). Their fear, she believed, stemmed from "their duty to protect me." Throughout our interview Kathleen stressed how well her parents took the news, given the times in which they grew up. She felt intense desire to protect her parents from being portrayed by others in a way that reinforced stereotypes of "the whole Irish Catholic bigotry."

Despite their initial trepidation, Kathleen's parents also expressed a liking for Robert and have since formed a very close relationship with him, perhaps making it easier for her to come to their defense. But even respondents whose parents never accepted their relationship tried to salvage their image of and relationship with their parents. Carrie Kashtan, a white woman now in her fifties, reflected on her father's rejection of her when she married an African American man:

> I was disowned, disinherited and treated horribly by my parents, by my father who maintained his position for twenty years . . . [I]t was very painful, very horrible . . . My father never in his whole life met my children and he just died last summer at the age of ninety seven. He never ever would meet them or meet my husband or anything and I've been divorced now a long time but, you know, my children are still my children. After twenty years I went back and finally tried to heal the rift and succeeded in becoming accepted back there, to just be there, as long as I didn't stir up any trouble or talk about anything controversial, I was just a good girl and just tried to be nice and not bring my family (pause). But that was always so hard, you know. But I did want to be with my family.

Carrie's desire to maintain a family connection was strong enough for her to meet their demands not to "stir up trouble," which entailed in part that she not bring her children on these visits.

How did you explain to your kids that they could not meet your family?

Well, I have not been one to really be bitter, you know, because I have made my choices and I was always happy with my choice. I was very happily married for many years. So I told my kids that my dad was afraid and I do see racism as a form of fear. And he was a very insecure man who himself was marginal . . . But, you know, his dad was Armenian and his mother was German. Therefore, he was very marginal and in World War II and the Great Depression and all that he desperately wanted to acculturate in to be a WASP. So he joined the Presbyterian church literally and dropped his foreign Armenian name and took on his mother's German name, Schmidt, changed from Katanian into Schmidt, and became a doctor. And you see, he wanted to be in that professional class so there's a lot of pressure to have certain appearances.

Carrie appeals to her own father's marginal ethnic and class position, and his desire to escape that position, as reasons for why he would not see or be seen with his multiracial grandchildren. Doing so would have threatened what Carrie suggests was his precarious position in the professional class. In suggesting that her father's "racism" was a form of fear, she makes him appear a vulnerable man, rather than the powerful father who once rejected her and caused her so much pain.

Respondents of color tended to invoke parents' experiences as victims of racial prejudice and discrimination to explain their reactions to outmarriage. Emma Russell, an African American woman in her early forties, grew up going to integrated schools and living in integrated neighborhoods. When she brought home Mike, who is white, Emma says her parents "were not happy at all."

> They did not come to our wedding. There was a period for like two or three years where I did not see them physically. We would communicate by letters. My mother said she was so hurt she thought she was going to die. I was making such a horrible mistake. This is a woman who was always saying brotherhood and togetherness and integration—as long as it doesn't include marriage and dating. And I've met people like that. They think we're all equal. It's just don't have babies, don't have sex, don't get married. Don't have any adult intimate relationship. I thought it was odd but I liked him and we dated anyway. We got married. They did not come to our wedding, [I] did not see my mother for three years after that, [she] would write me these letters, "He's going to leave—you should leave him" and all that and blah-blah-blah.

What was their reasoning? Why were they so upset about this?
> I think it's because of their background. Both of my parents are from Arkansas. You know, they had segregation there and she would tell us stories about how black people were treated and how they always got the worst of everything and they had separate everything. There were separate cemeteries and how black people—she said they were not seen as being human. I mean a white person could say something about you and there was not a whole lot you could do to fight it. You'd get into trouble. So I think being raised with that kind of attitude. She's not completely comfortable around white people now except maybe Mike. She's pretty comfortable in front of him. But the way she was raised in segregation I think had a lot to do with it.

Emma's mother invoked her experiences in the Jim Crow South to explain her opposition to Emma's marriage to Mike in much the same way as Ann Fox's parents used their experience as German Jews during World War II to explain their opposition to her wedding. Both Ann and Emma seem to have accepted these explanations and used them to repair their relationships with parents. It is interesting to note that among both respondents of color and whites, histories as victims of racial domination were just as often used to explain why their parents (or in-laws) seemed to readily *accept* their intermarriages.

Explanations that appealed to aspects of social location like generation, class, and race allowed the respondents to make sense of their parent's reactions to their marriages often in retrospect. They also allowed them to maintain an image of the essential integrity of a person they loved, which allowed them to forgive their parents any wrongdoing, and justify maintaining a relationship with them, even if that relationship was only in their heads.

Implications for Self-Identity

Marrying outside of one's racial category not only caused respondents to re-evaluate their family relationships, but it also prompted them to think about, and in some cases revise, their understandings of themselves, and in particular their racial identity. White women, in particular, talked about how marrying nonwhite men altered their self-identity. White women were quite aware of the stereotypes of white women who outmarry. One stereotype most often cited was that such women were usually "white trash," poor, who traded their higher racial position for the higher class position of their husbands. The "white trash" epithet has a double meaning, not only signifying a lower class position but loose sexual mores as well.

White respondents were much more likely than black respondents to talk about changes in their racial identity as a result of intermarriage. Kathleen Wong's response was typical: "When you're married interracially for a very long time your identity is quite multiracial after a while because you're no longer—I'm no longer just Irish in my perspective. In fact, it's probably not my core group any more."

For most white respondents in the sample, it was not until they married that they really began to see and *experience* for themselves a stigmatized racial status. Carrie Kashtan described what she became aware of:

> There were some aspects of it that were like completely mind boggling. I had to develop sensitivities and radar to scan and pick up who in the room—that kind of stuff—to walk into the store and be met with that suspicion or to have all eyes turn to my husband and have them—you know, that kind of stuff. You know, sales people that—the two of us would come in together and they

would say (snidely),"Can we help you," and just little subtle, pervasive racism was so—I'd never experienced anything like it. I grew up in a very white, very sheltered environment.

Often this intensified when they had children whom they feared would suffer the effects of discrimination. In this, their experience comes closer to that of nonwhite parents and is less like that of white counterparts. As one respondent put it, "I think a lot of the things I worry about black parents also worry about." That black parents did not talk about changes in their racial identity while white parents did is no doubt due to their familiarity with racial prejudice and exclusion.

Multiracial Families in Public

The stories described above deal with dilemmas that arise among family members when the monoracial family "becomes" multiracial. This section deals with dilemmas that emerge when interracial families are in public, among strangers. Both within their families and in public, respondents describe the difficulty others have in authenticating their families.

These respondents experienced varying degrees of hostility while in public with their families. The examples they offered ranged from threats of violence (being forced off the road by a group of angry white men shouting racial slurs at a white woman and her black husband) to less violent but still hostile actions (such as when one white female respondent who, when her black boyfriend went to the bathroom in a bar they were at, was subject to snide comments from the white men around her about her "poor taste" in men).

Several respondents talked of being stared at in public. Those who stare at multiracial families are not merely trying to reconcile differences in physical appearance, but also the different *statuses* ascribed to those appearances. Sometimes ascribed differences in status are so great as to prevent any granting of kinship whatsoever. One Japanese/white respondent tells the story of being at a PTA meeting in which his Japanese mother—an active member of the group—was standing with him at the door greeting guests as they arrived. As the community members filed in, they greeted him yet proceeded to hand their coats to his mother for coat checking. It soon became obvious that they had assumed she was the hired help, not a member of the PTA, and as such, not his parent. Another respondent, also with a Japanese mother, recalls when a co-worker called her home and left a message with her mother.

The co-worker, telling this respondents of his call to her house, offered this: "I think it must have been your maid who answered" (an impression formed with reference to her accent).

In both examples, neither the co-worker or the PTA meeting participants granted the status of family to these respondents and their mothers, precisely because they attributed to these mothers social statuses (that of maid or coat checker) based on racial signifiers—statuses that differed from those they granted their children (who did not have the same racial markers as their mothers). These examples, like staring incidents, reflect the reluctance and difficulty people have authenticating the multiracial family.

Varying degrees of public scorn were not the only reactions to multiracial families that people reported, however. Many individuals reported being the object of praise, affection, and desire precisely because they were from an interracial family. Staring incidents can also reflect a fascination with and desire for interracial sexuality, as well as a projection of interracial unity onto the racially ambiguous body. Many respondents reported often being told how "beautiful" their families were. One white respondent who described her parents as "very liberal" said they took her marriage to a black man as "a matter of pride."

Perhaps most common, however, were experiences where others just assumed that respondents and their children were not family members. Karen Britton, a white woman with two young children, recalled that once when picking up her daughter from school, school officials who had not seen her before, refused to allow her to take her daughter from the school. "They were arguing with me," she said, "whether I was the mother." Karen, like many other mothers, also recalled an incident where she was assumed to have adopted her children: "I mean I used to belong to a church and they were having an adoption thing and they called me to talk about being an adoptive mother. I've been at this church for years and my son looks dead on [like] me—I mean if you can get past the color of his skin. I was in shock. It was just so unfair."

Kinwork

Many of the dilemmas described by these multiracial families revolved around the difficulty extended family members had in acting and feeling in a "family way" toward persons outside their racial category. While many respondents initially described their families' reactions to their relationships in sweeping, general terms that emphasized the present state of family relations

("It all worked out in the end"), more probing usually revealed the active work that went into cultivating and sustaining what were, and in some cases still are, fragile connections. This "kinwork" was performed in intimate relations within individual families, but respondents also engaged in other forms of work—collective and symbolic—that served the same purpose, namely, to make multiracial families exist socially.

All monoracial parent respondents engaged in various practices to repair connections to family members, even when that proved difficult. As discussed above, much of that work was emotion work performed by respondents on their own feelings so as to maintain connection with parents.

Respondents engaged in other, more tangible practices as well—in ordinary, everyday acts of reciprocity and recognition, such as remembering to call in-laws to keep them abreast of the family's activities and visiting occasionally. Yet for several respondents, this work was performed specifically to counter racial barriers to family cohesion. For example, Eileen Sullivan's mother sees her grandchildren about once every three or four years, so Eileen sends her pictures of the kids "just to make sure she understands they're just people."

Often such work was performed at special family occasions. The wedding, perhaps the most important occasion symbolizing the establishment of family unity, was often a missed opportunity since family members often did not attend weddings or the couples eloped. Less symbolically loaded "family" events like birthdays, Christmas, and Hanukkah were often recognized in the form of cards between grandparents and children, gifts, and often gatherings at which many were present. Bobby Collins, an African American man in his late thirties, describes the conscious work he and his wife Christine put into maintaining ties with extended family: "Their entire environment, they see family, you know, black people and white people as family, a loving family. Because we do things—I know Christine and I, we go out of our way to do things—more so than our families do for us, such as celebrating birthdays, like gifts or being thoughtful like that." Bobby believes this kinwork is important for the psychological well-being of his girls.

Much of the work described by respondents focused on getting white parents to accept spouses, particularly black husbands. Monroe Fox emphasized the mutual interest that he and his father-in-law had in golf. Bobby Collins, emphasized his middle-class status: "I think I made it easier for them. I made it easier for them because I was not a threat. I don't think they tended to see me as someone who was just—I guess just a dumb guy, some dumb black guy who didn't have anything going for himself . . . I was smart, articulate, and nice, polite. I was not the stereotypical black male that they expected."

Like Bobby, Greg Douglas also emphasized his distance from stereotypical images of black men, instead emphasizing "intellectualism" in an effort to win over his Jewish in-laws:

> My wife's family's response—at first it was very cold because she had—I mean Jewish people want you to marry Jewish, a nice Jewish boy is going to be a doctor, da-da-da, and she was for one thing marrying a poet, a loud mouth type of guy, who was very intelligent they thought, but he's different . . . I would just overpower them with—I knew what they wanted. They wanted to see intellectualism. I gave it to them. I gave it to them so much that—all right, all right. He's okay. He's nice. And I am. I don't carry a radio on my shoulder; I'm not inarticulate; I don't want to do anything except live and let live, and I think they got that.

Negotiating family tensions.   In the stories respondents told of the work they put into building and maintaining family connections was an underlying theme of the hazards of navigating family relationships in the context of racial tension. Only a few respondents reported feeling acceptance from all extended family members. More often than not, there was at least one family member who did not approve of their relationship. Their stories reflected the subtleties of family acceptance and rejection imposed on people who had transgressed racial norms (either by being in interracial relationships or "being" multiracial). Several respondents spoke of their "acceptance" from family members as conditional. As Carrie Kashtan reported, as long as she did not rock the boat by talking about race in any way, she was tolerated at her parents' house. Many multiracial respondents spoke of being treated by relatives as "exceptions" from a (negative) norm ("you're not like other black people I know").

Many respondents found themselves in the position of family peacemaker and negotiator, trying to balance their desire to maintain connection to extended family with the impact that hostile relations potentially had on their spouses and children. Karen Britton, a white woman in her mid thirties, felt her grandmother's racist beliefs to be so odious that she could not expose her black/white children to their great grandmother. This became obvious to her when her grandmother refused to even look at her new grandchild at a family gathering. As a result, Karen no longer attends family reunions if her grandmother will be present.

In the course of one of the few group interviews I conducted, an exchange developed between Hank Gustafson, a white man in his forties married to a black woman, and their son, Brandon, a twenty-five-year-old student, that illustrates the working out of these family dilemmas:

Did you have relationships with your extended family?

Brandon: There weren't too many relationships. Like two of my uncles were very distant.

Hank: (slightly annoyed) One is dead now. That's one of them that you refer to as being distant.

Brandon: The other one is racist.

Hank: He said something about black people, about Rastas or something like that?

Brandon: No, he'll use the term "nigger." Being biracial and being among black people who call someone nigger is different than it is when a white person says it. (addressing me) And I did not like it—derogatory statements within earshot of my father—at all.

Hank: There's only so much I can do and people around this house who are Italian and they use the word all left and right. What am I going to do, go around to everybody and say, "What are you saying this for?" I have a choice as to who I can engage in conversation, so he sees me do things like that, thinking, well, I should stand up and get in people's face.

Brandon: But they're Caucasian. So we now have a [racial issue]—

Hank: I don't think that's even true with all of them. They see you coming out of college, both you and your sister, and many of them had trouble getting out of high school. Look at Tom, okay. They could barely get out of high school. Look at Sam, look at John and Sandy—didn't even get out of high school. So there's no way they could say that, well, John is more intelligent than you.

Brandon: (addressing me) I remember I was thirteen at the time and I had two cousins, Robbie and Kevin, and my grandmother gave them both pocket knives. They had the audacity to give me a balloon. After that I really didn't have too much feeling in my heart. Now I know how people think. I just said this is it.

Hank: (addressing me) And he doesn't understand my background either because when my father died everybody in my family got some sort of present from my mother to try to kind of ease the pain or the grief and I got nothing that was memorable. I remember going into the bathroom and crying my eyes out because I was so disappointed, because why was everybody else getting something so much more valuable than what I was getting. Mine was like nothing, you know, in comparison and being the youngest boy, I've always had to fight for my place, whether it's like attention or recreation or status, and it takes time because I'm more the peacemaker, you know. People come after you with words of war and I just kind of walked away. I've learned if I get into things I'm destroying myself and they're destroying me. They're about the business of destroying my spirit. So that's the reason why I ignore a lot of the stuff around. And then he doesn't know that I did write to my sister Louise and my brother-in-law a long letter, telling them, look, man, you guys are using these words around my family and I do not appreciate this. And it's a matter of respect. You're not respecting me. You're not respecting them. So he doesn't know that I have done that and taken more of a low key approach. I've talked to my brother John all the time and tried to iron out some issues. I've tried to pick my time to do those things. Hey, am I going to do this now or am I [going to wait for a better opportunity]? It's not the first time that we're in a situation, environment, where words are flying around. That's the way I felt about it. That's where I would say it's been a struggle socially and within the family.

In saying that one of the uncles to whom Brandon refers as distant is in fact dead, Hank implies that Brandon is exaggerating the claim that his family harbors prejudicial views of nonwhites. To buttress his point, Brandon brings up his uncles' use of racial slurs, not only within his presence, but also within the presence of his father. Brandon suggests that he holds his uncles responsible for subjecting his father to such insults, but Hank interprets Brandon's comment as an accusation that he ought to confront his brothers for insulting his wife and kids. In his own defense Hank offers a glimpse into his strategy of managing what are often tense family relations, presenting a picture wherein he waits for the appropriate time to address such matters, later revealing to his son for the first time that he has in fact stood up to his brothers and come to the defense of his family by writing letters and having individual conversations with them about their offensive language.

Hank presents an alternative interpretation of his brothers' use of racial slurs, suggesting that class jealousy, not racist beliefs, motivate their actions ("they had trouble getting out of high school") or perhaps that even if his family harbors prejudicial views, Brandon can take comfort in his superior education. During this exchange, Brandon became increasingly frustrated with his father's seeming avoidance of the "fact" that his cousins, uncles, and grandmother thought he was "less than" them because he is biracial. Annoyed, he offers the example of the less valuable gift given to him by his grandmother compared to the more valuable ones given to his (white) cousins, symbolic to him of the hierarchy of affection according to race in the family. Brandon sees his grandmother's lesser gift as racially motivated. For Hank, the meaning of the gift is not about race, but is an extension of his own mother's neglect of him.

Quite a few respondents reported that tension around racial issues was never really addressed in the family, leaving respondents to wonder how others felt about their intermarriage. Tiffany Jankowski claims that her parents never addressed the fact that her former husband was black, but she does suspect they may have had a little "bias." As evidence she offered a story of the advice her mother offered when Tiffany was in the process of getting a divorce: "My mother has twice said to me that in her opinion, just like Jewish men are more likely to cheat, so are black men likely to cheat, that they're predisposed to that. She didn't use that word. But [it's] some sort of a bias that she has."

Symbolizing Solidarity

The context in which multiracial families live denaturalizes them as families. The work they do to make multiracial families exist is an effort to *naturalize* them. To do this, respondents engage in a variety of acts designed to symbolize their union and solidarity with each other. For many parents, racial classification was an important means through which their status as family could be legitimated and recognized. For most, this meant that they should be able to declare a multiracial identity both officially (on state forms—even if very few of these parents were actively involved in the lobby effort to do this) and in everyday life. Many explained their opinions with reference to nature and biology. As one respondent described her son, "he's 100 percent me, 100 percent my husband." Related to naturalized ideas about racial identity was the common perception that there can be a truthfulness to racial identity, encapsulated in this statement by a white parent: "Multiracial Americans have been forced by our government to commit perjury."

Most parent respondents understood the racial classification and identity of their children as symbolic of their psychological connectedness. This was often expressed in statements about denial of parents. Many parents interpret how their children racially identify as a barometer of their identity and self-esteem. Lynn Miller, a black woman married to a white man, believes that people with differently raced parents who do not identify themselves as multiracial is "okay." "But," she adds, "technically it's like denying the mother, technically it's really denying . . . They must not feel that good about that." Emma Russell felt strongly that her children should identify as multiracial since if they identified as white "it's not recognizing that I'm mother." Tiffany Jankowski felt differently and attributes this to her status as a single mother:

> As far as I'm concerned, she's multiracial but I want her to be able to choose and if she wants to call herself black that's fine with me. I don't have any personal ego involved in that. I'm white. And I know there are white mothers who feel that way. I've had discussions with them. Whatever she chooses herself will never negate the fact that I'm her mother and I'm probably more secure in that because I am her sole provider, I am her sole caregiver, I am the one that she is going to most identify with, even during her rebellious years.

Intermarried partners, however, did not always agree on issues of classification. Eileen Sullivan said: "I think they're biracial or interracial or multiracial so I kind of push that a little bit and he really pushes more that they're black. He and I have some very light discussion about it because I don't really care one way or the other. It's not something I feel very strong about."

Yet despite the value most parents placed on their children choosing to identify as multiracial, most recognized that the "choice" was between identifying as multiracial or nonwhite. When explaining how they talked to their children about racial identity, nearly all parent respondents did so by marking their kids as the logical cross between their parents (for example, "Daddy's X, I'm Y, you're XY"). In cases where children expressed an identity as white, most would tell them of the unlikelihood that others would validate that identity. Carrie Kashtan made a distinction between the public and private identities of her children:

> Well, for me it always was that they were black. They were black. Their dad was black and so they were black in the public sense. In the private sense they were mixed because they were both—you know, we were—they got input from both cultures and both sides, so they weren't just black. So that was the whole thing, that they could be who they wanted to be and they could be who they were in their family.

Out of Place in Family

Like their parents, mixed race respondents felt their families were "out of place" in the culture at large. Unlike their parents, they also understood themselves to be out of place *within* their own families of origin as well. Multiracial respondents described their experiences within their own families as different *from those of other family members* in significant ways. In particular, multiracial respondents marked that difference in relation to their monoracial parents and extended relatives, and at times in relation to their siblings (Wallace 2001).

Dealing with identity. Given multiracial families' peculiar place in U.S. understandings of family, a surprising number of respondents told me that their parents never openly discussed racial identity. While this could be taken as a sign that there were no problems concerning race in the family, the stories multiracial respondents told about their families suggest otherwise. Vicki Reynolds, a thirty-six-year-old black/white woman, remembers her parents actively ignoring the discomfort she and her sister sometimes felt when people would stare at their family in public.

> My sister would say—she would cry and she would say, everybody's looking at me. Everybody's looking at me. And my parents said, "No, they're not. Nobody's looking at you." Nobody would acknowledge it. And when I think about it now, of course, they were looking at us. I mean people were always looking at us. But my parents were so—they had this incredible like normalizing, you know—there was incredible normalizing support.

Vicki's parents dealt with race by ignoring it. That they were ignoring it, however, was not lost on Vicki and shaped how she thought about her racial identity. She went on to link this kind of experience with the reason she and her sister never talked about their racial identity despite "struggling" with it.

> I would say I'm both or I'm half black, half white. I never liked saying that I was half black, half white but that's how I used to describe myself when people would ask me or I would identify my racial categories, like talking about my parents. It was as if I didn't have a racial category. I was just a product of my parents and one was black and one was white and that meant that I was neither black nor white. Right? So it was like identifying yourself somehow in this negative state. I did see it as negative . . . I felt it would be so much easier if I

was one or the other and I think, too, because I sensed my mother's resistance to us being black.

Racial difference from parent.　In talking about their family experiences, several respondents relayed stories having to do with how they felt about the different ways they and their parents were racially positioned by others. Many commented on the tendency of strangers to assume that they were unrelated to their parents, a fact that bothered some (especially when they were young) but was considered relatively unimportant or at least reasonable to expect by most.

The racialized difference between parent and child was most deeply felt in those instances when it highlighted a different set of privileges and constraints that racial membership entailed. Brenda Jackson recalled how she felt when as a teenager she and her mother went to a public pool and a guard said she could enter but her Asian American mother could not:

Having to watch one or both of your parents be antagonized verbally or physically, especially when one of your parents is a person of color, I think that there are hard feelings that go with that 'cause I felt like I could pass but my mother definitely couldn't and so when she was being antagonized it made me very angry and guilty because I could go and she could not.

While several respondents talked about their parents being targets of racial antagonism, the starkness of Brenda's example is unusual. The sense of being distanced and treated differently from one's parent, however, is not. Nor are the kinds of emotions she describes feeling. Brenda feels guilt because she was spared the mistreatment her mother faced. Why guilt? Another respondent who recalls when her father was called "chink" by some neighborhood kids also felt "guilty" because "there's a part of you that's sort of grateful that it doesn't happen to you, that he looks like that to them, that they don't see you as being so different [from them], you know." The guilt these respondents describe stems from *wanting* to be spared racialized humiliation, as well as embarrassment of and on behalf of a parent who is supposed to represent dignity, authority, and control.

Coming to terms with parents' understandings of the meaning of race.　Respondents' sense that they had to think about race in their relations with family members emerged strongly from the interviews. For them, "race relations" were not simply relations between themselves and strangers, but between themselves and those on whom they were dependent materially and emotionally. A common way in which race became an issue within the family had to do with the meaning of physical difference between respondents and family members, especially their parents. One black/white respondent recalled that her white mother did not want her to straighten her tightly curled hair or style it like other black girls. Looking back, she felt this was because doing so would have emphasized a racial difference between mother and daughter. Of her mother she said, "She didn't see us as black girls. We were her daughters." This respondent suggests that for her mother, to see her daughters as black girls would have made it feel as if they were a little less her own.

Mimi Sherwood, a thirty-five-year-old Japanese/white woman, told a story that illustrates the ways that she internalized a series of racial distinctions in thinking about herself and her relationship to her father. Explaining her father's negative reactions when she began to date a black/white man, Mimi said:

I think deep down inside I knew [there would be] negative reactions, because even though we say, "Oh, when we grew up on those military bases, we all got along and everybody loved each other and, oh, we were all mixed," clearly when I reflect back there is a hierarchy. You know, the Japanese women who dated the African American servicemen, [people said] "Oh, they're so pretty and why are they with them?" "So and so is half Japanese but her dad is black." Half Japanese and yet sort of a different half category of half Japanese. And so on. So I think there's some part of me deep down inside that knew that my choice [to be] with this person, people from my community, quote, unquote, might see me differently because of that choice. That's all that stuff about she's tainted, she's now not a nice girl, you know.

Did your parents react that way as well?

I think so. My dad was hurt, I think, more than anything else. And I know it was hard for him to have to admit that. My parents were sort of liberal—I don't know if it's a facade. I think they really believe people are people, da-da-da, but it's one thing about dating my daughter, that's a problem. I wanted him to know I wasn't doing this to hurt him—I mean there was a lot of pain there, a very painful time, for me, for my parents . . . I think he felt like I was rejecting him as well, that I was choosing to be with what my father had grown up learning as the taboo. I think he felt that I was rejecting him as a European American person.

What was it like for you to deal with that?

It was a very angry time in my life. I was very angry. In fact, I just wanted to go after everybody, I think, anyone who represented injustice, I mean I really wanted to go after them—not go after them like physically or anything, but I wanted to challenge them and I wanted to hold them accountable. That's why I really, really empathize with students, university students, and that passion, that pain, that anger. Also the feeling of betrayal. I felt betrayed, even though probably I knew deep down inside, I mean, what could I expect. I mean I grew up with this and I knew this at some subconscious level. But having it—sort of being confronted by it personally, I felt very betrayed.

Mimi's story points out the tricky set of dilemmas facing multiracials within their own families. Like intermarried respondents, several multiracial respondents talked about coming to terms with parents who harbor racially prejudiced views. For multiracials, this takes on a particularly personalized dimension. While Mimi's father was "hurt" by her dating a black (even if only "part" black) man, she felt personally betrayed and rejected. Her father's attitudes toward dating someone not of her own ancestry suggests the limits of his racial tolerance and opens the door for her to suspect the limits of his tolerance of *her* racial difference.

Loyalty to parents.   Mimi's story also illustrates that the logic that equates ethnicity with social relatedness is at work in multiracial families as well. Several respondents told similar stories in which the race of their sexual partners and spouses was interpreted by their parents as a sign of acceptance or rejection of them. Just as one's choice of marriage partners is often interpreted as an indicator of one's ethnic affinity (or lack thereof), it is also interpreted as a sign of how close and loyal one is to one's parents. Charlene Nieda, who dated only white boys in high school, recalls her Japanese American father saying, "Aren't you ever going to date an Asian boy?" and being "hurt" that she did not. She also suspected that her mother would have felt "alienated" if she had married someone Asian. For Charlene, this understanding of her parents' feelings about the race of men she dated was "frustrating" because she had always felt uncomfortable "choosing sides."

Charlene was not alone in feeling the need to negotiate ethnic affiliation and expression in relation to her parents. While many spoke of their desire to use ethnic identification to signal their affiliation with their parents, a few commented on the usefulness of ethnic identification to mark a sense of alienation and distance from family. Majeeda Kibri, a twenty-year-old Persian/

Mexican woman, believes her brother's decision to change his last name to something less-identifiably Persian while a soldier in the Gulf War was motivated not only by a desire to distance himself from the "enemy," but because he felt "neglected" by his father.

Relations between siblings. In talking about their families, relationships between siblings were frequently mentioned as important in shaping how respondents thought about race. Older siblings were often talked about as role models for learning how to negotiate racial issues, while younger siblings were sometimes talked about as those whom respondents could help navigate those same issues. While not all respondents reported talking about racial identity with their siblings, all made assessments of how they thought their experiences may be similar and different from those of their siblings. When talking about difference, physical appearance was mentioned as particularly salient. Robin Peters felt the reason her brother identified so strongly as Japanese was due to being dark skinned and the negative experiences he had because of it while growing up.

Physical appearance was sometimes used in childhood struggles between siblings. Majeeda Kibri recalls that people would tease her white-looking sister saying "Oh, you must have been switched at birth." Majeeda remembers her sister commenting on her color: "[W]hen I was little she used to come in—she denies it now because she thinks I'm saying this because I want to feel like I was being oppressed when I was a kid—she would come in and you know how sometimes when you scratch your skin it gets whiter?" "Yes," I responded. "She'd say, 'Oh, look, it's just dirt, it's just dirt.'"

Discussions among siblings about phenotype and identity were particularly interesting because they often led to discussions of the future ethnoracial identity of the family as a unit. The race of siblings' marriage partners—because the children of those unions represented the next generation of the family—were often talked about as indicators of degrees of likeness between siblings and harbingers of future relations. Majeeda worried that the children her sister had with her white husband would not look like her, and the consequences of that for their relationship as a family:

> I think it's to be able to look at the kids and they're not going to be able to look like me. And that's why I'm afraid, I'm really afraid of having a baby—I mean I'm not attracted to white men but I'm probably going to marry like black or brown or yellow, or whatever color, but it's having that—I want the kids to be

able to look like me . . . I mean my sister looks light—she'll marry somebody like the color of her skin just because that's what she's been attracted to. So I think that the fear is because they're going to look white. Well, how can they accept their ethnic identity and will they do like a lot of biracial people do and say since I look white just forget about it because I won't be accepted anyway? My nieces and nephews are going to be Chicano, Persian, and white, you know, and they shouldn't have to choose, so that's what I want to be able to tell them.

Parents just don't understand.   In general, respondents expressed the sense that their parents could not fully understand their dilemmas. Jade Wolkoff, a nineteen-year-old black/Jewish woman, felt that because of the "racial difference" between herself and her (white Jewish) father, her father "has such a different life from me." Mandy Rodriguez echoed this belief saying, "I felt that my parents—they knew what they were and we were something else that they couldn't quite understand."

What is it that they could not understand? Monique LeBlanc, a twenty-year-old college student, believes parents "won't know what it's like to like always be looking for your place, your space, sort of." Of his African American mother, Kanji Uyematsu, a twenty-year-old black/Japanese man, said:

> She talks about race a lot and she knows about race but I think she kind of tends to translate her knowledge of race and the fact that she interracially married into an assumption that she has knowledge about what it's like to grow up with an interracial identity. You don't know, you know. And I think that happens to a lot of parents. They tend to think because they have an interracial child they know—just because you have a interracial relationship doesn't mean you have an interracial relationship within yourself.

Charlene Nieda was more specific. To illustrate the difference race makes in how she, part Japanese, and her mother and husband, both white, see the world, Charlene told the story of an incident involving her six-year-old daughter in which some girls at school were "doing the Chinese eyes thing."

> I cried so much about this period of time. It was so shocking to me that I had such a strong emotional reaction to it because I thought I had worked through any kinds of self-hatreds . . . so I don't know if it was tapping into some old childhood, unresolved issues or what, but I was so emotional about it . . .

But it was funny because I came home that day and I was so sad and I called [my parents] up and one of the things my mom said right in the beginning was, "Well, they don't probably mean it at her. I mean they probably weren't trying to hurt *her* feelings." And I was like, Mom, it doesn't matter. I don't care. Actually I do care if they were trying to hurt her feelings but that wasn't the point. That wasn't why Pam [her daughter] was upset, you know. And Dan [her husband] said the same thing, you know. And it was important to them to tell themselves that Pam wasn't getting this personally because she's a person of color—you know what I mean—and that just wasn't what I needed. It wasn't like I was mad at them or anything. I just couldn't get from them what I needed. So I called my brother and I told him and we talked for hours and I cried and he was perfect for me to talk to because he was as upset as I was for the same kind of reasons and it was like—He just understood it in this complex way like I was and was hurt in the same way and also, you know, was thinking about Pam in that context and assuming that she was, in fact, a person of color, not mostly white or anything like that. So that was another one of those experiences where these things re-emerged.

As Charlene tells it, her mother (Jessica) and husband (Dan) were relieved because they felt these children's insults could not have been targeted at Pam because Pam looks white. Thus reassured, they were able to dismiss the importance of the incident. Charlene, however, cannot, since it is clear to her that indeed her daughter had taken this incident personally. Charlene described being upset at the thought of her six-year-old daughter having to fend off racialized assaults to her sense of self much like she had had to do as a child. But Charlene was also upset at the response of her mother and husband. To Charlene, Jessica and Dan revealed that they thought of Pam as exempt from the Asian category. To Charlene, this amounted to saying Pam was not really one of "them." It also suggests that in their minds Pam (and for that matter, Charlene) are exceptions to the "them." This was painful for Charlene because it exposed a gap in understanding between herself and her mother and husband.

Jessica and Dan's rationale (that Pam is only a little Japanese and not really one of the "them"), though intended as something to take comfort in (because it could protect Pam from racial slurs), is disturbing to Charlene precisely *because* it is intended as a source of comfort. It echoes what several respondents reported white people had at times said to them as a means of making them feel accepted (such as "you're okay 'cause you're only half-black"), which were experienced as "you're tainted, but only a little." Vicki Reynolds described the confusing meanings of such messages:

> [W]ith white friends there's this way in which you get to be a human (unintelligible). They don't identify you racially because it's not something that's important to them. I mean it's a strange thing because like a lot of people of mixed race—and a lot of black people, too—have had experiences of being told by whites, "oh, you don't seem black to me." And to them that means I can relate to you as if you're like me . . . It's like when you're accepted in a white world or in a white context, when people treat you as if you are white, you know, it's like—a good friend of mine said, it fucks with your mind because it's very different to be treated as if you're white than to be treated as if you're black by many, many white people.

Though ostensibly intended as tokens of acceptance, claims to "not see" racial difference come off as measures of acceptability. As such, rather than giving comfort such statements emphasize the tenuous and limited nature of that acceptance (even if one "looks white"). Claims of not seeing racial difference, like being marked as the exception, far from reassuring one that racial difference does not matter, suggest instead that racial difference *cannot* be seen if the degree of comfort in the relationship is to continue.

Relationships with extended family.   Being mixed set apart respondents from extended families in various ways. Despite the drama and tension that sometimes accompanies intermarriage, multiracial respondents' relations with extended family members are not universally negative. While a few respondents reported feeling that their racial difference was a source of tension in relations with cousins or grandparents, most felt it was not. For Mia Guimond, being mixed indeed set her apart from her Chinese and Haitian relatives, she said, "but I always used it in my favor . . . I was always like the oddity that everybody wanted around because, you know, 'well she's the prettiest one in the family, she's the artsyfartsy one in the family.' So they always wanted me around."

Nearly all multiracial respondents reported having contact with their extended families, and most report those relationships to be amicable, and even openly loving and affectionate. But whether or not issues of race are positive or negative within the family is, in some way, beside the point (although certainly it is important). The fact that respondents must think about how race shapes their relationships with family members is the point. It is dealing with the manifestations of racial division, both subtle and obvious, in the context of relationships that are expected to be free of such concerns that form the ground of a common multiracial experience.

The Costs of Interracial Kinship

Most of my respondents reported having maintained relations with (and some still received economic support from) their families. Some, however, were "disowned" from their families of origin. When family ties were cut off, so too was economic support. Since most of these respondents lived in either integrated or mostly white neighborhoods, they avoided many of the costs of segregation that eventually have economic impacts, like poor schools, reduced housing values, and fewer jobs. The "costs" to them were less obviously economic, more often psychical. Within their communities, their families were different, even stigmatized. Most intermarried respondents felt they had to be cautious and even vigilant to protect their children from the disadvantages that might come from being both of African descent and multiracial.

Having a "normal" family makes the individual appear normal as well—and that has political consequences in other realms of life beyond the family or personal identity. One can imagine ways in which being in a multiracial family could have economic consequences of which respondents were not, and perhaps could not be, aware. For example, housing discrimination in the form of redlining on the basis of interracial couple status has been documented, yet is quite difficult to prove and sometimes difficult to detect.[8] In business arenas where one's spouse is an integral part of the path to power (for example, as host[ess] at functions that facilitate rapport and demonstrate one's partner's suitability for the position), being part of an intermarried couple may be a barrier to establishing such rapport.

These kinds of "costs," material, psychical, and social, explain why the legitimization of the family is the avenue sought by respondents. What makes their attempts to challenge their stigmatization possible are, ironically, the very things that mark them as privileged in other realms. Their intermarriages are facilitated by their access to a college education, for example. Most married respondents met their spouses in college. As I noted earlier in the book, respondents are overwhelmingly middle class, and many could be classified as upper middle class and are employed in skilled, white-collar occupations. Perhaps even more ironic is that their position of relative privilege also shapes their grievances. Whites, unused to experiencing racial prejudice and discrimination up close, face new forms of exclusion when they outmarry. For these women, but for some black women as well, this exclusion manifests itself in a lack of social recognition of their mothering relationship to their children. Their inauthenticated relationship to their children is at odds with the sense of connection they feel to their children. While such conditions challenge these women's status as *mother*, for white women, they make more apparent their whiteness and the disadvantages of nonwhite status (Twine 1996).

Although some of the experiences mothers talked about as important for why they joined multiracial organizations were unique to the experience of mothering "transracially," others were the outcome of structural conditions, like divorce, facing women generally. For divorced mothers, multiracial organizations provided a community of support that could provide kids with a connection to the culture of their ex-spouse, while it offered mothers support for childbearing concerns beyond race. It is not surprising that members join and are most active in these organizations during peak childbearing and childrearing years, while participation tends to drop off as children enter their teenage years.

While many of the parents in the family organizations have been only tangentially active in issues of official classification, this does not mean they are unconcerned about how they classify their children racially. As we saw earlier, parents identified their children using the state's racial categories. Seldom did they refuse those categories in crafting their conceptions of multiraciality. Several spoke of "accuracy" in racial classification. For them, however, racial accuracy was a stand-in for recognition of their relationships with their kids.

Collective Solutions to Family Problems

The emotional work these respondents invest in developing and sustaining family feeling within their own extended families is mirrored in the activities they engaged in with other interracial families. Multiracial family organizations counter the forces of fission that obscure and make difficult interracial kinship by creating a family of families. Through this collective work they seek to obtain what is not always granted to their individual families—recognition and legitimacy.

Multiracial family organizations are first and foremost social support groups, more interested in the pragmatics of parenting multiracial children and dealing with issues in interracial families than census classification. Of I-Pride, Eileen Sullivan, an active member said:

It's been beneficial for us as a way of providing contact for our children to be around other biracial children. That's really the motivation. And we have fun. And we're not joiners or activists. We're not trying to change the world. I think it's changing the world in a much smaller way deciding to be married biracially. But that's really what the organization is for. It's not a political thing. We just want to have a way that our kids can meet other biracial kids. If they did have a question—they may not—but they see it. It's a common occurrence. They see a whole big group of people having a good time of all mixtures.

Carrie Kashtan, a founding member of I-Pride, described her motivation to form the group:

My most pressing issue was [the rejection of] my family . . . [I]t was very helpful to me to see that in I-Pride most families after that initial—at the marriage, blowout and rejection and scandalous behavior and all of this stuff—would come back together and in particular around the birth of the kids. [But] my family didn't. There were a lot of families who didn't, too, but mostly they did. So it let me see that what I thought was so extreme in my family actually *was* so extreme, and most people didn't have that much of a rift created between themselves and their families.

The kind of support that the group provided Carrie was often cited by other respondents as the main reason they were involved in the groups. While this support was important for them personally, as Carrie suggests, it was also important for, and explicitly geared toward, counteracting negative public perceptions of multiracial families. Said Harmony Spencer, a black woman married to a white man and expecting her first child at the time of the interview, "I joined the group so that my family would no longer be considered weird."

Several white parents sought groups soon after, or in anticipation of, becoming parents. Karen Britton said she joined a local group because she "didn't know what to expect" with raising mixed children. Peggy Walters says she "anticipated there would be challenges to raising biracial children."

As a way to deal with those "challenges," many cited the importance of their kids knowing other mixed kids, so they had someone to compare notes with on their experiences. Lynn Miller felt this would "enhance self-esteem" for her daughter. Yet for many mothers, especially white mothers, the organizations provided a structure to allow them to interact with at least some children of color, something their mostly white neighborhoods could not provide. At the annual Halloween party thrown by I-Pride, the mothers hired a deejay who it seemed may have been one of their sons, who spun hip-hop music exclusively.

The importance of the organizations was heightened for divorced mothers who had limited contact with ex-spouses' extended families. In a particularly poignant story, Carrie Kashtan described the fallout of her parent's rejection and the divorce from her husband on her kids:

> [My mother] would visit once or twice a year. Then as she got older she wasn't able to travel so there were years where [the kids] couldn't see her. But they had my husband's family and he has brothers and sisters. So they had cousins and aunties and uncles and a grandpa for a short time. Then at one point my youngest son went down the street and asked this old man that used to garden out on the sidewalk—he was riding his tricycle and asked if he'd be his grandpa because he didn't have one. So it was hurtful to my kids and, you know, as years went on my older son said, you know, well, it doesn't matter to me because I never knew him [Carrie's father] and it was making me feel so bad. It was incredible to me that the racism, the most feared—my mother used to say, well, honey, you do that marriage then people will reject you. They'll feel sorry for you. And here's my own parent doing that more than anybody. It's like the irony.

Those involved in family-based organizations understand what they do as helpful to their children, themselves, and to others in intermarriages and families. Most believed they were changing public perceptions of multiracial families, changing the perception of them as oddities ("like when the circus comes to town," said one respondent) to families that are "another way, but still legitimate."

Organizations created many activities toward this end, sponsoring such events as "Family Photo Day" in which people brought in and passed around pictures of their families *as* families. In Interracial Family Circle's newsletter there was a regular feature to introduce new members, which includes pictures and brief bios of the families as a unit. In the book review section of one issue, Patt Silverthorn, the president, writes, "When IFC parents get together, it's not unusual for us to talk about what kids' books we like: which have positive role images [of] multiracial families."[9]

In this their efforts are aligned with those emerging in other public contexts, from other sources. Tawonga, an organization for Jewish families, for example, sponsors "a Jewish Weekend for Multiracial Families," while an organization called Fusion runs a summer camp for mixed race children in the San Francisco Bay Area. The publishers of *Interrace* magazine, now defunct, understood its mission as that of trying to alter the stereotyped images of multiracial families. "We created *Interrace*," the editors wrote in 1993, "not to challenge a racist society or to validate interracial relationships but to bring balance to the negative depictions of our families and children in the mass media."

In 1999, PBS aired *An American Love Story*, a multiepisode documentary about the everyday life of a black/white couple and their children. The uniqueness of the series (it is the only documentary depicting the home life of such a family), and the director's desire to depict such a subject, confirm the novelty of interracial families in American cultural consciousness. But even more telling of their position is the reaction audiences had to the film. In online chats held with the family, several people evinced a somewhat startled recognition that the family was "just like them," a recognition that the director herself experienced and admitted to being relatively unprepared for. The realization that "they're just like me" speaks volumes about just how far apart and essentialized notions of race can become. It also suggests that images of family are important means through which such essentialized differences can be challenged.

Attempts to normalize interracial kinship are ongoing. In 2004 Jen Chau, founder of the Swirl organization of community groups, and Carmen Van Kerckhove of EurasianNation.com, formed Mixed Media Watch, a Web site that tracks representations of mixed race people and families in the media. Both Chau and Van Kerckhove are critical of the portrayal of interracial families in the media, which too often "continues to exploit fear and stereotypes," such as the "tragic-mulatto-raised-by-single-white-mother" story. "These contemporary tragic mulatto stories are subtle cautionary tales against interracial relationships," writes Van Kerckhove (2005). "Contrary to popular belief, not every interracial couple is doomed to a life of tragedy, nor is every couple a happy, smiley United Colors of Benetton ad. The truth lies somewhere in between, but that's something we rarely get to see in the media."

In 2005, Harvard's Remixed student organization sponsored a photo exhibit of interracial families ("Genealogies: An Unfamiliar Exhibition of Familial Compositions"), inspired, its organizers said, by the noticeable absence of such images in the media. "Even as there is a growing trend toward exoticizing mixed race models and actors, society has yet to embrace the source of these 'racially ambiguous' people." Depictions of interracial couples and their children in contexts symbolic of family (like the home, family portraits) are attempts to normalize interracial kinship and are an integral part of the making of multiracials.

5 Creating Multiracial Identity and Community

[W]hat does somebody who looks like a white Hispanic . . . really have in common with someone who's say, Filipino and black? Do they really have more in common than someone who's white and someone who's black? The fact that you have two parents that come from different racial backgrounds doesn't automatically mean anything so the assumption that just because you do come from that background you have something in common is another stereotype. It's another racism, if you will, because you're basically saying that based on your biology we have something in common.

—Mitch Russell, forty-six years old, black/Japanese

[P]artly what led me to I-Pride was looking for a bunch of people who said, "Well, we're all different races but we're mixed. That's our name. We have a theme. We belong." That's what I wanted for my son [a place where] automatically he belonged . . . It's weird that even though you're into like different races and all that stuff you really do want people like you. We really want diversity? We want people like us. Let's admit it.

—Mandy Rodriguez, forty-five years old,
Japanese/white, identifies as Latina

THROUGHOUT THE COURSE OF MY RESEARCH, activists, the media, and respondents talked about "the multiracial community." This has only intensified since the U.S. Census Bureau began keeping data on the multirace population. But as the above quotes attest, the notion of "multiracial community" is contested even by those who are organizing collectively on the basis of multiracial identity. How then do respondents think about multiracial identity and community? Who do mixed race people say they are? In what ways do they talk about a "we"? In what ways do multiracials differentiate among themselves, and why are some distinctions relevant at certain times and not at other times?

These questions are important because they get at the heart of group-making processes. Deciding just who is "like us" involves erecting a boundary between us and them. Examining on what basis likeness (and thus difference) is determined provides insight into how racial differentiation works. In this chapter, I address these various issues. First, I examine the centripetal forces that bring multiracials together—what comprises the sense that they may be alike in important, basic ways and what leads them to feel this way. But I also examine the centrifugal forces that *undermine* the construction of group solidarity. Even as multiracials feel they share important experiences and consciously attempt to elaborate what those are, they question whether those experiences are enough to warrant social and political action as a group.

Marking a Boundary: Who Is Mixed?

Central to understanding how "multiracial community" is being constructed is understanding just how people define who is a member of the group. In the course of my research, it became clear that deciding who is a member of "the multiracial community" was not the same issue as defining "who is multiracial." When respondents spoke of "multiracials" ("mixed people," "biracials") they were almost always referring to people whose *parents* were of different racial categories.[1] Multiracials were defined in contrast to those whom respondents called "monoracials." One was monoracial if both of the person's biological parents were of the same racial category, even if those groups were understood to have "mixed" origins (such as African Americans or Latinos).[2]

Reflecting the extent to which the paradigm of the social constructedness of race had permeated their understandings, however, most respondents qualified their definitions of who is mixed with statements like, "well, everyone is mixed depending on how you define race."

How people think about "who is mixed" is central to understanding how a sense of collective multiracial identity is being constructed. The boundary that respondents draw around mixedness is intended to mark a category of persons who *share* something more than just an externally imposed designation and suggests the foundations on which an understanding of collective identity is built. The grounds for distinguishing multiracials from monoracials lay in what most respondents felt was the unique experience of having *parents* of different races.

Deciding "who is mixed," then, also had implications for how people thought about membership in multiracial community. There was a general sense that "multiracial community" encompassed parents of multiracial kids and persons of mixed descent, no matter how "removed" that mixed ancestry. Yet it was the experiences of multiracial adults who had been raised in families with differently raced parents (not the experiences of parents or the "generationally mixed") that defined discussions about the content of collective multiracial identity.[3] For this reason, in this chapter I spend the most time analyzing the observations of multiracial adults. Mixed race adults, not the parents of multiracial kids, talked about the *content* of multiracial identity—its meaning for understanding themselves and their relationship to others. The elaboration of a notion of multiracial community predicated on a sense of a shared multiracial identity was also most prevalent in these respondents' interviews[4].

What Unites

Multiracial respondents drew the boundary between multiracial and monoracial on the basis of a set of experiences that had to do with having differently raced *parents*. As we saw in the previous chapter, dealing with the manifestations of racial division in relationships with family members is a central feature of a common multiracial experience. Mixed race respondents mark as especially salient experiences that gave them the sense that they are "out of place" in their families. But their sense of dislocation within their own families does not fully explain their mobilization. Just as important in motivating their attempts at collective identification is the sense that they are "out of place" in the ethnoracial communities of their parents. This sense of being an outsider gives rise to the desire to create "multiracial community."

Racial Belonging

Multiracials must deal with understandings of race that entail requirements of authenticity and loyalty and that leave those who fall outside prevailing modes of acceptable behavior vulnerable to accusations of being traitors or disloyal. Like intermarried respondents, multiracials talk about feeling that they are sometimes seen as traitors. Unlike these parents, however, mixed race respondents believed the source of their transgression is located by others not in what they do (that is, intermarry), but in *who they are*. This was indicated in the ways respondents suspected others thought of them. When I asked them if there were stereotypes of mixed descent persons, each agreed there were, and used words like "mutt," "mongrel," "traitor," "confused," "mixed up," "tragic"—images that link ambiguous physical appearance and mixed ancestry to a diminished character of the self. As such, it is not surprising that adjudication over their belonging in ethnoracial communities often concerned physical appearance, parents, friends, and dress—the very things that tend to signal ethnoracial identity. Vicki Reynolds's description of how being mixed felt while growing up in the 1970s typifies the kinds of feelings other multiracial respondents expressed.

[I] think when you're a child of mixed race—and this was the case for me as a child of mixed race—I was hyper aware of being mixed from the time I was young. And I felt—I always felt the potential to be rejected because of this and I felt—yeah, you know, I felt my difference and I felt nervous because of it. It's like the nervous condition of the colonized, you know. I felt that it was a nervous condition for me, too.

"What are you?"   Much as other researchers have found, nearly every respondent reported experiences where others could not "accurately" categorize them racially (G. H. Williams 1996; Gibel-Azoulay 1997). The "what are you" question is so common that one enterprising respondent, Jamie Tibbetts, sells T-shirts with the retort "What are YOU?" Ambiguous physical appearance was significant for respondents for several reasons. Phenotypical ambiguity often marked them outside ethnic communities. Several respondents reported feeling (and being made to feel) a little less authentic and a little less a part of ethnic communities because they did not look like a "real" member of the group. This phenotypical mismatch between their appearance and prevailing standards of ethnoracial embodiment was sometimes taken as a signal to both them and others that they might not possess the requisite cultural credentials to fit in, and it prompted Jade Wolkoff to reflect "there were times I wish I were darker." At the same time, those with a racially ambiguous appearance said they often felt "put to the test" to declare their loyalty to communities of color. Despite feeling that black Americans were "always ready to include" her, one respondent said: "I really look at my interaction with black people and I can sort of see, you know, that—if you're passing someone in the street they look at you and you can see, is she going to say anything? Is she going to slip by? I know she's not white, you know. Is she going to pretend?"

Majeeda Kibri pointed out, however, that what marked one as "other" in one context was the very thing that could secure belonging in another. Fitting into the Chicano theme dormitory in college was for her "easy, I pass. People don't question if I'm other. Sometimes people say, 'Oh, you have an interesting look to you, are you really Chicana?'" Majeeda says, however, that those who are Mexican and white "are more questioned." Moving from her hometown—where she felt that being brown was a liability—to college changed the value she placed on her skin color: "I'm on this level of brown pride now, you know, because I'm taking that anger and resentment of being brown and I'm turning it to something I can love now and something—like this brownness can't be taken away from me because I have it and I love it every day. And before I could have shied away from it."

At the same time, those multiracials who thought they did not look mixed enough sometimes felt that their sense of belonging to multiple ethnoracial groups was often not recognized by others.

Mandy Rodriguez, forty-five years old, explained that her racially ambiguous appearance caused problems for her when dealing with Japanese Americans, whom she believed are "really into racial purity," while growing up in Berkeley in the 1960s and the consequences it had for how she identifies herself racially:

> I realized everybody's racist. There's no shelter anywhere. So I guess it made me somewhat bitter, even at ten maybe. My two brothers learned how to fight because they had to fight to defend me. It made me very wary of Asian people. To this day I don't have a lot of Asian friends. I don't, and I don't align myself with the Asian community, and I don't feel very Asian American. I feel the way most people perceive me, which is as a Latina, and that's become my identity. It's not as unusual as I thought. For me it was like the white—the two races that I am were the two that were the least accepting of who we were. White people—I mean we moved next to these white people and all they could do every day, they're screaming at us, go back to Japan . . . Then the Japanese people were very cruel. The people that weren't cruel were the blacks and the Latino . . . Latino kids thought that me and my brothers were Mexican so of course they always gravitated to us and that's how—like I learned Spanish, and to me that was my culture because people always thought I was Mexican. And it's such a warm and embracing culture. They don't ask questions. They're all mixed. They don't give a shit . . . And that was great, to find a place where nobody cared.

Symbolism of parent.   Respondents with foreign-born parents, many of whom spoke the language of that parent or practiced their cultural traditions, conveyed the sense that they are closer to the culture because of their parental connection and recency of immigration. Having a foreign-born parent, especially a foreign-born mother, was considered a plus in the evaluation of one's cultural authenticity because of a general belief that mothers, not fathers, pass on cultural traditions. This logic was encapsulated in the shorthand phrase used by several mixed Asian respondents with non-Asian fathers, "Keep the name, lose the culture."[5]

While one's parents could symbolize authenticity in one ethnic realm, they could also mark one as counterfeit in another. Aware of the shifting meanings of one's parents for negotiating ethnic belonging, many multiracial respondents reported at times going out of their way to make known their kin ties to their parents in public and at other times downplaying those connections. In general, they downplayed connections to parents in situations where they felt it would threaten their belonging in racially charged settings. Monique LeBlanc admitted that "I've had to deny my parents—I don't know whether I've had to—but there are times—not really my dad but my mom, like I can't really deny my dad, but like my mom more so, either I won't speak up on something, you know, or I won't come out—"I'm black and white"—especially if I'm in a black setting or a black community." For Monique, having a white mother potentially threatened her belonging among black women, and she believes it did for her sister as well. Monique described what it was like for her sister when she considered joining a black sorority at the University of California, Berkeley:

When she came to Cal she like made an effort to go out and like seek black people . . . she was like Miss Black and it was really interesting because she was thinking of pledging Delta, right. So she went with her friend who is black, and she said to this other girl that was already in the sorority "Are you mixed?" because the girl was black and Asian, and the girl said "Yeah," but she was like "Don't talk about that," you know . . . And I was like I can understand like in a black sorority trying to be as black as possible. You don't want like your Asian mom to come up and be like acknowledged. So I guess it's just like in that kind of situation like I've got to be especially black or the girls won't invite me and won't want me to be in the organization.

Stephanie Williams, a forty-year-old black/white woman, recalls the tensions that arose around her having a white mother while growing up in a black neighborhood in Los Angeles in the late 1960s and 1970s: "I got beat up every day for having a white mother. I got beat up a lot, especially in my early teens. All the girls would catch me in the bathroom and beat me up. It was a very ugly business."

To the kids at school, Stephanie says, white people were not to be trusted, and by association, neither was she. In an effort to deflect that hostility, she cut off the symbol that most obviously connected her to whiteness—her long hair: "I went through a period where I cut my hair off, and I had my little afro, and it fell down in my face every day, and it was just an awful time for me, attempting to identify with only the black race and not associate with anyone that was white, anything that was white. It was a very, very hard time."

While it was the younger college-age respondents who were grappling most immediately and regularly with issues of authenticity and their relationships with their parents, older respondents discussed having felt similarly when they were younger. Although Robin Peters was president of the Asian Students Association at her college, she recalled an incident when her belonging in the organization was questioned because she had a white parent. While debating whether or not to prevent white students from attending the group's meetings, another member said:

Well, then, if we [don't allow white students] then technically you couldn't be here." So I was like floored. Whoa, I couldn't believe, I was absolutely shocked that she said that to me. What do you mean, I can't be here? I'm the president. I might be half. So that was very shocking to me, and Jennifer who was my co-president, I think, was really grappling with her issues of identification, and it was like, wow, maybe she's right. And I was like, no, she's not, because I was mad that she could—I couldn't believe that she would ask the question, the fact that I was part white did not mean, well, that means you sort of can't be here because you're not full was what she was telling me.

While these incidents happened years before, that they were still remembered by respondents indicates their salience in shaping how they thought about racial identity.

Many of my respondents measured their degree of cultural authenticity by the depths of contact they had with their extended families. When respondents did not have contact with their extended families, they used the language of race to describe that distance. Monique LeBlanc said she often worried that she was "not black enough"—that she would not talk the right way or listen to the right music. She speculated that this might be due to the fact that "all my dad's family is on the East Coast."

Friends and lovers.   Just as their choice of romantic partner was sometimes interpreted as a sign of how one felt about one's parents, it had the power to signal how one felt about ethnic groups. As one respondent told it, his parents were waiting to see the race of his girlfriend to figure out "which way I'll swing." Respondents also described their choice of friends as having similar telltale potential, but not in the enduring way that romantic, sexual, and *family* partners did. Much like Twine (1996) found, respondents felt that others were interested in the race of their romantic partners to gauge their ethnic identification and commitment. They also felt that the race of romantic partners portended the identification and commitment of their future children. In such a formulation, one's children are not merely carriers of the family tradition, but ethnic symbols—future recruits for the collectivity. Their children, most felt, were seen by others as indicative of a decisive stance on identity.

Mixed descent respondents were themselves also susceptible to that logic. When Charlene Nieda was thinking about the children she would have with her white husband, she confessed that she was unsure she wanted to "cast my whole genetic future" with whites. Her language is striking in the extent to which it links the body, race, and time. Charlene conveys the sense that the race of one's partner, inasmuch as it determines the race of one's children, marks a turning point that will determine the path she and future generations will take.

Others felt that whatever the race of their partner, any resultant children they had would be multiracial. More typically, mixed descent respondents said that how they would racially identify their children would depend on the race of their partner. In general, respondents felt it would be more difficult to sustain a mixed identity over generations if future partners were of the same monoracial category. Multiracials of African descent felt it would be especially difficult to sustain a mixed identity if their partners were black. All multiracial respondents, however, found it hard to think of their children as white, even when their real or imagined partner was white and they themselves had a white parent. All felt it was particularly important that their children feel a connection to nonwhite people (and said they would expose them to cultural traditions like dancing and language toward that end). It was as if an identification of their children as white really would be a significant break in relations with nonwhite families and communities.

Dressing the part.   Part of securing belonging in a group is knowing the appropriate means by which to signal membership. All multiracial respondents were quite aware of the subtle ways that authenticity could be conveyed.

In describing her observations of a mixed woman's attempt to fit into the Chicano theme house at school, Majeeda Kibri explained these subtleties:

> She would try to buy culture if that makes sense. [S]he would try and make herself look more ethnic and try to put on culture, try to buy material items so she could be part of the group. And there was like this front she was putting up like she's really down for whatever—like the cause and the movement. She'd always try to like make herself look like Frida Kahlo, and I'm like girl you don't have to do that . . . I think a lot of her issues were because she looked so white. Being in the community she felt like she would have to speak Spanglish. She would buy—God, the jewelry that was ethnic looking. People would say wow, that's cool. You're really down, huh, you're buying turquoise so you believe in indigenous people, you know. But she'd end up buying it at an art gallery, spending tons of money. And I'm just like, what are you trying to do, buy culture? [Culture's] something you live and you practice. If you go in museums and you buy it in galleries for a hundred dollars, you know, what's the purpose?

Majeeda portrays this girl's attempt "to put on culture" as, well, a "put-on"—a sham ("front") designed to gain acceptance as Chicana from other Chicanos despite her white appearance. Although Majeeda empathizes with the girl, noting that this sham is well intended, she believes it is a sham nonetheless. Majeeda recognizes a set of legitimate and illegitimate means through which culture is acquired and through which an authentication of one's ethnic identity is granted. For her, "buying culture" is style without substance—inauthentic to the extent that it is not "lived and practiced." While most respondents of mixed descent felt conflicted about these calls to demonstrate their authenticity, and aware of the artificiality of such tests, most also recalled attempting live up to them. When I asked Kanji Uyematsu to describe what it felt like when he first went to a Black Students Union (BSU) meeting, he said:

> Intimidated, because really—and I feel comfortable saying it now but back then it was just kind of, "Oh, so this is what it means to be black," so I tried to conform myself to fit into what people with issues were defining as black. This is where the "I'm black and you're not," the BSU, "if you don't follow these rules then you're not black" [comes from].
>
> Q. What were some of those rules?

A. Oh, gosh. Talking trash about people, I think. You know, you had to talk the right talk about certain people and about the administration . . . Whoever happens to be in charge decides what blackness is. Walking the walk, talking the talk, sitting, you know, in the black section of our dining hall. [A]nd walking the walk and talking the talk was pretty ridiculous to me, because most of these kids are from upper-middle-class families. And I realized pretty quickly that these fools didn't know what they were doing because they were about as enlightened as any white boy watching a music video, watching BET [television] for like a few days can be . . . I think me proving myself was getting the [BSU] board position and once I got the board position and served then I felt like, okay, I've proven myself. I guess that was what being black was, just doing the same stupid things that everybody else was.

Kanji is typical of the ways mixed descent respondents understand the rules of the ethnic game. Though critical of the rules, they find themselves playing just the same—wearing certain hairstyles, emphasizing brownness, adorning walls with nationalist posters, and feeling truly invested in it because they want to belong. Exploring and expressing ethnic affiliation in part helps to secure it. Yet their sense that the rules of ethnic belonging are, in fact, contrived underscores the extent to which they are out of place.

Coming Together

Being out of place from both family and ethnic community are the grounds from which the desire to explore what multiracial people have in common springs, and lead multiracial respondents to join organizations. The experiences respondents described in which they were out of place in their families and in ethnoracially defined settings are meaningful precisely because family and ethnic groups are institutions culturally sanctioned to give individuals a sense of communal solidarity—to bind them to a collectivity. The "we" feeling ethnic membership provides is "derived from associating with others perceived as like oneself in important basic ways" (Blu 1980). The same can be said of families. What multiracial respondents describe, however, are the various ways, some harsher than others, in which they have felt distanced from that "we" feeling.

Thus it is not surprising that when I asked multiracial respondents to describe what it was like to get together with other multiracials, their descriptions centered on how they *felt* (rather than what they thought) about the experience. The metaphors they used to describe their feelings are striking

Rather than suggesting shared racial identity, they evoke a kind of romantic sensibility—expressing a palpable desire for connection with others like them, in a space set apart from the everyday world where they could feel at home.

The desire for community. "I had that mixed person's radar," said Kanji Uyematsu "where I would just leave my shit if I found somebody that was mixed. I just went up to them, "Oh my God, you know what it's like." Kanji's 'radar" was tuned to pick up the signals of other mixed people in public. That his radar was tuned in this way is telling of the extent to which he was seeking similarly situated others whom he felt would understand him. Charlene Nieda describes how she felt as a child when she saw other mixed people in public: "You would think about it. You would go away and think about it. And you would tell someone else who was interested. You would make a laundry list—(mimics counting on fingers) I saw a hapa at the shoe store, and a family at the restaurant…"

Both Kanji and Charlene, like nearly all other respondents of mixed descent, describe being drawn to other multiracials, captured in stories of not being able to take their eyes off the multiracials they saw in public or finding multiracial celebrities particularly interesting (not for what they do but for their family background). One respondent said she "loved looking at [other] multiracials." Another said that talking to other multiracials when she went to college was "addicting." This sense of being drawn to other multiracials has the character of longing—which itself suggests something is missing. The thing longed for in this instance is understanding and a sense of community. These are, at bottom, longings for "place" in the here and now, but also, as Charlene Nieda explains below, a link between themselves, a past and a future. Explaining why she felt drawn to other multiracials she said:

[I]t must be partially because when you spend all these years not seeing really anybody that's like you, hardly ever, never seeing families that look like yours, never getting to talk to people about—it's just cumulative, you know. Then when you get the chance it's just so great. But not to say that I sat around thinking about, "Gee, if I could just see [another mixed person]"—I don't think I really noticed that I didn't—I had different little epiphanies like where—when I first met a woman, Rose Stone who was in her eighties and she was Asian and white, it was really emotional, and I realized this was the first time I had seen an old person who is like racially quote unquote like myself. This is maybe what I would look like as an older person. And that seemed like something that was in my subconscious but I had never consciously realized . . . My God, all that emotion, because I had never seen anybody who's old, elderly, and who is Asian and white. But now actually the one group that I am kind of like always excited to see is when I see kids who are like my daughter, you know, one quarter Japanese and the rest white, just sort of that whole spectrum of looks is sort of fairly interesting to me. But it's still not the same as that original feeling of hunger.

Q. Can you say a little bit more about the feelings that were involved?

A. It's kind of like happiness and sadness at the same time, you know, because you're so happy and it's fun and it's happiness, but then there's this other thing, like pain that sort of comes out a little bit that you become aware of, of never having had that option, I guess, before. So it's a funny sort of bittersweet thing. And then at the same time, you know, like with the Rose Stone thing I was sort of old enough, and I had been thinking about race identity and mixed race long enough that I was kind of disturbed by the fact that I even cared. I'm always uneasy with this idea of being too attached to other people simply because of shared ancestry, because it doesn't seem like a good enough reason to feel connected to people. And yet, you know, I'm aware that the impact is on that level.

Despite feeling that shared ancestry is "not a good enough reason to feel connected to people," this respondent understands that indeed she does "feel connected" to this woman whom she had only just met. For Charlene, this older Asian/white woman serves as a reflection of what she might become in the future while at the same time she symbolizes a past that Charlene has felt cut off from, or more to the point, that does not exist for her. The old woman also appears in this story as a kind of grandmother, related to Charlene through the "same" racialized ancestry.

Homecoming. The tales multiracials told of how they felt when getting together with other multiracials contrasted sharply with their experiences in monoracial settings. Instead of feeling like strangers and outsiders, being with other multiracials was often described as like "coming home" to a place where one truly belonged. "I've gotten to be close friends with a few [mixed race people] and it's so great," gushed one. "I mean I love it. I do. I feel like the way I felt when—like when I became a feminist. I felt like this is it you know. This is where I belong." Mia Guimond (Chinese/Haitian) described the feeling of being with other multiracials in a group setting as "very family-like," that she was with people "that had something in common with me. Like I didn't have to explain."

It is fitting that having felt out of place in family and ethnic community that respondents used the language of home and family to describe what they found (and thus what was once missing) in dialogue with other multiracials. The metaphor of home carries with it meanings of safety, acceptance, and comfort, and was often described as what respondents wanted out of multiracial organizations. "It was important that the group be a safe space," said Majeeda Kibri of her college mixed race group. Mandy Rodriguez wanted "a sense of comfort, a sense of understanding" from I-Pride. For Mandy, joining with other multiracials in a group provided what her parents could not—a community of people who understood her experiences as a mixed person— and highlighted for her what she could offer her son: "I just remember being so relieved and happy, realizing that when you are a mixed race person you have this wonderful family that your parents didn't have. We have a kid who's like [us], you know, you have a mixed race kid. I always told [my son] that I'm racially mixed, you're racially mixed, we're so lucky, we have each other and we understand each other."

Reflecting the felt sense of home that they shared with people of a variety of ethnoracial "mixes," more than one respondent referred to other multiracials as "my brothers and sisters." The kind of emotionality respondents expressed about being with other multiracials is aptly described in what Turner (1969) calls *communitas*, an intense emotional fusion among members of the same group. Respondents put forth a vision of sociality in multiracial community that was organic rather than forced. Instead of (monoracial) places where they felt "nervous," they sought a space to "relax"; rather than experiencing rejection, they would find acceptance; in place of isolation, mutuality. Overall, respondents described being among other multiracials as times and places where they feel they can, as one respondent put it, "just be."

Exploring commonality. While in the previous sections we saw the similarities in the ways respondents experienced being mixed, such similarities do not constitute group identity if they are not understood by multiracials as part of what binds them to a collectivity. A class in itself, to paraphrase Marx, is not necessarily a class *for* itself. "Being mixed," however mixedness is defined, is not enough to constitute a group. Mixedness must first be meaningfully con-stituted. A key way through which a sense of shared mixedness is developed is through the telling of stories to other persons of mixed descent about growing up mixed. Telling these stories, often in group settings, produces what Kanji described as "a bonding kind of experience."

> I think the commonalities are that growing up, more likely than not, you're going to be faced with that question, "What are you?" It is definitely a bonding kind of experience. I think, also, we tend to have the same kind of issues about—well, similarities in issues about dating, for instance, where whoever you date—I mean if you don't choose for yourself, you know, I'm going to go this way or that way, people usually date which way they're going to swing. We dealt with that—you're trying to make topics that apply to everybody like interracial dating and growing up, where you sit in the dining hall, things like that. I think that's where the biggest commonality comes. We're still kind of exploring that. We're still trying to see if it's something that works and if it will fit together.

Who to affiliate with according to race (encapsulated in the dilemma of where to sit in the dining hall), questions about "what are you," and dating are some of the things multiracials described as having in common with other multiracials. Brenda Jackson described what she thought other multiracials shared:

> I want to think that there are certain experiences that people who are mixed race have in common, and one of them is having to fill out an ethnic survey and the feelings that go with that. Having to watch one or both of your parents be antagonized verbally or physically . . . Being asked "what are you," like "you're not like any black person I've ever known," those kinds of remarks. So I think in handling those and going on to try and preserve self in some ways [other mixed race people] have had similar experiences because of the way race is constructed. So I believe that there is kind of a core experience of which, of course, there are many variations. I've never met anyone who is mixed that didn't recognize [these sorts of experiences].

Key in both these accounts is *how* multiracial respondents learn of their commonalities. Storytelling is part of an enactment of mixed identity through which multiracials come to feel part of a group. In this, "talking about being mixed" with other mixed people takes on the character of a ritual. Durkheim noted that in place of feelings of isolation, rituals collectively renew the individual's connection to the group. Telling stories that are often very emotionally charged creates a shared sense of "we," where group members learn what binds them together as a group. But this initial sense of euphoria is not enough to keep the group together. This is reflected in the common observation respondents made that once people had told their stories (again and again) at group meetings, interest in the group tends to wane. Longer-tenured members of the group described reacting to the stories of newcomers with a "been there, done that" attitude.

Sustaining a sense of groupness (and keeping the group itself alive) requires active work, a fact that was not lost on the leaders of multiracial organizations. Of the groups respondents were involved in, those oriented toward *particular* issues and demographics groups (for example, classification, inclusion in the Japanese American community, families with young children) retain members for a longer period of time and, in so doing, solidify bonds of solidarity.

Brenda compares HIF (a group first focused on mixed race Japanese Americans) to Miscellaneous (MISC) (a campus pan-multiracial organization), which she describes as having difficulty retaining consistent membership. HIF is successful in organizing:

> [B]ecause they have a community to focus on that they want to be incorporated into. MISC doesn't really have a common racial ancestry bringing them together, so they don't have a common community to deal with or interact with. So that's the main difference. Also HIF's focus seems to be on promoting awareness within the Japanese American community of us [mixed race people] and also the wider community to let them know that this is going to be an issue they have to deal with. Whereas MISC seems to be primarily interested in being a kind of support group for one another, Hapa seems more serious. Students are the same students, the turnover doesn't seem to be as high, there's a core group of people that come back and do all the work, whereas MISC seems like a lot of people are floating in and out.

Like the work that goes into making multiracial families exist, multiracials engage in symbolic work to make a sense of collective multiracial identity exist. The symbols by which multiracials were marked by others and which many saw as characteristic of mixed experience were also self-consciously used to elaborate what mixed people share. For example, while looking racially ambiguous was one way in which multiracials were positioned outside racialized communities, it was also a way through which they constructed a sense of commonality with each other. Several respondents of African descent spoke of the problems associated with having "multiracial hair" (such as dealing with hairstylists who were unaccustomed to and unskilled at styling their texture of hair). Using the term "multiracial hair" served to distinguish multiracials from monoracials both in phenotypical terms and by delineating a characteristic experience that only they really understood.

One indicator of the extent to which ambiguous appearance was seen as emblematic of mixed experience is evidenced by the frequency with which respondents described someone as "typically mixed looking," which for many meant being unable to easily situate that person in dominant racial categories based on what they look like. The experiences stemming from this ambiguity were the stuff of many support group meetings on college campuses and ritualized through the telling of stories about what Teresa Williams (1996) dubs "what are you encounters." The "chameleon factor," as Steve Tomita called it—the ability to blend into multiple ethnic communities depending on context—was cited by several respondents as something they shared with other multiracials regardless of their "mix." I was reminded of the degree to which physical ambiguity has come to be seen as emblematic of mixed experience when one woman of Mexican/Korean descent remarked that she sometimes felt like an outsider at multiracial group meetings because she did not look ambiguous *enough*.

Respondents also distinguished mixed identity on grounds of culture. As with physical appearance, the salient dimensions of that cultural experience lay not in a specific set of traditions but in the ambiguity and blending of cultural traditions. Typically cited were the combinations of foods one ate on a regular basis, like the "sushi and grits" of Mariko Frazier's childhood, or everyday practices in which one engaged, such as taking off shoes in the house. The members of HIF institutionalized the blending of cultural characteristics by publishing a regular feature in their newsletter called "Hapa Grub." In it were recipes for such tasty concoctions as "shoyu hotdogs" and "sushi burritos," often accompanied with stories of childhood memories that linked the blending of food to family relationships and cultural belonging.

Several respondents used the ways in which multiracials had been marked by others to construct a set of behavioral and moral characteristics that they believed delineated mixed identity. In contrast to monoracials, according to Charlene Nieda, multiracials were "flexible, easygoing, cosmopolitan," and unconcerned with authenticity requirements for membership, while Steve

Tomita felt multiracials had "fewer hangups about race" than monoracials. Mandy Rodriguez described mixed identity as at its core, a "way of thinking" that was not "uptight and boring" but "organic," that comes from experiences in which one has to synthesize multiple cultural styles: "because you're used to pulling in, say, your white Anglo-Saxon Protestant grandmother who was very regimented, somehow you internalize that and you are able to get your homework done. But then your Native American grandfather over here knew how to intuit, and both of those are important." Mitch Russell described as typically Japanese the ways he interacts with his students—asking them questions instead of just talking—while what was characteristically African American about him, he said, was "worldview stuff—kind of like the need for certain kinds of contact, music, food—in terms of feeling, you know? When I hear stuff on TV about black people it's about me. Those kinds of things where there's a link between me and this group of people."

What Separates

Respondents' conception of a shared multiracial identity is predicated on a set of shared experiences with respect to monoracial understandings of race. Yet despite feeling a sense of commonality with other multiracials, most were quite reflexive about, and even critical of, their desire for community based on a shared mixed position. Like Mitch Russell (quoted at the beginning of this chapter), many respondents wondered if what multiracials share constitutes enough of a shared *interest* to warrant coalescing as a group.

Despite the efforts of the most overtly politicized activists to highlight multiracials' shared fate, most respondents were quick to point out how their experience differed from other multiracials. The axes along which multiracials elaborated their differences have tended to follow the same categories that other political movements have divided along and by which Americans tend to organize subjective experience, namely race, ethnicity, generation, and gender.[6] In this, the politics of multiraciality are in keeping with the practice of identity politics developed in the 1980s generally, in which people became disenchanted with concepts of identity and community that obscured differences among them and began to organize along ever-narrower loci of identity.

Chief among the ways multiracials differentiate their experience is by ethnoracial category. Just as notions of mixedness rely on accepted ethnoracial boundaries (even though they are constructed against those boundaries), respondents differentiate among themselves according to those same boundaries. Such a differentiation is reflected in the pattern of organizational creation. Multiracial organizations have tended to form along currently recognized ethnoracial divisions, most notably with multiracials of Asian descent forming organizations separate from what might be called "pan-multiracial" organizations. The founders of HIF, for example, knew there were other ethnically nonspecific mixed race groups on the University of California–Berkeley's campus and in the local San Francisco Bay Area, but they believed that Asians had grievances that were unique to them (like exclusion from Japanese American basketball leagues) that an ethnically specific multiracial organization was best suited to address. According to HIF's founders, the delineation of hapas apart from a general notion of mixedness was prompted as well by the tendency of the concept of mixed race to suggest a black/white person, an extension of the tendency of the black/white divide to dominate discussion of race in the United States.

The skepticism about the content and significance of what multiracials share reflected the same kinds of uncertainties about shared racial location and interests evident in currently recognized ethnoracial groups. For example, uncertainty over the meaning of "Asian American" was reflected in debates over the meaning of "hapa." Although HIF was first created by a group of students at Berkeley with one Japanese or Japanese American parent, and oriented toward particular concerns within the Japanese American community, almost immediately participants in the organization questioned the exclusively Japanese focus, arguing for a broader pan-Asian focus. "I was one of the first to integrate the organization," quipped Lief Hogan (Chinese and white), only partly in jest. Discussions over whether and how to include in HIF part-Asian multiracials from Asian groups who immigrated post-1965 have been debated often among HIF members. Some members of HIF were concerned that biracials from these groups might not necessarily share the experiences of Japanese and Chinese Americans around whom the pan-Asian concept has been constituted.

Questions about just who was "hapa," like the question of who is "mixed," were present from the outset of the organization and signal a general concern among multiracials over the legitimacy of racial distinctions as the basis of sameness. These uncertainties about the shared location and interests of hapas were crystallized in an incident I observed at the annual meeting of the Asian American Studies Association in 1996. The term *hapa* comes from a Hawaiian phrase "hapa haole" (half white or foreigner), which HIF founders adopted as a reappropriation of a label once used to denigrate persons of mixed Asian ancestry (the use of which one respondent likened to "calling someone a dog"). At this conference, two women of Hawaiian ancestry raised vociferous objection to "Asian Americans" using a Hawaiian term. Underscoring the schisms within the constructed category of Asian Americans (which includes Hawaiians as Pacific Islanders), to these women, this amounted to a colonialist taking by Japanese Americans of yet another piece of native Hawaiian culture.

"Is Halle Berry hapa?" Organizational creation along racially specific lines suggests which social categories respondents understood to be salient in marking their identity. Most part-Asian respondents felt that the Asian focus of HIF made sense to them experientially. Yet even as they said this many questioned the legitimacy of such a distinction. Thinking about the rationale for limiting an understanding of "hapa" along "Asian" ethnicities prompted Robin Peters to ask rhetorically, "Is Halle Berry hapa?" referring to the black/white actress. The question might just as well be asked, why *isn't* Halle Berry hapa? The common sense answer is, of course, because she is not Asian. Defining "hapa" as those with partial Asian ancestry necessarily highlights experiences as Asian as the glue that holds the group together. But since delineating a "we" always entails defining who is *not* "we," the effort to construct a unified concept of hapa always threatened to collapse. This is because in practice, the kinds of experiences respondents believed defined hapa experience were, according to nonwhite (or "double minority") hapas, more accurately described as experiences particular to Asian/white multiracials because they did not consider the unique position of nonwhite hapas. Elaine Johnson (Japanese/black) remarked that "even within the multiracial community there is a problem related to blackness," one that she found especially in activism around hapa issues. "[I]f the white/Asians are saying, you know, that our agendas aren't addressed in the organizations that focus on black/white mixtures, they turn around and they do the same thing. They form an organization and they don't focus on Afro/Asian issues and Latino/Asian issues. They focus on white/Asian issues."

According to Elaine, being black made her experience substantially different from white hapas. For Mitch Russell, the significance of that difference lay in skin color and the negative stereotypes of black people. Kanji Uyematsu positioned black/Asians as having more challenges than Asian/white multiracials, an issue he said he felt "nervous" to bring up at group meetings:

I can't help feel a bit of resentment towards like the Asian/whites . . . It's easy. When you're black/Asian it's not easy. It's like a double minority, you know, and it feels like you don't get any of the perks of either because I think it's harder—I think we feel it's harder because—I'm not saying it's true or anything—but we feel it's harder to gain acceptance in either—it's hard to gain acceptance in the Asian community. And it's hard as hell to get accepted in the white community, and the black community is like—you can get acceptance but you have to deny the other side.

He then positioned black/whites as having a particularly "hard time" because "I think I can claim both, and it's still kind of problematic but white/black, they can't claim both because those are warring sides."

These kinds of divisions are not unique to hapa organization but are a general difficulty in constructing new hybrid social categories (racial or otherwise). In this instance, the difficulty stems from perceptions of the relative positon of racial groups in a hierarchy. While hapas were defining what marked their experience in different and significant ways from nonhapas, multiracials of African descent were doing the same. Several said that being of African descent afforded them a unique set of challenges in negotiating racial matters, not merely in terms of fitting into the black community but in relation to other multiracials.

Majeeda Kibri demonstrated how one symbol of race (skin color) that is a source of conflict within monoracial communities was equally salient in navigating relations between multiracials. "I don't want to make the issue of color such a big deal but it is because it's even in—it's like, honestly—I know this is all confidential—but it's like I even deal with people that typically look whiter than me so being angry at them, you know, because it's like you're not Chicano and white, you're white."

The reticence that Majeeda and Kanji showed toward revealing these schisms among multiracials is interesting because it suggests a sense of group reputation that they feel invested in protecting. Majeeda said that while she wanted to bring up these issues in her organization, she was "afraid" because she did not want to "make it a people of color mixed group and separate us even more."

Multiracials have been unable to avoid reproducing the same kinds of divisions that lead them to organize together in the first place. The separation of organizations along a black or Asian axis puts "double minority" multiracials in the position of choosing between what are structured (intentionally or not) as mutually exclusive alternatives. At the same time, the kinds of uncertainties about what individuals within panethnic groups (for example, among Asian Americans) and between ethnoracial groups (Asian and blacks) share, are the very things that separate multiracials.

Hierarchies of Relatedness

The distinctions among multiracials that respondents spoke of comprise a hierarchy of relatedness—a continuum defined by poles of proximity and distance that follows dominant understandings of race. In this hierarchy, one feels more of a sense of belonging, affinity, and closeness with those who are of their same mix, where "same" is defined in racially and ethnically specific terms. "You know, for me to talk to someone who's black and white, I don't feel as close to that person as I do [to someone] who is black and Asian," said Mitch Russell (black/Japanese American). "And in terms of linking up with someone who is Latino and white, I don't feel very close to them at all, especially if they're light skinned, you know. So there's a hierarchy of sorts."

Mitch's response typifies the nested distinctions in this hierarchy that other multiracials talked about. He feels closest to someone of the same ethnoracial combination than someone with whom he partially shares ancestry and not at all close to someone with whom he shares no ancestry, even if that person is mixed. This distance is exacerbated by the other's light skin.

Several respondents articulated hierarchies of relatedness refined along multiple axes of differentiation. Gender was often added in the hierarchy of relatedness, especially by women. The national origin of one's parents was also frequently named. While Vicki Reynolds described feeling a sense of belonging with "all different kinds" of multiracial people, she went on to say:

I certainly have more in common—I mean I have the most in common with people who have a background exactly like me, which is to be African American and white, to have a white mother. I actually have a couple of friends now who have a white French mother and an African American father and that's the thing I never had when I was growing up, somebody who was precisely like me. So even like I have two friends who have a French white mother from France and an African American father from the south of the U.S.

Although Vicki's hierarchy of relatedness was slightly more differentiated than Mitch's, it followed the same logic in which "closeness" is grounded in ancestry. Likeness is conceptualized according to broad categories of race, gender, and national origin. Most respondents expressed similar understandings of relatedness that drew upon symbols of ancestry, blood, and gender as well. This hierarchy of relatedness relies on the same logic as the broader cultural system embedded in the familization of race and the racialization of the family.

The hierarchy of relatedness demonstrated by respondents should not be mistaken for a rigid set of rules that describe with whom respondents can and do associate. Mitch's wife, for example, is neither black nor Japanese. Rather, the hierarchy demonstrates the cultural categories we use to think of strangers, persons in the abstract, whom we do not know personally, rather than those we know personally. This hierarchy suggests the likelihood that we will seek to develop relationships with and an understanding of the stranger. It defines a kind of circle of affection. Those within our circle we feel obligated to care for and about. Those outside our circle we feel less obligated to and may likely abandon.

This distinction between the stranger and someone known personally is important to help understand what may seem like contradictions in respondents' thinking. For example, many respondents reported feeling resentment toward whites, and even at seeing interracial couples, despite having intermarried parents. Respondents tended to exempt parents, whom they know intimately, from the abstract category of white people.

How Multiracial Community Is Constituted

In the first part of the chapter we saw the ways that multiracials draw the boundary between themselves and others. The sense of "we" they report focuses on a common set of experiences—experiences that stem from the ways that normative families have been constructed along racially exclusionary lines and understandings of race that downgrade interracialism. Multiracial respondents believe these experiences set them apart from their parents and "monoracial" people generally. It is their sense that they are out of place in racialized families and racialized communities that gives rise to the desire to create multiracial community.

Yet while the understanding of community put forth by multiracials refers to a sense of belonging with one's own kind, "one's own kind" varies depending on context. Notions of multiracial community rest on variable interpretations of identity, each one more or less salient depending on context. Moreover when I asked respondents if they thought there was a multiracial community they gave varied responses. Some respondents had in mind explicit criteria for determining whether or not a multiracial community existed. Pedro Santana was reluctant to say a multiracial community existed because multiracials did not practice endogamy. Steve Tomita believed a multiracial community existed and located that community in the realm of activism, among people who were "active and working on" issues of multiracial inclusion. For Paula Kane, the multiracial community was a "virtual community," existing in the written dialogues between people interested in talking about classification and identity. Others felt conflicted about just where the "there" of multiracial community lay. Said Monique LeBlanc, "There's nothing like distinctive that holds us together." At the same time she believes that a pan-multiracial identity exists. Mia Guimond said that whether or not she felt a sense of connection to another multiracial person depended on "if they identify with being multiracial." Matt Kelley, director of the Mavin Foundation asserts that it is time to "stop questioning the obvious: a mixed race community exists."[7]

The shifting salience of multiracial identifications and the different understandings of community make it clear that rather than investigate whether or not a multiracial community exists (which presumes one can define its limits and count its members), multiracial community is best understood as a cultural category people use to *develop* collective identity and think about relationships to others. In their negotiations with each other (and within themselves) over the meaning of being multiracial and what they do and do not share with other mixed race people, the notion of a multiracial collective identity takes shape. Yet in this process two seemingly contradictory impulses are at work. At the same time as they elaborate a sense of shared groupness, multiracials are deconstructing the basis upon which racial membership has been erected.

Like all identities, multiracial identity is constructed in relation to other groups. In particular, the meaning of mulitracial identity is elaborated in a social and cultural system where understandings of race and family are intertwined. Prevailing assumptions about racial membership in the United States liken it to a kin relationship, with all the attendant expectations that such relations entail: loyalty to the group and standards for determining who belongs. According to this logic, multiracials are considered disloyal if they express a mixed racial identity, and inauthentic if they do not possess or cannot perform cultural requirements. Aware of this cultural logic, multiracials have joined collectively in part to make sense of the ways that logic makes them feel, and to transform both their feelings and the conditions that make them feel that way, such that being mixed feels and is perceived by others as authentic.

Table 5.1 Cultural Logic

Cultural Logic (normative)	According to which multiracials are:	Through collective efforts multiracials seek to become:
Race as quasi-family	Disloyal, inauthentic	Authentic
Family members share same race	Outsider, stranger	Insider

In order to do this given dominant understanding about race, multiracials must think about the symbols that are commonly taken to indicate racial membership in ways that differ from dominant modes. In what ways do they do this?

"Race ain't your face."   Many respondents call into question the association of racial identification with a certain type of physical appearance. Mandy Rodriguez posed perhaps the most thorough rejection of the correspondence between racial identification and ancestry. She identifies not with the ethnoracial groups of her parents (Japanese and white), but as Latina, and more particularly as mestiza because:

> [F]or me it kind of embraces the idea of a big ball of everything and my little credo is that the race ain't your face. I say this all the time. It's who you believe yourself to be and how you can shape the world. Because of racism, because of the lack of understanding of what being mixed is I've basically adopted an identity that has nothing to do with my race.

Both/and.   Many multiracials try to refuse the choices between what are posited as mutually exclusive alternatives in dominant ways of thinking about race. Says one respondent:

> In the meantime, what's the big deal? We know that we are parts, also, even if we are an ethnic community, we also have ties and connections to other ethnic communities and that's important to us, not unimportant. [It's not] an either/or proposition. I do not see the contradiction between identifying as a multiethnic person, unified synthesis, at the same time as I identify with my roots. That's the old Greek antithesis/synthesis. There's a unity there. I don't see any problem with that. I don't know why we have to divorce the concept at all.

By asserting that one can "be" more than one race, multiracials assert an essential integrity to themselves. One respondent was particularly fond of saying "I'm 100 percent black and 100 percent Japanese," refusing to split his sense of self along ethnoracial lines in an effort to convey his sense of undivided loyalty to both groups.

Something else. At times multiracials expressed a conception of identity that was different from either of the ethnoracial groups of their parents. As Jade Wolkoff put it:

> Now I recognize that both of my parents are different from me . . . For my mother I'm black and for my father I'm Jewish, and I think of myself more as like a full person now. I'm a mix of these two. You know what I mean. I don't look at it like—I mean yes, I'm a product of my parents but I'm a black Jew—you know, it's not so much about me choosing.

This conception of multiracial identity as a "third" space defies the parental matching rule that underlies fractional ("I'm half white, half Asian") as well as both/and identities. While Jade is a black Jew because one parent is black, the other Jewish, the meaning of that identity is for her something different from either of its constituent parts.

While multiracials' understandings of race, identity, and community diverge from dominant understandings of race, they are also continuous with those understandings in important ways. In elaborating a notion of collective multiracial identity, multiracials still draw upon the same pool of symbols that are understood to indicate race in the United States (blood, ancestry, skin color, eye shape, hair texture, and language), even if they invest them with different meanings than in dominant racial understandings. Ironically, their elaboration of a different way of racial thinking makes more obvious the hierarchies of affection, likeness, and difference that racial differentiation has wrought.

While multiracials attempt to talk about race and construct a sense of community that challenges existing modes of racial affiliation, they do not depart from the underlying bases upon which race and kinship are constructed. Most still grant notions of blood and ancestry the power to signify social relatedness. The differences among multiracials are too often the divisions that mark them in the first place and threaten the possibility of community across these divisions.

Using the symbols of racial membership in ways different from the dominant modes is a daunting task, difficult both in logic and in practice. This is because success in doing so has at least as much to do with how *others* think about race as it does with how one identifies oneself. So while Mandy Rodriguez thinks of herself as Latina, speaks Spanish, is married to a Puerto Rican man, and participates in Latino political organizations, if she does not possess the criteria others deem necessary for legitimate membership, she will not be fully authenticated as a member, at least not without hiding just a little. Mandy was glad our interview was confidential, she said, because her co-workers "think I'm Mexican and I haven't—they never asked and I never said. We're all operating on an assumption, but I know if they found out that I wasn't really a Hispanic Latina they would dump me. They have their own racism, too."

It is also difficult to fully challenge American concepts of race because of the temptation to use the same means by which they are excluded from ethnic communities to establish their own sense of shared identity. For example, in their critique of authenticity tests for granting racial inclusion, some multiracials have substituted their own understandings of an authentically *mixed* position. One respondent described as "blackwashed" mixed descent persons of African descent who identify themselves as black, standing on its head the more familiar epithet "whitewashed" used to describe a nonwhite person who has adopted the attitudes and behavior of a white person. In a community meeting, one activist described mixed descent persons who identify monoracially as indicative of "racism within the multiracial community." The idea that asserting a mixed identity reflects a truthfulness to the self suggests not only that there can be an authentic position, but that authenticity resides in ethnoracial affiliations. Lurking within these ideas is not merely description of what is, but what *ought* to be—a moral prescription about how one should racially identify oneself.

Others have tried to sidestep these dilemmas of authenticity and membership criteria by abandoning the notion of identity-based community altogether and attempting to avoid social categorization with the individualist claim "I am who I am."

The Dilemmas of Community

Getting together with other multiracials provided a place of understanding, to feel "safe" and "relax," in direct contrast to the isolation, sense of loneliness, and perception that they were invisible. In this sense, multiracial community was thought about in relation to "monoracial" community. In their classificatory schema of mixedness, multiracial is to monoracial as close is to distant, home is to isolation, and same is to different. These distinctions refer to a sense of commonality multiracials felt among themselves. Yet while respondents talked about feeling a sense of commonality with other multiracials, there is wide variation both in whether or not respondents felt this comprised a community and what they meant by "community."

Most respondents rejected the sameness implicit in general notions of community, and attributed a special importance to exploring and identifying with one's specific ethnic and cultural heritage. This was reflected in the very few number of respondents who thought the promotion of a "pan" mixed identity symbolized in a multiracial category with no elaboration of ancestry was a good idea. Even so, most who understood themselves as say "Persian and Mexican first" also felt they had significant commonalities with persons of mixed descent who were not of their "mix," and they saw as important the exploration, if not elaboration, of a sense of "we" among multiracials.

This apparent paradox reflects the distinction most respondents made between personal identity and politicized identity. For some this connection with other multiracials was important for what they described as "personal" reasons—a sense of well-being and self-esteem. Even Mitch Russell, who critiqued the idea of political organization along the principle of multiraciality, thought that getting together with other multiracials was "wonderful" on a "personal level."

Many multiracials voiced a desire for a kind of community founded on the premise of shared positioning *between* racial categories, the content of which was unspecific. This vision was constructed in relation to how respondents felt they were included (or not) in ethnic communities. Multiracial community could not reproduce, some contended, the problematic divisions (manifest in membership criteria and authenticity tests) that prompted the formation of multiracial community in the first place. Instead, multiracial community could offer its members the sense of belonging and acceptance they did not find among monoracials, while maintaining a fluid conception of what it meant to be a member.

Yet others were wary of the notion of mixed racial community, afraid that it might reproduce the very categories they seek to challenge. "I'm very wary of the so-called multiracial movement," said a student of Wesleyan University who founded a magazine on "the mixed-race experience." "It seems to me more intent on creating a new race than people who have the wholeness of their heritage . . . Aren't we simply replicating the same exclusive ideas of community we in the past had been criticizing?"[8] These multiracials reject the analogies some activists have drawn between multiracial politics and other movements organized along racial lines, where group members are treated as fairly homogeneous, and a particular code of conduct was said to define an authentic experience of group members. For multiracials who could not or did not want to conform their behavior in order to fit into prevailing standards of membership, multiracial identity was a way to challenge the presumptions of a unified experience that prevailed in these understandings of community.

Commentators on mulitracial activists' claims to represent a community have questioned that assertion, skeptical that multiracials have much in common. Echoing the sentiments of Mitch Russell, quoted at the beginning of this chapter, novelist Danzy Senna writes, "But we've decided on this one word, 'multiracial,' to describe, in effect, a whole nation of diverse people who have absolutely no relation, cultural or otherwise, to one another" (Senna 1998, 23).

Yet some multiracials are indeed inventing a collective vision of themselves. And that is exactly the point. All ethnic self-understandings are invented. They are perspectives on the world—a way of seeing rather than things in and of themselves. Rather than chastise them for it, my goal has been to understand both why and in what ways they are doing so and to show the contested nature of that process. Perhaps the most interesting facet of this phenomenon is that even those most committed to making multiracials exist socially seek to undermine the very foundations upon which this identity rests. As Carlos Fernandez, founding member of AMEA noted:

There is the possibility that a mixed race "community" may never fully develop as a separate community because it will become American society and even what it means to be a global citizen. And that will define what the culture is. We will become the majority. And whether people interracially marry or not, it is a fact that already this culture is a multiculture. And really that's the most important thing of all, in the sense that what sets people apart—culture—not skin color but culture—will be neutralized and distinctions will be at the level of individuals as opposed to the artificial lines of culture.

The manner in which multiracial community develops (or not) will not be determined by the intentions or actions of multiracial actors alone. Due in large part to the advocacy for social and statistical "recognition" of mixed race people and the release of census multirace data, multiracials are no longer statistically or socially invisible. In the next chapter, I explore how that newfound visibility is being put to use in an arena with far-reaching capacity to shape the meaning of race—the marketplace.

6 Consuming Multiracials

Strange to wake up and realize you're in style.

—Danzy Senna[1]

IN THE LATE 1990S I WAS A TEACHING ASSISTANT in a course on the family at the University of California–Berkeley. In beginning a lecture on interracial families, I asked the students, "If you saw an ad for a minivan featuring a black father, a white mother, and their two children, would you focus on the car or the family?" Nearly every student (about one hundred) said "the family." My intention at the time was to get students to think more deeply about the cognitive dissonance that interracial families provoke and to begin a dialogue about racialized conceptions of the family. The fact that interracial families were virtually never used in advertisements[2] and seldom seen in the media was secondary to me at the time, merely support to the contention that such families were outside the cultural mainstream.

Fast forward to 2004 when Verizon, the telecommunications company, airs a series of seven commercials featuring "the Elliotts," a fictional interracial family with a white dad and Latina mom. The ads depict scenes of family life (dad trying to decipher the mysteries of e-mail or cell phones, for example, while the kids interpret for him). In the commercials, ethnicity is never mentioned though present nonetheless. The first commercials to air included only the white father and the darker-skinned, curlier-haired kids, leaving curious viewers to wonder just who (or rather what *race*) mom was. "The Elliotts" series is part of a discernible trend in which images of interracial families and mixed race people are increasingly used in advertising and marketing campaigns. The growth of this trend is so noticeable that the question I asked Berkeley students only a few years ago no longer resonates. Depictions of interracial families and mixed race people in advertisements are no longer rare

Moreover, images of interracialism have moved from being taboo in mainstream ads to being increasingly sought after. According to a Verizon spokesman, for example, "the Elliotts" commercials were explicitly designed to appeal to *mass market* consumers (Texeira 2005).

As we saw in previous chapters, state institutions, multiracial activists, and people involved in mixed race organizations have been crucial in the making of multiracials, particularly in the years leading up to the 2000 census. In the post-Census 2000 period, however, the contours of mixed race identification and community are increasingly being forged in the marketplace. When the Census 2000 multirace data was released to the public (U.S. Census Bureau 2001), marketing industry professionals wasted no time in accessing and interpreting it. In 2001, the marketing magazine *American Demographics* began a series of articles examining and interpreting the new multirace numbers. Marketers are keen to understand the significance of a range of characteristics that delineate this demographic, most notably its largely urban and coastal geographic dispersal, its ethnic patterning, and its relatively young age.

Not surprisingly, marketers are also interested in the buying power of multiracials. According to a report by the Selig Center for Economic Growth, at $148 billion, the buying power of multiracials is about one-quarter that of African Americans but over three times that of Native Americans. Multiracial buying power is expected to increase at a faster rate than that of blacks or whites in the next few years.[3]

Currently, marketers know only the broadest demographic characteristics of the multiracial population. What they seek to find out is who "the multiracial consumer" is—her tastes, habits, and beliefs—in order to market *to* her. According to one marketing analyst, "the growth of multiracial America . . . means that the time to figure out what multiracial means to today's consumers, whether it creates specific consumer marketing or communication needs, and exactly how to tap into the market was about five minutes ago, and it's time to catch up fast" (Wellner, 2001, 2).

Not only have corporate marketers been devising strategies to identify and target messages at "the multiracial consumer," entrepreneurs have also begun to develop products designed to appeal to multiracials.[4] These entrepreneurs are largely of mixed descent or live in interracial families. They are selling items like shampoo and greeting cards, each tailored to the specific "needs" of multiracial consumers. This marketing *by* multiracials, like the marketing *to* multiracials by mainstream companies, is about selling for profit. It is also motivated by—according to its purveyors—a desire for social recognition. The creation of products for and the development of consumer profiles about multiracials is a new phenomenon. A relationship between marketing and multiracials, however, predates the ability to count this population. During the 1990s, racially ambiguous-looking people and even interracially intimate scenes began to appear in advertisements designed to appeal to a broad, ethnically nonspecific audience. The construction of such images requires no knowledge about multiracials and their putatively unique habits and needs. Rather, their impact, and advertisers' motivation for using such images, lies in their symbolism—the ability to evoke for a viewer positive qualities, feelings, or desires. Of course, multiracialism's capacity to invoke such desirable qualities, and even what is considered "desirable," are historically and context specific.

Danzy Senna is right. Multiracials are indeed in style. But *why* are they "in style"? What role does marketing play in the making of multiracials? And what does the marketing of multiraciality imply about contemporary modes of racial formation? Social scientists have long looked at consumption as a major means through which Americans define their identities and compete for social status (Bourdieu [1984] 1988, DiMaggio 1994). Recently, researchers have turned their attention to the consumer culture's role in ethnic identity formation. Marilyn Halter demonstrates marketers' increasing reliance on ethnicity as a hook to stimulate demand for their products and develop brand loyalty. Moreover, she argues that the marketplace is a site through which people learn representations of ethnic groups (their own and others) and through which they can participate and enact culture. "Ethnicity," writes Halter, "is increasingly manifest through self-conscious consumption of goods and services and, at the same time, these commodities assist in negotiating and enforcing identity differences" (2000, 7). Arlene Davila (2001) argues that marketers shape public perceptions of the culture as well as the relevance and influence of racial groups by determining the kinds of racialized images we see. Joane Nagel (1996) and others have examined how culture industries centered on art and tourism in American Indian communities provide economic support as they encourage cultural renewal and shape (for good or ill) the kinds of cultural expressions artists produce.

In this chapter, I explore the marriage of multiracials and the market. I use the term *marketing multiraciality* to refer to a broad set of practices that include marketing to, by, and of multiracials. My intention is to show how the marketing of multiraciality is both similar and different from the ethnic target marketing that has developed over the last several years. I describe early developments in marketing *to* multiracials and the ways that firms are developing an understanding of multiracials as consumers. I also analyze examples of marketing messages and products created by multiracials for multiracials. By conducting and using the research available on this newly discernible statistical population, marketers give shape and substance to a multiracial market and contribute to creating an image of multiracials as a group. Next I look at the marketing *of* multiracials, in which images of multiracials are used to appeal to a broad audience. Finally, I discuss what marketing and consumption have to do with racial justice.

Marketing Multiraciality in the Age of Target Marketing

Mass marketing—crafting one size fits all messages—reached its peak near mid-twentieth century. Since the 1940s, segmented marketing has steadily supplanted it. The difference between the two strategies, simply put, is that mass marketing approaches differentiate between products, while market segmentation differentiates between consumers.[5]

Segmentation by race and ethnicity did not begin to gather momentum in the industry until the late 1960s. As early as the 1940s, however, companies began to recognize the money to be made by getting African Americans to buy their products. To capture black dollars, they began to advertise their products in black-owned and black-consumed media outlets. Cohen (2003) dubs these early attempts to reach African Americans "color blind advertising" because the ads used were largely the same as those featured in mainstream media outlets. Many African Americans saw the mere fact that companies were advertising in black media outlets as a symbol of greater social acceptance. Gradually, African Americans called for advertisements that included black people and reflected their culture. In response, companies began to craft messages and products specifically designed to reach African American consumers.

Ethnic target marketing is currently one of the fastest growing segments of the advertising industry. Businesses are responding to shifting demographics that predict whites will make up less than half of the U.S. population by 2050 and substantial increases over the already-substantial buying power of Asians, Latinos, and African Americans (Humphreys 2002). Major companies like

Ford, Pepsico, and Proctor & Gamble are devoting significantly more of their ad dollars toward reaching these markets than ever before (Garcia 2004).

From one vantage point, marketers' interest in multiracials looks like just another manifestation of the ethnic target marketing in which they have engaged for years. Recognizing a growing multiracial population with purchasing power, marketers seek to attract their dollars and so begin to market to this population. From another point of view, the marketing of multiraciality appears different from marketing toward other ethnic groups. When marketers began to court African American dollars, African Americans were already defined as a distinct social group with distinctive values and ways of thinking and acting. Multiracials are not yet so clearly defined. The category "multiracial" encompasses people of a broad range of racial and ethnic ancestry combinations. One could argue that this is no different from the construction of Latinos and Asian Americans as racialized groups in which diverse immigrant populations are lumped into overarching categories on the basis of language difference (for example, Spanish) or the logic of racial sameness (for example, Asian). The "lumping" of a diverse group of multiracials, however, is predicated on the logic of *multi*raciality, within which language, tradition, *and* racial identification are variable.

This variability poses a challenge for marketers in figuring out just who "the multiracial consumer" is. The challenge, however, is not insurmountable. To a considerable degree, when marketers recognize and cater to market segments, they have contributed to reinforcing those divisions (Cohen 2003; Davila 2001). As a sort of self-fulfilling prophecy, they create what they appear to only reflect and feed back to consumers an image of what they are supposed to be (Frank 2000). In this respect as well, however, multiracial marketing may prove to work differently. As I discuss in more detail later, some marketers do indeed emphasize the commonalities among multiracials and their collective *difference from* "monoracials." This will likely strengthen some segment of the population's sense that multiracials are a distinct class of people. On the other hand, much of the marketing of multiraciality emphasizes an ideal of racial harmony and the transcendence of racial division through racial blending and cultural hybridity.

Defining the Multiracial Consumer and Identifying Her Needs

Despite the diversity of the multiracial population, marketers appear to be developing a profile of just who the multiracial consumer is. Much of that profile is driven by demographic data. In an early article on the multirace data published in *Forecast*, a marketing magazine, the concentration of multiracials in Hawaii is highlighted. Hawaii, we are told, "is home to the nation's largest share of multiracial consumers." The author goes on to characterize the Hawaii data as the "first look at the multiracial market" and informs us that multiracials in Hawaii are "more likely to live with family than average." In subsequent articles in *American Demographics*, researchers pay more attention to the racial breakdown of this population and delineate multiracial buying power by ethnic subgroup (the greatest of which, according to industry analyses, is that of Asian/white biracials) (See Table 6.1). They are particularly attuned to the age of multiracials who are disproportionately young. Of the two-or-more-races population, 42 percent is under age eighteen compared to 25 percent of those who indicated one race only (U.S. Census Bureau 2001).

Demographics, however, merely sketch the contours of a multiracial market, alerting marketers to its statistical existence and general characteristics. They do not by themselves constitute markets. The creation of a market requires some interpretation of what those numbers mean—of what makes this demographic different from others. To get a better sense of how a multiracial market is being constructed, a good place to look is at the companies developing products specifically for multiracial consumers. Since 2000, several such ventures have developed. "Multiracial Apparel: the mixed race experience" and "Likemindedpeople" sell clothing, mostly T-shirts with pithy sayings reflecting an aspect of the mixed race people's common experiences ("Team Hapa," "Beautifully Blended") or employing symbols to convey hybridity (the

Table 6.1 Selected Population and Economic Characteristics by Race

	*Multiracial**	*Black*	*Asian*	*White*
2000 population (in millions)	6.8	34.7	10.2	211.5
Percent U.S. population	2.4	12.3	3.6	75.1
Under 18 years old	41.9%	31.4%	—	23.5%
Geographic dominance	40% West	54.8% South	48.8% West	34.4% South
Buying power (in billions)**	148.1	588.7	254.6	5,800

*"Multiracial" refers to those who marked more than one race on the census. All other race figures are for those who chose single race responses.

**Buying power is another term for disposable personal income, defined as "the share of total personal income that is available for spending on personal consumption, personal interest payments, and savings" (Humphreys 2002, 8).

SOURCES: Data from U.S. Census Bureau 2001, 2002 and Humphreys 2002.

El Camino car/truck popular in the 1970s). RealKidz Biracial Dolls sells plush toys marketed to parents of mixed race kids.

Purveyors of the various products developed specifically for multiracial consumers—be they books, conditioners, or cards—emphasize a special need that they claim multiracial consumers share. The owners of Melting Pot Gifts, for example, have developed a line of interracially themed greeting cards and other tchotchkes like wedding cake toppers.[6] They assert that the need for such products arises from the "substantial number of interracial families and couples," many of whom, they claim, "want cards that look like them. Children of these couples are reassured by cards with pictures of children that reflect their identity."[7] Curls, a hair care company, bills itself as "a premium, ethnic hair care company whose purpose is to deliver quality products that cater to the unique needs of today's multi-ethnic market." The company tagline reads "Curls . . . Because your curly hair is different from the rest."[8]

"Need" is a relative concept. Making decisions about what we buy often involves distinguishing between our need for the thing purchased and our desire for it. In some cases, like clean water and food, most of us can agree we need such things, for without them long enough we will die. In other cases, like when a child claims he "needs" the latest electronic game, most of us would agree this is not a need, but rather a desire. Needs and desires, of course, are not always so clearly distinguishable. What we strongly desire we often feel we desperately need. It is standard operating procedure in the marketing arena to make desires feel like needs. The rationale of need serves a twofold purpose. First, claiming people need a particular item is intended to make the case that the product is performing a service. Second, claiming that a group has needs to be met reinforces the idea that the group is distinctive from others as it stimulates demand. In the world of advertising, the delineation of needs goes hand in hand with the construction of a market.[9]

The promotions for Curls delineate a market of "bi/multi racial women and girls with naturally curly hair" for whom Curls was "truly created especially for." According to Curls, *Women's Wear Daily* was set to focus a "spotlight" on the company in the December 2003 issue, which would discuss "the needs of multi ethnic hair care, and how CURLS is fulfilling an unfulfilled need in an overlooked market." In an example of even more specific market segmentation, Curls has created a line of products marketed specifically to "racially mixed *girls* with naturally curly hair"(my emphasis). It is called "Curly Q's."

Source: Mahisha Dellinger

Products Catering to Mixed Race People

What, then, are the needs of multiracial women and girls as seen through the marketing department at Curls? While the supposedly unique needs of racially mixed girls and women are not explicitly stated in the ad copy, a set of "needs" are delineated nonetheless through the vehicle of "customer reviews." The most often repeated "need" is for a way to control, make shiny, and moisturize one's curls.

A common advertising strategy is to establish (or make claims about) the superiority of one's product—why this shampoo and not others, for example, will do the job. In the testimonials used and company claims made by Curls, however, seldom are the particular ingredients in Curls or Curly Q's discussed. Instead, the market at which the products are pitched is meant to serve as endorsement enough for the product itself. This is why in almost every testimonial, the customer's relationship to multiracialism is communicated. Sometimes this relationship to multiracialism is conveyed subtly as in the following testimonials. C. Donnow writes:

I can't tell you how happy I am with your products. They "understand" my hair. After trying product after product for as long as I can remember, I was thrilled to find Curls. Curls products bring out the best in my hair without weighing my curls down or leaving my hair greasy or "heavy" feeling . . . Curls lets my hair retain it's own "happy spirit" without taking time out of my busy schedule . . . Thanks so much for developing a product that knows my hair![10]

One customer writes, "I absolutely LOVE the products! My hair is moisturized without feeling greasy, and it's soft and swingy—yet the curls and waves are defined. I'm thrilled. Thanks for thinking outside of the box. It's refreshing to be able to use products that are more specific to my hair type, instead of my constant experimental mix-n-match routine."[11]

These descriptions accomplish several tasks at once. First, they establish that mixed race women share a common dilemma in finding the right
products for their hair type. Moreover, the statement that the company "understands" a customer's hair implies that the company—whose president,
Mahisha Dellinger, is of mixed descent—has an insider's knowledge of that
presumably unique experience and which allowed her to develop the products. At the same time, such descriptions conjure up an image of the characteristics that typify "mixed hair" (defined, shiny curls and waves, not coarse,
dull kinks or frizz)—if only the right products are used.

Finally, in these testimonials, racially mixed women's hair is implicitly,
and sometimes explicitly, contrasted to that of African American women.
About Curly Q's, one mother writes:

> [W]e are amazed at the difference the products have made in the texture of
> our daughter's hair. We have tried just about every African-American hair
> care product in the market place for children. We have a bi-racial (Black/
> Caucasian) child and this is the first product in the market place that we have
> come across that unequivocally has made it easier to maintain our child's
> hair. We highly recommend the Curly Q's products to all parents of bi-racial
> children.[12]

In order to accept the rationale that mixed race women have unique hair
care needs, one must believe that the kind of curly hair such women have
is different *in a generalizable way* from the curly hair of *non*racially mixed
women and girls. As we know, however, lots of women (including African
American women) have curly hair and have managed to "care" for it all these
years without Curls or the statistics necessary to identify a multiracial market.
Such a claim relies for its impact on the folk belief that there is an inherent
bodily difference between the races that expresses itself in *predictable* ways
when the races mix (without ever needing to say so directly).[13] While it may
be true that many people of partial African descent have corkscrew curls, it's
also true that many do not.

I assume that that the intention of Curls's founder is not to reinscribe
biological notions of race, but rather to delineate a characteristic fairly widespread among people of partial African descent (curly hair), package it as a
point of cultural uniqueness that unites the racially mixed together, and use
that to sell them hair care products. Curls is also capitalizing on the desire of
those who purchase it to believe that they are part of a definable, knowable
group of women.

Many of the entrepreneurs who are creating products for mixed race people see the market as a community-building tool. Writes Rudy Guevarra, creator of Multiracial Apparel, "I wanted to create and share a clothing line that acknowledged and celebrated our experiences as multiracial/multiethnic people and families" a venture that he regards as consistent with "our desire to have representation. The goal of Multiracial Apparel is to address these experiences and share them with the world."[14] Guevarra has written for *Mavin* magazine and counts on his board of advisors Maria Root and Reginald Daniel, two academic activists long associated with multiracial mobilization.

Attempts to delineate what is unique about multiracial consumers and the creation of products for mixed race consumers are important aspects of group making among multiracials. In this sense, they are cultural constructions— means through which groups create shared meanings, define membership, and create a shared symbolic vocabulary.

Multiracials as Branding Tool

Even before Census 2000 reported multirace statistics, images of multiracials were used to sell things. While certainly not ubiquitous,[15] depictions of multiracials *as such* began to appear with some regularity during the 1990s. Advertisements for items like jeans, sneakers, laundry detergent, and pain reliever depicted mixed race people both well known and anonymous. Multiraciality itself is becoming a branding tool. Unlike target marketing, in which a message or product is created to appeal to a particular demographic, this kind of marketing uses multiracialism to appeal to a mass audience. By definition, such images created before there were statistics and industry research reports on multiracials, rely on stereotypes, cliches, and dominant ideas of racial mixedness. This is not to suggest that the market research currently proceeding (in large part because statistical data on multiracials is now readily available) will result in more "accurate" depictions of multiracials. Rather, without any empirical information about basic demographic characteristics of this "group," the image of multiracials *can only be* based on culturally dominant or resonant ideas about this population.

In the United States, the multiracial body has often served as a resonant symbol for Americans' racial anxieties. At times multiracials have been vilified as harbingers of the death of particular cultural communities, depicted as manifestations of the degeneracy of human populations, or as evidence of their parents' traitorous disloyalties. They have also been celebrated as "bridges" of racial harmony and unity, possessors of an inherent disposition against prejudice, and a maverick, new people. It probably will surprise no one to learn that advertisements depicting multiracials nearly always employ the latter symbolism. To do the former would be unwise, to say the least, if trying to appeal to a mass audience that includes a near majority nonwhite population. But the growing use of such multiracial images has more to do with convergences between trends in advertising generally and the cultural and social position of multiracials.

Multiracials' demographics and the symbolism of racial mixedness fit very nicely into an advertising model that has dominated the industry since the 1970s. "Hip consumerism," as cultural critic Thomas Frank dubs it, is defined by advertising that draws from the symbols of 1960s' counterculture and offers to "help consumers overcome their alienation, to facilitate their nonconformity and . . . celebrate[s] rule breaking and insurrection." As a commercial style, Frank argues, hip is everywhere—"a staple of advertising that promises to deliver the consumer form the dreary nightmare of square consumerism" (Frank 1997, 28, 32).

Much of the content of this "hip" consumerism draws from and seeks to appeal to youth. Since the mid-1940s when the teenage demographic began to be recognized as a unique stage of life "with its own language, customs, and emotional traumas" (Cohen 2003, 319), marketing to teens has expanded exponentially (Linn 2004). Other forms of segmented marketing, not only by race and ethnicity, but also age and gender, have as well. For an industry whose modus operandi is to craft "hip" messages, target ethnic audiences, and appeal to the young, multiracialism must seem a tailor-made marketing vehicle. First, as industry reports always point out, multiracials are disproportionately young. Forty-two percent of multiracials were born after 1982.[16] In some regions, like parts of Hawaii and the San Francisco Bay Area, they make up a substantial proportion of the local population. The overall growth in interracial births suggests that younger audiences may have more familiarity and comfort with multiracials, particularly in those areas where they are a significant demographic presence.

Packaged Rebellion

One of the earliest ad campaigns to use interracialism to craft a hip brand image was Benetton. Seeking to associate its brand with a fight against racism, this late 1980s campaign featured a racially mixed cast of models—a relatively rare phenomenon in fashion advertising at the time.[17] The models were often arranged in ways to visually heighten their physical differences—very dark skin, hair, and eyes, next to very light. Their attack on social convention was made in the form of posing models in interracially intimate scenes. The campaign garnered the company praise and criticism. The most controversial ad featured a bare-chested black woman breastfeeding a naked white baby. From one perspective the image depicts cross-racial nurturance, caring, and bonding. From another it recalls African American women's use as wet nurses to white children under slavery.

The Benetton campaign pushed the limits of the public's tolerance for interracially intimate imagery back in 1988 (Blum 2000). Given the debate it stirred back then, it might be surprising to learn that two decades earlier Mattel created a mixed race doll and marketed her as Barbie's cousin. "Colored Francie" was at once ahead of and behind her time, as her name (outdated even forty years ago) makes clear. Brought to market in 1967, company officials misread the demand for such a doll. She was discontinued after poor sales and concerns that she promoted interracialism (DuCille 1996, Halter 2000). Ironically, her unpopularity forty years ago has resulted in her being a very hot (and pricey) collectors item among doll enthusiasts.[18] Currently there is no Barbie explicitly marketed as a multiracial doll, but Mattel has developed a line of racially ambiguous friends of Barbie (that's *friends*, not cousins).

A decade after the Benetton campaign, Levi Strauss and Company began a new campaign to bolster flagging sales of Levis jeans. To do so, they sought to appeal to young consumers. How? By crafting a campaign that centered on "assertions of the brand's authenticity," that used images that were "familiar yet utterly surprising" (Kane 1998a). As part of that effort, the creative people at TBWA Chiat/Day in San Francisco (Levi Strauss's ad firm) published an ad showing a brown-skinned woman with a golden afro holding a sign that read, "I can't be prejudice [*sic*], I'm mulatto." The ad uses discursively familiar elements of racial mixedness. Decked out in flared low-riding (or "hip-hugging") jeans, her image recalls the 1960s' counterculture.

According to its creators, the campaign of which this ad was a part sought to craft an "unconventional, streetwise attitude . . . to take fashion ads from the catwalk to the sidewalk" (Kane 1998b). Mixed ethnicity symbolized this "attitude" as many of the ads, some illustrations, "blend ethnicities and blur racial definitions." According to the ad manager on the project, the campaign is "a virtual melting pot of cultures and races linked by similar interests and diversity." While the "mulatto" ad is supposed to be streetwise, authentic, and hip, the mixed race character's use of an outdated, even offensive, term to refer to herself belies such assertions. The notion that multiracials cannot be prejudiced is a recurring (if absurd) conceit about multiracialism. Finally, the misspelling of "prejudiced" is, I suspect, included for an added dose of "streetwise authenticity." According to a marketer working on a related Levi's campaign at the time, the creators of the ad seemed unaware of what she called the "ridiculous" and "offensive" nature of the ad. The creators, she said, "didn't get it." She attributed their lack of sensitivity to the fact that all of them were white. Whether or not their whiteness explains the content of the ad, I do not know. Neither do I know if the Levi's marketers "didn't get it." But maybe they did not have to. Advertisements sell fantasy, not necessarily reality. The image of the "mulatto" used in this ad represents what people (or at least the makers of the image) want to believe and communicate about multiracials.

"I am Tiger Woods": Multiracials as Symbols of the "New Economy"

Levi Strauss was not the only company to capitalize on the symbolism of multiracials for marketing. Since the mid-1990s, companies like Ikea, Tylenol, Nike, Verizon, and General Electric have featured multiracials in their ads. While multiracials were sometimes used to convey authenticity or rebellion, they were also used as symbols of the "new." The "unexpected" that marketers in the age of hip consumerism were after is embodied in the juxtaposition of racialized physical features in one body. This "look" has been particularly sought after in an era of technological change and globalization. According to one casting agent, "'The multiracial look screams 'current, youthful, and urban.' And it also evokes a certain authenticity . . . Eight strawberry blondes in a cyber-cafe wouldn't be realistic."[19] I think it is safe to assume that if this advertiser saw several redheads in a café sipping lattes while surfing the Internet he would find this *perfectly* realistic. What he means, rather, is that commercials with all-white casts are conventional, but so too are those with integrated casts. We have seen such images too often for them to signal something new. Images of multiracial people, on the other hand, have been relatively rare in media until now and thus awaken the viewer to a change because of their difference. Says another casting agent, "The mix of Asian facial features and kinky hair . . . conjures up an immediate sense of both globalization and technology. The blended look says 'we're all in this together' and that the 'world's getting smaller.'"[20]

It is perhaps not surprising that in the 1990s when the rapid development of internet commerce was hailed as the beginning of a "new economy" in which the old rules no longer applied that multiracials as a "new people" were chosen symbols. Perhaps the best known example of the marriage of multiracials and markets is the relationship between Nike and Tiger Woods. After becoming the youngest golfer to win the Masters Tournament in 1997, commentators prophesied that Tiger would democratize the elitist and racially exclusionary game of golf. People of color, they reported, would now become interested in golf. Children from all walks of life would be able to compete on the green unfettered by old rules about money and pedigree (Dorman 1996).

Soon thereafter, Woods signed an endorsement deal with Nike worth an estimated $30 million. Nike enlisted Woods at a time when it was suffering serious attacks to its public reputation. During the 1990s, Nike had shipped most of its manufacturing jobs overseas to factories in which its employees labored in sweatshop conditions.[21] Nike's public relations offensive sought to rebuild its public image from that of ruthless profit maximizer to that of a "democratized, soulful corporation"—a strategy pursued by many firms at the time (Frank 2000, 252). One of the earliest Nike ads using Tiger's image featured children—boys and girls—of a wide variety of ethnicities on a misty golf course, clubs in hand looking earnestly into the camera while each uttered in succession, "I am Tiger Woods." Every child, the ad implied, could be Tiger because Tiger was a little bit of everybody. By this time, Tiger's mixed ethnicity was quite well reported. In the Nike ads, Tiger's racial mixedness is positioned as a democratizing, unifying force.

Contrast this portrayal to the use of another famous athlete's image in advertising. Michael Jordan has received perhaps more endorsement deals than any other athlete. Jordan's black silhouette soaring to the hole is immediately associated with Nike.[22] In many of those ads, however, Jordan's athletic accomplishments are portrayed as almost superhuman. While everyone may have wanted to "be like Mike," such a possibility was merely a fantasy.[23] On the other hand, "I *am* Tiger Woods" says we already are like Tiger, notwithstanding his extraordinary athletic accomplishments. While those achievements may be as out of reach for us as those of Jordan, Tiger's racial mixedness makes him accessible to all.

Woods is popular as an endorser because of his mixedness, not in spite of it—a point his father Earl Woods recognized early on. Commenting on Tiger's popularity with companies looking for endorsers, Earl Woods told a *Newsweek* reporter, "For marketing purposes, Tiger's mixed heritage goes off the charts" (Leland 1997). The market appeal of mixed race persons extends beyond Woods himself, however. According to one of my contacts who manages talent featured in ad campaigns, he now receives many requests for so-called "ethnically ambiguous" actors. This practice is either widespread enough, sexy enough, or both to have warranted an article in a recent Sunday *New York Times* (La Ferla, 2003). Why the appeal? Says one executive of an advertising and trend research company, "Both in the mainstream and at the high end of the marketplace, what is perceived as good, desirable, and successful is often a face whose heritage is hard to pin down."

Consumer Culture, Racial Formation, and Racial Justice

The marriage of the market and multiraciality raises several questions about the relationship between consumption, racial formation, and racial justice. What does it say about contemporary modes of racial domination that images invoking interracial mixing are increasingly sought after while just a few years ago they were rare and when used, as in the Benetton ad, employed as much for their ability to shock as to "fight racism"? Is multiracials' quest for representation in the marketplace significantly different from that of other ethnoracial groups? What does the focus on representation obscure about other aspects of racial inequality?

Racialized groups have long understood the connections between consumption and racial justice. Organizers of the sit-ins of the civil rights movement, for example, recognized that access to white consumer establishments was essential to ensure blacks' access to a full range of goods and services. They understood as well that the conditions of such access (segregated vs. integrated) were symbolic of the level of dignity and respect afforded African Americans in the society at large. Moreover, civil rights organizers understood that owners respond when their profits or livelihoods are threatened. Their actions politicized consumption in order to achieve social justice.

Racialized groups have also understood the importance of representation in media in their quest for full and equal citizenship. Advertising's scope and reach is so extensive that it has the power to shape public perceptions of social groupings: which ones exist, their relevance, and their influence. As such, civil rights organizations like the NAACP and La Raza monitor the degree and kind of representations of African Americans and Latinos in advertisements.

Moreover, in public discourse of late, politicians explicitly equate consumption with democratic participation and good citizenship. Increasingly, they encourage citizens to view themselves in a market relationship to government. We are encouraged to shop around for social services and to "vote with our pocketbooks" to signal our political preferences and beliefs. In times of economic downturn, politicians and economic analysts encourage Americans to consume more as a means of doing our part for the country by way of stimulating the economy.[24]

Like other racialized groups in the United States who couch their demands for full recognition as citizens with calls for companies to recognize them as a market, multiracials are doing the same. Mary Murchison-Edwards of the Interracial Club of Buffalo, for example, encourages people to buy products with multiracial themes whether or not they reflect one's family background. She says, "We need to show there's a market for these products by supporting the companies that make them."[25]

One could assume that Murchison-Edwards believes recognition as a market is a proxy for greater social recognition as a group. Given advertising media's reach, this is likely. The question then becomes whether or not social recognition is equivalent to social justice. It strikes me as an ironic twist of the politics of consumption that racialized groups not only welcome, but also seek out, the opportunity to be pitched to—to be *sold*, as it were. The danger in the marketing of multiracialism (or any other ethnoracial identity) is not that mixed race people will receive social recognition. Rather, it is when "recognition" (be it in the form of representation in advertisements or in the census) is substituted for a politics of civic and economic equality. Boycotts and representation in advertisements are not the same thing. The former uses consumption as a leverage point to secure something else—access to institutions, fair wages, respect, for example. The latter treats consumption as a political end in itself and is oriented toward the right to consume more—to be marketed to—and is delinked from broader social concerns.

In the ways that multiraciality is being marketed, there is cause for both optimism and concern. A commercial for a pain reliever in which a white father stays home from work to care for his ailing Asian son[26] is a welcome representation of interracial intimacy. The decision to use a white mother and her daughter of African descent in an ad for pain reliever[27] when interracialism is not the focus of the message is a subtle recognition of changing social norms concerning race. Yet, while there are more representations of interracial intimacy in popular culture than in the past, many companies are reluctant to use such images, concerned that they are inconsistent with their brand's image or that they will offend their customer base.[28] Others do not yet consider images of interracial families as realistic. Of Anheuser-Busch's decision to use an all-white cast in an ad, run during the Super Bowl football game, which featured pop star Justin Timberlake knocking on a fan's door, the brand manager said, "It didn't lend itself to multicultural images necessarily, because it was at someone's house" (Texeira 2005).

Currently, advertisers use interracial imagery in a limited set of lifestyle contexts and to invoke a rather narrow set of feelings. Too often, advertisements featuring images of multiraciality repeat rather than challenge racial stereotypes. The images of multiracials now put forth by advertisers echo older images of the mulatto, but include only those elements that are putatively positive in the age of hip consumerism. The multiracial is a bridge between racial groups, one who goes against social convention, and signals the future. Like the image of the Hispanic consumer generated by advertisers, the image of the multiracial is "not altogether an original development. Instead, it is better regarded as an archetype, constituted by motifs that, while adaptable, persist across generations" (Davila 2001, 61).[29]

Such "archetypes" obscure more about social reality than they illuminate. While some analysts would like to claim that the marketing of multiraciality reflects a trend toward a "post-racial America" (Walker 2003; Wynter 2002), this assessment is premature. Note that nearly every article about multiracial public figures, be it Tiger Woods, Vin Diesel, or Mariah Carey, says something about the significance of their racial mixedness. That which receives so much attention can hardly have been transcended. Rather, I think it more accurate to say that the interest in mixed race bodies, and particularly in multiracial celebrities, is an example of what Thomas Holt has identified as "a shift in the terrain of 'racism.'" "Could it be," he asks, "that the issue now is less the utter ignorance of other cultures, as in times past, but too great a surface (sound-bite) familiarity; less stereotypes of the other than the voracious consumption of its metonymic parts?" (2000, 108).

Additionally, the popularity of images of racial hybridity, coupled with the trend toward using racially integrated casts in television commercials, present an image of a racial utopia that does not quite exist. Nearly 80 percent of whites, for example, live in neighborhoods where 95 percent of their neighbors are white, and as we have seen, racial intermarriage is a relatively rare occurrence.[30] The increasingly integrated world of television ads against the backdrop of racial segregation in real life prompted sociologist Charles Gallagher to comment, "The lens through which people learn about other races is absolutely through TV, not through human interaction and contact. Here, we're getting a lens of racial interaction that is far afield from reality" (Texeira 2005). To marketers, that's just the point. Advertisers use fantasy and appeal to our aspirations. In the current climate, according to some advertisers, multiculturalism is socially desirable (Garcia 2004). Some mixed race advocates, however, eschew both the exoticization of mixed race bodies that advertisers trade in, as well as the suggestion that interracial images distort reality. Jen Chau (2005) of Mixed Media Watch writes:

> What about the families and people for which these images ring true? While it is clear that this is not reality for many, these images reflect a reality that *does* exist for many others. This is the very thing that we here at Mixed Media Watch are fighting for—representation of mixed individuals and mixed families . . . Let's think positively. Perhaps those who are not seeing in their real life what is represented on their TV screens will be given a head-start in thinking about this growing demographic before it actually shows up in their neighborhoods (or dare I say families?).[31]

The implications of the marketing of multiraciality are not only about the politics of representation but are also economic. Some analysts suggest that the "ethnically ambiguous" trend signals the impending decline of niche marketing. The multiracial data, says one marketer, "takes the pressure off agencies to play it ethnically" (Whelan 2001). If many consumers connect with and respond to a multiracial actor, the logic goes, why craft several different campaigns targeted toward discrete ethnic communities (Walker 2003)? In trying to develop consumers' identification with a message, some advertisers see the racial ambiguity of multiracial bodies as an asset because, it is presumed, viewers from many ethnoracial groups will search for and usually find something in an ambiguous appearance with which they can identify.[32] In other words, multiracials are potentially useful in companies' quests to capture market share while simultaneously lowering their costs.

Attention to issues of multiculturalism and cultural hybridity is also influencing advertising firm creation. Firms specializing in ethnic markets have tended to specialize in one ethnic group (that is, Asian American *or* African American consumers). These firms have tended to have a subcontractual relationship with what are known in the industry as "general market" (that is, white) firms. Recently, however, ethnic niche firms have joined forces to combine their expertise in order to compete for a wider range of business.

One such firm—GlobalHue—formed in 1999. Its CEO Don Coleman merged his African American urban market agency (DCA) with that of Montemayor Asociados, a Hispanic firm based in San Antonio, and Innovasia, an Asian American firm in Los Angeles. In 2003 it was ranked the top ethnic advertising agency in *Black Enterprise*'s annual survey (based on annual billings) (Hughes 2003). At the same time, other firms are positioning themselves to reach consumers who cross traditional ethnic boundaries. The True Agency, formed in 2000, has published its own book that details its marketing philosophy and strategy. They call it "Transculturalism." Despite the growth in multicultural marketing, however, the reality of racial segregation in the United States means that those companies who primarily advertise through direct mail or local media will continue to craft messages specific to one ethnoracial group (Wellner 2002).

Marketers explain their interest in multiracials as simply another form of ethnic target marketing, and that it is. But it is also part and parcel of a process of group making. Marketers have become aware of a multiracial market in large part because this population is now statistically visible. Ever in search of new markets, they will proceed by conducting research on this population so as to understand better how to appeal to its desires. Whether or not they actually uncover anything unique about this demographic's tastes, values, practices, or beliefs, with the knowledge that this population is growing, marketers will continue to use images of multiracials in their advertising.[33]

In the world of advertising, increasingly marketers describe their research efforts as "ethnography," which implies that they have identified a social group whose habits and lifeways they seek to uncover. What this portrayal leaves out is the extent to which the cultures that marketers claim to merely represent are in part their own creations. The issue is not that marketers fabricate their messages independent of social context. Quite the contrary. They draw on existing culturally resonant narratives of the meaning of racial mixedness for the purpose of selling stuff. In so doing, they shape social perceptions that multiracial exist as such. Through the marketplace, multiracials are being constituted a subjects.

7 Redrawing the Color-Line?: The Problems and Possibilities of Multiracial Families and Group Making

It is my belief that the next generation's principal task will be the hard and painful one of destroying color-caste in the United States.

—W. Lloyd Warner[1]

AFTER TIGER WOODS WON THE 1997 MASTERS TOURNAMENT, he quickly became the poster boy of multiracialism—the well-adjusted, hugely successful, mixed race child with two devoted, loving, and *married* parents. Woods's rising public profile mirrored and symbolized the increasingly public profile of mixed descent persons. By the 1990s, multiracial families and multiracial identity were given more attention in the media, portrayed in such a positive way that one could be excused if one forgot the powerful stigma previously heaped upon intermarried couples and their families. Woods's success and embrace by the American public lent credibility to assertions that multiraciality was "old news"—that this had been going on for centuries (by which people usually meant interracial sex, not family), and that Americans were no longer shocked by this anymore.

Yet the emergence of multiracial families represents a significant historical shift, particularly when we consider the efforts made to prevent and conceal family ties across racial boundaries. The emergence of a multiracial identity as the expression of such family ties is a major shift as well. Given that race as a mark of identity (rather than a uncomplicated descriptor of a biological reality) only developed in the twentieth century, and that the major period of growth in marriages across racial categories did not begin until the 1960s, this shift has taken place in a relatively short period of time. In the last decade, the idea of "multiracial community" has developed a social and cultural presence in the United States. Since the struggle over the census in the 1990s, references to "multiracials" regularly appear in the popular press, in academic literature, and in the marketplace, and the creation of multiracial organizations has continued unabated. Due to the efforts of people in those organizations, in conjunction with increasing rates of intermarriage, the multiracial family is no longer a contradiction in terms. Rather than "melting" into traditional racial groups, people of mixed race are elaborating a distinct sense of groupness as "multiracial." At the same time, they are asserting specific mixed ethnoracial identifications such as "Japanese and Mexican" or "black and Irish."

How then should we evaluate the impact and significance of multiracial group making? How is the color line being redrawn? The definition of race—a basic concept for describing social differences and inequalities in the United States—is in the process of changing. But in what ways and with what impact?

It is impossible to evaluate the impact of multiracial politics without attention to historical and social contexts. Without such contexts, it is tempting to conclude, as many have, that the collective efforts of multiracials are inherently progressive, inherently regressive, or even irrelevant. Appearing on the Oprah Winfrey show, for example, a black/white woman explains to the audience that as a multiracial person she can be a bridge to promote understanding between racial groups. In hearings over changes to racial classification, opponents to the possibility of the state enumerating mixed descent persons invoke the specter of apartheid South Africa, suggesting that new categories will create an escape hatch from blackness. At around the same time, some scholars claim that Asian outmarriage reflects Asian self-hatred and is an attempt to leave behind a stigmatized group. Still others state that the issue is "old news," not important enough to waste time commenting on it.

In this book I have tried to offer the social and historical contexts that will allow us to make sense of what multiracials are doing today and that make such blanket assessments of multiracial politics less defensible. For the multiracial movement is about race and family—cultural categories, not static institutions—the meanings of which depend on context. This being the case, there can be no definitive answer to the question "are multiracial politics progressive or regressive?" Such evaluations will differ according to individual identities and political intentions. More useful than evaluations of the logic of racial categories or intermarriage in the abstract, then, are historically grounded and ethnographically parsed accounts that show us what is different between now and the past and that ask what these categories mean to the people who feel invested in organizing around them.

Family Matters

According to Drake and Cayton (1993 [1945]), "Social segregation is maintained, in the final analysis, by endogamy—the rule that Negroes must marry Negroes, and whites must marry whites—and by its corollary that when an intermarriage does "accidentally" occur, the child must automatically be classed as a Negro no matter how white his skin color." [2]

I have argued that in order to understand multiracial group making—its rise, shape, contents, and possible impact—one must not only denaturalize race but denaturalize the family, for the construction of the American family and race are joint historical and cultural processes that are mutually determinative. Racial classifications and antimiscegenation policies facilitated the creation of sharp divisions between social groups, defined them as racially different, and in so doing shaped the cultural common sense in which racial difference and the division of families along racial lines appears to be natural. Despite the possibility of legal marriage across racial boundaries, the normative family is still monoracial, and racial affiliation exacts a kind of loyalty that disqualifies intimate connections across racial categories. The realization that they are misfits in this context motivates multiracial actors to challenge the prevailing race/family nexus.

This struggle is apparent in the stories told by my respondents. While the interracial unions in my respondents' families were legally sanctioned, some struggled with the discretionary acts of disowning by their monoracial parents that mimicked the economic impacts that antimiscegenation laws once had. For most intermarried couples and families, however, what is at stake lies in the terrain of relatedness, emotional connection, the sense of cultural loss and gain, and the recognized reflection of the self in one's child—all structured by the racial dimension of the normative family.

The legalization of intermarriage, along with popular representations of multiracial families as heterosexual and nuclear leads to interpretations of multiracial families as an interesting "flavor" of the normative family. While it is clear that the heterosexual nuclear family is accorded material and social privilege in U.S. society, and that most of the contemporary discussion of multiracial families concerns heterosexual couplings, it misses the point to see multiracial families as an interesting variation on the theme of the heterosexual nuclear family. Rather, multiracial families—and multiracial politics broadly conceived—should be understood as part of an historical transformation in kinship, ideology, and social relations that have come about as the result of conflict, contradiction, and struggle.

Yet just how far we have come is a matter of debate. Although antimisce-genation laws are unconstitutional, intermarriage remains rare, especially so between blacks and whites. Moreover, a nontrivial percentage of people (of all racial groups) still disapprove of intermarriage. While the social climate for intermarried couples and families has certainly improved in the last several decades, Drake and Cayton's observations of Chicago in the 1930s describe all too well the state of intermarriage today, especially for blacks. They found that while blacks had made gains in governmental and economic areas, only "very moderate" gains had been made in "spatial and family relations." They concluded that while intermarriage is legally permitted, "it is generally dis-couraged." "[I]nformal social controls among both Negroes and whites," they wrote, "keep the number of such marriages small despite the fact there are no legal prohibitions against them" (1993 [1945], 127).

Of course, the same degree of separation is not found between Asian and whites and Latinos and whites. Intermarriage rates with whites for Asians, La-tinos, and Native Americans are comparable to those of Southern and Eastern European immigrants in the early twentieth century who, through intermar-riage with American-born whites, expanded the definition of who is white. With each generation in the United States and as income and education levels rise, Latinos and Asians are more likely to marry whites. This has prompted Roger Sanjek (1994) to argue that we may be seeing a "race-to-ethnicity" con-version for Hispanics and Asians, but not for African Americans.

Despite very low intermarriage rates for blacks, which testify to a firmer racialized boundary separating blacks from other groups, assertions by mul-tiracials—even those of African descent—that they are not "just black" con-founds that once defining feature of the color line to which DuBois ([1903] 1996) referred a century ago. Multiracial activists' demand for a recognition of mixedness challenges the categorical nature of the American racial classifica-tion system which, until 1997, recognized membership in only one category. As such, it is in direct opposition to the logic of the one-drop rule—the key mechanism that maintained that color line. Moreover, their efforts disrupt what the one-drop rule firmly established, namely the racial basis of kinship in which relatedness across racial boundaries is not socially recognized.

In everyday life, not just in official categories, the definition of blackness (and consequentially of white, Asian, Indian, and Latino identities) is shifting as well. So while in the 1930s Drake and Cayton (1993 [1945]) observed that the "children of mixed matings" are "always defined as Negroes," an understanding that prevailed through the 1980s, this is no longer as certain as it once was. Mariah Carey, for example, is not understood (or marketed) as a black singer, despite being of African descent, just as respondents with an ambiguous physical appearance and who lack cultural credentials are not necessarily accepted by blacks as (authentically) black, nor are they necessarily seen as sharply different by nonblacks despite knowledge of their African ancestry.

Racial Options?: Choice and the Limits of Choice

Twenty-six years ago, in the conclusion of her study on the Lumbee Indians of Robeson County, North Carolina, Karen Blu stated that "there is no 'right' to choose one's 'racial' ancestry, as race is currently conceived, but if race and ethnicity become progressively intertwined in a new way, it is possible that being Black will, in years to come, be more a matter of individual choice and less a matter of assignment by others" (1980, 210). Students of race and ethnicity in the United States often note that a key difference between the ways Americans experience ethnic and racial identities is the degree of choice one has to identify (or not) in ethnic or racial terms. This distinction is based on the historical experience of European immigrants. As the voluntary and involuntary factors that held together European immigrant ethnic communities (for example, residential segregation, discrimination, prejudice, religious affiliation) have declined, so too has the salience of ethnicity in the lives of their descendants (Alba 1990; Gans 1979; Lieberson 1985; Waters 1990). For these white ethnics, ethnicity is chosen rather than ascribed and expressions of ethnic identity are largely symbolic in content.

In her often-cited book *Ethnic Options: Choosing Identities in America*, Mary Waters (1990) found that not only did her white respondents choose which ethnicity to be, but also whether to be ethnic *at all*. Moreover, ethnic identity held few negative consequences for her respondents. It did not limit whom they could marry, determine where they could live, their employment prospects, or who their friends were. In contrast, the literature is replete with examples showing the continued prevalence and salience of ethnoracial ascription for nonwhites. The third and fourth generation Japanese and Chinese Americans Mia Tuan studied report that "others consistently expect them to identify ethnically (e.g., as Chinese or Japanese) or racially as Asian and be knowledgeable about Chinese or Japanese 'things' and express dissatisfaction when they are not" (Tuan 1998, 156). Attributions of racial difference are consequential for African Americans whether or not they choose to assert a racial identity, even for middle-class blacks who conform to white middle-class norms of behavior (Bell 1992; Cose 1992; Fordham 1997).[3] Racial options—the ability to choose whether to identify or be identified in racial terms—have been elusive.

Events of the last decade, however, suggest that we need to revisit the question of whether or not "racial options" are in the making. The institutionalized option to choose multiple racial affiliations in official race counts represents a racial option "on paper." The flexibility exhibited by respondents in how they describe, display, and perform their ethnoracial identities makes clear that indeed racial identification and categorization are somewhat malleable. But how much can this be said to approximate the kind of symbolic ethnicity found among white ethnics?

In all the ways ethnic identity did not matter for Waters's respondents, racial identity *did* matter for mine. Regardless of how much they chose to identify themselves as mixed, they faced resistance from institutions, peers, and even family members. When they wished not to have to identify themselves in racial terms, others *did* classify them in racial terms, and not necessarily in the ways they wished to be classified. Moreover, *how* they looked mattered very much in what types of identity expressions were likely to be authenticated by others. The dark-skinned person who identifies as white—or even mixed—must still work very hard to get others to treat him as such. In other words, not all heritages can equally be chosen or discarded at will. That their efforts have been met with suspicion and resistance is telling of lingering opposition to treating what are considered racial distinctions as just another form of ethnicity.

A key aspect of the optional character of white ethnicity is its costlessness. Unlike the ethnic identifications of white ethnics, for my respondents "being" mixed race or marrying someone of a different race had significant costs. Some intermarried respondents were "disowned" by their parents. For others, racial difference within the family was sometimes a source of tension that distorted emotional connections between family members. Moreover, for mixed descent respondents, asserting a mixed racial identification threatened their belonging within ethnic communities.

Yet while racial identification for multiracials is not entirely voluntary or costless, there is a way in which multiracial identification looks like the symbolic ethnicity of whites. Waters (1990) explains the apparent paradox that while ethnicity is a matter of choice, relatively costless and inconsequential in her respondents' lives, her respondents "cling tenaciously to their ethnic identities." They do so, she argues, because symbolic ethnicity actually reconciles two contradictory impulses in the American character—the desire for both individuality *and* conformity. " Having an ethnic identity is something that makes you both special and simultaneously part of a community. It is something that comes to you involuntarily through heredity, and at the same time it is a personal choice. And it allows you to express your individuality in a way that does not make you stand out as in any way different from all kinds of other people" (Waters, 1990, 150).

Similarly, the idea that racial identity can be freely chosen appeals to the high value Americans place on individualism. The novelty of a mixed racial identity makes one stand out against dominant modes of identification. At the same time, the elaboration of a sense of multiracial group identity makes one feel as if one belongs to a community where one is, if only in one's perceived marginality, just like everyone else. The irony here is that while the discourse of choice in racial identification suggests we as individuals are determining for ourselves who we want to be, in fact we are "choosing" within a given set of epistemological, social, and political conditions that make only certain choices possible.

Scholars have sometimes described the trajectory of white ethnicity from a consequential group affiliation to a largely symbolic one as a transition from "being" to "feeling" ethnic (Bakalian 1993). "People desperately wish to 'feel' ethnic," Steinberg argues, "precisely because they have all but lost the prerequisites of 'being' ethnic." (1989, 63). In this respect, the multiracial example is perhaps best understood as a move in the opposite direction. Elaborations of multiracial collective identification represent an attempt to move *from* "feeling" *to* "being" multiracial. For some of my respondents, that feeling of being mixed race was largely a feeling of not fitting into any ethnoracial community. For others it was based on a feeling of being a part of both. The construction of multiracial organizations, the push for official designation of mixed race status—these are moves to make multiracials appear more real in a culture that elevates ethnicity and race as primary markers of personhood—to not only feel multiracial, but also to "be" multiracial in civic and social life.

The dividing line between what constitutes racial versus ethnic difference in the United States has always fallen fairly close to the line marking whom one would consider marrying and what ancestry one would publicly claim. Yet according to this barometer, some racialized distinctions—particularly American Indian status—have also been treated as "ethnic" ones—interesting "decorations" to the family tree that have little consequence in everyday life. Of course, the symbolic aspect of American Indian identity has only been inconsequential for persons of mixed background, whose native ancestry is generations removed, and who do not live on reservations. While to date visible non-European ancestry has been consequential, particularly for persons of African descent, one can certainly imagine a time in the not too distant future where being Asian, Mexican, and even black will increasingly be treated and *experienced* (much like American Indian ancestry is currently treated by whites who claim it)—symbolically. As this generation of mixed descent persons have children of their own, who may cross even more racialized boundaries, they are likely to encourage their children to "embrace" all of their ancestry. As such, the proliferation of racial identifiers that individuals use is likely to expand. The consequences of such racial identifications and the nature of the connections to those racialized communities, however, will largely depend on where they live, whom they live with, and what they look like.

The Future of Multiracial Group Making

I have discussed in detail how the multiracial example draws our attention to the hegemonic, yet hidden assumptions about the American family—namely that families are monoracial—and how racial homogeneity has been fundamental to how families are constructed. But what does the multiracial example teach us about ethnoracial group making? In the process of elaborating what they share with each other, and seeking public recognition for themselves, multiracials make the mixed position a socially recognizable one. As the idea that multiracials exist is further institutionalized, it is appropriate to evaluate in what sense this "group" will come to be like traditional ethnoracial groups.

Like panethnic formations among Latinos, Asian Americans, and American Indians in the United States, the construction of multiracial community is profoundly shaped by state policies. These panethnic formations arose out of a context in which the state "lumped" together groups who consider themselves to be distinct on some basis deemed salient (such as shared language or presumed racial similarity). In response, these distinct cultural and linguistic groups began to assert a common identification (Espiritu 1992; Nagel 1995; Omi and Winant 1994). Collective identification, generally speaking, followed categorization.

The assertion of a collective identification among "multiracials" emerges out of a different relationship to the state. Unlike Latinos, Asians, and American Indians, "multiracials" have not been lumped together for the purposes of racial classification or the administration of social policies. Neither were they counted separately in racial statistics nor was social policy developed to deal with them as a class of people. Multiracials began to coalesce in response to social and cultural pressures that defined them as misfits and that stigmatized interracial families. They *sought* a state classification as a remedy to those grievances.

Now that the state classifies mixed race people as such, one of the key factors motivating multiracial mobilization in the 1990s is no longer available. Additionally, the prejudice and stigma associated with interracial marriage and families has declined significantly. Even in the absence of those initial motivating factors, however, it seems likely that collective mobilization around multiracial identification will continue for the foreseeable future.

First, mixed race organizations have become increasingly institutionalized. The Mavin Foundation has professionalized what began as grassroots, minimally organized community building efforts. Matt Kelley, its founder and president, has assembled a paid staff that operates a Web site, runs community outreach activities, and acts as a kind of clearinghouse for information on mixed race people and issues of race and social justice. The foundation publishes a quarterly magazine (*Mavin: the Mixed Race Experience*), the production values of which rival those of most national monthlies—a far cry from the photocopied newsletters irregularly produced by local community organizations in the 1990s. Moreover, through its Campus Awareness and Compliance Initiative, sponsored jointly with HIF, AMEA, and the Level Playing Field Institute, it aims to ensure that the MOOM option is fully institutionalized in federal agencies.[4]

Groups like Mavin, as well as campus organizations and academic classes, focused on mixed race people are manifestations of ongoing attempts to create and sustain mixed race community. Once established, people have vested interests in maintaining them, as they provide jobs, income, and a public platform for members. These venues for expressing and exploring multiracial identity are likely to thrive, as the "two or more races" population is expected to grow significantly in the next decade. Recent population estimates show the "two or more races" population was the third fastest growing group between 2003 and 2004 (behind Hispanics and Asians) (Files 2005). While demographic statistics cannot predict whether multiracial collective identification will be meaningful to this population, the ongoing institutionaliza-

While in Washington, D.C., the Mavin Foundation Generation MIX Crew interviewed U.S. Senator Barack Obama (D-IL). Himself biracial, Sen. Obama cautioned mixed race people to avoid focusing so narrowly on their own experiences that they become detached from larger struggles of racism and inequality.

tion of mixed race identity will encourage such an identification. For example, schools are required to ask students if they are "of two or more races," and given the opportunity to identify themselves this way, many people will. With statistics on this population, school administration will likely craft programs for such students, further encouraging such an identification. Indeed this is already happening. In 1988 when students at Harvard formed a discussion group for mixed race students, they knew of no other such group. By 2005, the ninth annual Pan-Collegiate Mixed Race Conference took place while one of the largest professional associations of student affairs personnel inaugurated a standing committee on multiracial student affairs, alongside its committees for Asian, African American, Latino, and Native American students.[5]

While the educational arena will likely encourage multiracial identification, so too will the market. The juggernaut of consumer capitalism has taken up multiracialism. As long as mixed race retains its air of hipness and authenticity, marketers will continue to exploit it. As long as the population that identifies itself as mixed race continues to grow, businesses will court "it," developing products to meet its putative needs and helping to make multiracials in the process. Five years after Census 2000, multiracial community is increasingly translocal, Web based, and media driven. The advent of high-speed global communications technology in the 1990s has allowed those previously isolated by geography to "come together" virtually. These virtual communities are cheap to start up and to run and so will likely continue. Not incidentally, the low cost and wide reach of Web communications has greatly facilitated the creation of companies selling mixed race consumer products. Increasingly, mixed race organizations, Web communities, and entrepreneurs engage in a symbiotic relationship, with each Web site giving links to each other, and in so doing reinforcing their raison d'etre.

While mixed racial identifications have become further institutionalized through state codification, it is not clear to what extent "multiracials" will make demands on the state on behalf of multiracials as a group. To date, self-appointed spokespersons for multiracials limit themselves to ensuring that federal agencies collect multirace data and to calls to investigate the extent to which multiracials have unique health care needs.[6] At this time, the multiple race population is not a protected class for the purposes of antidiscrimination efforts, which may be the next battle multiracial activists wage. The political commitments of younger organized multiracials, however, appear to be left leaning. Participants in Mavin, the leaders of Mixed Media Watch, and my respondents largely consider themselves to be politically progressive and antiracist. They are skeptical of the claims that race does not matter by conservatives who point to their multiple racial identifications as proof of its irrelevance. There is a strong impulse among these respondents to avoid essentializing a set of differences that distinguish multiracials from others. Yet through the debate over official classification and the organizations in which they explore what they share as a group, racial mixedness is constituted as an adequate principle upon which to act.

There is an inescapable irony of group making that in seeking to undermine the foundations of American racial thinking, they reaffirm racial thinking as well. While activists and parents describe their use of multiple terms for indicating their racial identity as "revolutionary" or simply "accurate," it is also true that the logic of mixed race stems from the same underlying logic that preceded it—that individuals have race, and when they combine sexually we get "racial mixture." Both ideas assume there is race, it is carried in the body, and its mixed through sexual reproduction.

While those who fought official enumeration of mixed race status challenged the prevailing way that race was categorized, they stopped short of challenging the principle of racial classification itself. While seeming to challenge the racial state, multiracial activists *affirmed* the right of the state to label individuals in racial terms by arguing that it has a *duty* to label them in ways that fully recognize the possibility of boundary crossing. This can only entrench the underlying notion that individuals are made of "racial stuff" (albeit of more than one type) and that their racial composition ought to be recognized by that ultimate symbolic agency—the state. Their activism recognizes, indeed *welcomes* the right of the state to record a race for each of its members (even if individuals "self-identify"). This is a striking acceptance of the racial state, in and through which the category of race was created and through which it is reproduced.

Yet this irony is not limited to this movement. "The reproduction of ethnicity and the reinforcement of its pragmatic salience," writes Comaroff, "is as much a function of efforts directed at its erosion as it is of activities that assert its positive value" (Comaroff 1987, 315). If race is where you locate your difficulties, race is where you look for solutions. "Race" seems like an efficacious basis upon which to act.

The construction of multiracial community, like panethnic constructions and movements for ethnic renewal, is a flexible, sometimes strategic and sometimes contradictory phenomenon. It creates new racial subjects while conforming to the preexisting U.S, racial order, as it provides a crucial consciousness-raising tool with which to make demands on the state. It undermines rigid modes of racial thinking in the United States while multiplying the available ways of naming racial difference. While mixed race people may identify *with* each other, they eschew the notions of racial sameness that racial identity usually entails. While a collective mixed race identity is potentially subversive, it may be readily absorbed into the existing racial order, in which multiraciality comes to be seen as simply another racial category, robbed of its critical content.[7] The meaning of multiracial will be affected by the political alignments, demographics, and economic pressures of all other groups.

Critics of the group-making project among multiracials claim that "the multiracial community" is a fabrication. After all, mixed race people come in a variety of "mixes." As such, as a group they share no ancestry in common Nor do they necessarily share language, religion, or culture. They are not, in other words, a "real" ethnic group. Yet the fabricated aspect of multiracial group making that its critics find so troubling is precisely what makes studying this phenomenon so valuable. The notion of "fabrication" has a double meaning, signifying both an act of creation (which captures the constructed nature of groups) and a *deception*, in which the ways we tend to perceive groups in everyday life (as durable, real, substantial entities) masks the reality that groups do not exist as such, but rather are the products of a complex work of *group making*. All ethnoracial groups are constructed. In the project of making multiracials, however, the ways in which such construction proceeds are just more obvious.

The Family's Role in Racial Change

The trouble with family.   Multiracial activists have used the state as a means through which to gain symbolic recognition not only of their racial identity, but of their families as well. The multiracial family, some believe, serves as proof that America's racial problems can be overcome. I dub this the "family thesis," inspired by Benjamin DeMott's critique of contemporary racial politics. In his book, *The Trouble With Friendship*, DeMott (1998 [1995]) critiques what he calls "the friendship thesis" that underlies many putative solutions offered in culture and politics for healing racial division. According to DeMott, embedded within the "friendship thesis" is the "certainty that one-on-one, black-white relations can be relied on to resolve race problems". In a similar vein, the "family thesis" suggests that if we all just intermarried and had children together our problems would be resolved.

Historical and cross-cultural analyses show the problems with such an idea. First, rather than bringing about social equality, intermarriage tends to follow other indicators of social equality (such as educational achievement) between groups. But more to the point, it is questionable that personal relations can resolve what is wrought institutionally with the help of the state, no matter how intimate and caring those personal relations are. The hierarchies of relatedness that my respondents hold, which structure their sense of trust, affinity, and beliefs about others (despite growing up in interracial families), suggest that more than intimate and empathetic relations between individuals are needed to bring about social change. Empathy is limited in its capacities to bring about social change, since people can cultivate empathy for specific individuals while keeping intact their basic (negative) beliefs about the categories of people from which those individuals come. This is why assertions that people in intermarriages and multiracial individuals are less prejudiced natural bridges across the racial divide are problematic. It is easy to make exceptions for one's kin, marking them as the exception to the negative rule for others of a particular group, thus leaving the line of demarcation intact.

The complexities of interracial intimacy revealed through the stories of my respondents are cautionary tales with implications for how we interpret intermarriage statistics as barometers of racial change. In his influential study of white ethnicity Richard Alba writes, "By far the most impressive evidence of the diminishing power of ethnicity among whites is the rising tide of interethnic marriage. Marriage is a sensitive barometer of social integration because it involves great social intimacy" and links together members of families in regular contact (1990, 11–12). In contemporary interpretations of intermarriage patterns, families are assumed to engage in regular contact and to be intimate—to care for one another in a variety of ways (physically, financially, and emotionally). In the process, children are assimilated into one ethnic group (usually the dominant one) or act as bridges between those of their parents. This formulation imagines intermarriage as the sine qua non of assimilation: a cultural merger that produces children who embody that merging.

While interracial families are imagined as sites where racial differences meet and melt (away), racialized differences among family members create variable experiences for the members of such families. The family, as feminist scholars have argued for decades, is not a monolithic unit, and members within families have divergent and competing interests. For my respondents, race often formed the ground of those competing interests. In other words, while intermarriage may be common for some groups, it does not follow that it is either preferred or without controversy for either the partners in a marriage or their children, to say nothing of the ethnoracial communities with which they are engaged.

While invaluable for helping us understand changes in identification and marriage patterns, such statistics are very crude instruments for understanding meaning and tell us very little about practice—how and why people think of themselves in such terms and how they behave on the basis of them. When we rely on demographics to tell our stories we are merely recording and elaborating the preconstructed categories of the state and of social movements and are unable to say anything about whether and in what ways such categories are meaningful.

My point here is both methodological and epistemological. We need qualitative ethnographic work to understand meaning and process and we also need to question on what basis the assortment of people who marked boxes on the census can be considered a social group. Analyzing the statistics on racial identification tells us about patterns, but before we begin to make inferences about what those patterns say about group boundaries, the existence of groups, or the "groupness" of groups, we need to know something about meaning and practice.

Family's Radical Potential

All this is not to say that interracial kinship lacks a radical *potential*. Though I am cautious about interpreting multiracial identification and rising rates of intermarriage as signs of fading ethnoracial boundaries, I do believe that these developments, along with a growing public discussion of interracial intimacy, reflect and signal significant changes in the nature of racial division in the United States. The attempt to obtain some form of multiracial classification grew out of a desire to make visible those bonds that are easily elided—a recognition of not only a varied racial heritage, but of *relationships*. The MOOM option institutionalizes and records in statistical form a trace of those relationships.

For many of my respondents, parenting mixed race kids provided a powerful means through which they were able to extend their sense of obligation, empathy, and likeness beyond the circle of their ethnic group of origin. The notion that one can change one's people, to embrace the "other," is a potentially powerful tool to begin healing social divisions because it says that such social boundaries are artificial, and despite the very real consequences of those boundaries, through love and work they can be overcome.

The experience of living within interracial families allowed many of my respondents to overcome the racial categories that have almost always served to mark others outside one's moral domain, emphasizing the difference, and even the inhumanity, of the Other. It strikes me that the multiracial movement has its most radical potential in this vein. Presentations of multiracial family *as* families lessen the presumed distance across racial categories. Kinship symbolically bridges the imagined distance between racial groups. I am reminded of Patricia Williams's observation of a white woman suckling a black child. She writes:

Is there not something unseemly in our society about the spectacle of a white woman mothering a black child? A white woman giving totally to a black child;

a black child totally and demandingly dependent for everything, sustenance itself, from a white woman. The image of a white woman suckling a black child . . . Such a picture says, there is no difference; it places the hope of continuous generation of immortality of the white self in a little black face.

Given the pitfalls of family imagery mentioned earlier, images of the family are only truly transformative if they extend the cultural obligation to care for and about others *outside* the limits of both genealogical relatives *and* racial groups. One respondent tried to put into words how he saw this potential:

The way that a multiracial person sees the world—we come in so many different shades that I realize I can't look at someone and tell what they are any more. They could be black and white. They could be the same mixture that I am and look totally different or look very similar. So walking down the street, I can't look at someone and immediately conclude that I'm not related to them in some way, maybe not immediately but somewhere back in history we probably had some common ancestors, you know. Who knows? I really don't know. I can't say as a fact. So in a sense you start walking down the street and you look at everyone and see everyone as being related to you. Now, if you do that how can you discriminate against someone if you acknowledge that they're related to you? You can't discriminate against your brother or sister. What line, what rules—what lines of demarcation are you going to use to say this is us, this is them, these are the haves, these are the have-nots. You start to break them down. So the people can then start seeing or recognizing that—we are talking about the whole idea of one common humanity, you know, and I think that's a part of multiracial identity. The more you learn about multiracial people you just see multiracial people. This is what they look like. They're not so different as I thought. You know, so-and-so might not be so different. So that's why I really like to promote a multiracial outlook.

Seeing oneself in the other, as Jessica Benjamin (1988) argued, opposes the breakdown of mutual recognition that allows members of one category to see themselves as apart and above (or below) that leads to domination. It is this sense—that they are visible yet not seen—that motivates the action of the people who have been most involved in the multiracial movement. An acknowledgment of their social existence is something they understand to be crucial to eroding the color line. The issue is as much emotional as it is structural.

Understanding the emergence of multiracial families as a politicization of kinship helps clarify, if not the political implications of multiracial politics, then how multiracials understand the meaning of the actions in which they are engaged. The meaning of multiracial movement for its participants cannot be grasped merely at the cognitive level, where analysts of multiracial politics insist on grounding their critiques (for example, chastizing notions of racial accuracy or the use of fractional language as a reification of race). The notion of racial coherence put forth by respondents and evident in the idea that multiracial identification is expressive of a "whole self," should be understood not as a ground of politics, but as its effect—a response to the social conditions that create, sustain, and reproduce racial division.

The opposition between race and mixed race reaffirms boundaries between categories (white/black/Asian and so forth) even as the vocabulary of kinship brings together categories of bodies previously isolated outside of the sphere of family. So while multiracialism may reinscribe racial thinking by leaving intact the idea of race, it also calls attention to the peculiar history of the United States that denies social and sexual mixing across boundaries and helps us understand the role of such denial in supporting white domination.

The notion that one can choose one's racial identification disrupts the notion of genealogical descent as well. Such a notion says that people can choose *not* to identify with one of their ancestors' categories, or may choose to identify with a group to which none of their ancestors belonged, as did Mandy Rodriguez. Moreover, while some people might claim a multiracial identity, their children might not necessarily retain such an understanding of themselves.

While perhaps not revolutionary, the emergence of multiracial families as such represents a significant transformation in the logic (or illogic) underpinning dominant American racial discourse. The increasing prevalence and acceptance of intermarriage is a redefinition of permissible objects of sexual passion, as well as a redefinition of kinship. Multiracial families (and multiracial politics more broadly) do not necessarily challenge the biologistic and genealogical logic of race or family. Instead, they undercut the twin pillars of racial formation—hypodescent and antimiscegenation—creating the space by which the racialized family and familized notions of race are undermined.

While the multiracial family has long been a cultural contradiction in terms, that is no longer the case. The formation of collective organizations for multiracial families and their assertions that they are indeed families challenges a fundamental feature of American racial domination, yet its implications are not entirely clear. Intermarriage patterns and the political and cultural response to them and to mixed racial identity have always been linked to the broader system of racial domination that demarcates white from black (and less rigidly, white from other ethnoracial groups), and the fates of those of African descent (whether one is putatively "mixed" or not) have always been linked. While the possibility exists that the greater visibility of multiracial families will lead to more acceptability of all kinds of relations across racial boundaries—beginning with intimate and familial ones and corresponding with spatial and social ones—this does not mean, of course, that the problem that defined America in the twentieth century—the color line—has not followed us into the twenty-first.

Appendixes

List of Respondents

Name*	Age Category	Race/Ethnicity**	Occupation	Marital Status***
Vicki Reynolds	Mid 30s	White (French, I)/Black	Graduate Student	Single
Charlene Nieda	Early 30s	White/Asian (Japanese)	Graduate Student	Married (White)
Xavier Upton	Late 40s	Black (African, European, Indian)	Academic	Single
Mitch Russell	Mid 40s	Asian (Japanese)/Black	Academic	Married (Dominican)
Paula Kane	Early 40s	Asian (Filipina)/White	Psychologist	Married (Jewish)
Lareina Williams	Late 40s	White (Portuguese)/Black, Indian	Sales	Single
Steve Tomita	Late 20s	White/Asian (Japanese)	Law Student	Single
Pedro Santana	Declined	White/Mexican	Lawyer	Married (White)
Ben Cohen	Early 40s	White (Jewish)	Lawyer	Married (Trinidadian)
Marie Braxton	Mid 40s	Black (Jamaican)	Homemaker	Married (Jewish)
Stephanie Williams	Early 40s	White/Black	Psychotherapist	Married (White)
Elaine Johnson	Late 30s	Asian (Japanese, I)/Black	Playwright	Single
Mimi Sherwood	Mid 30s	Asian (Japanese, I)/White	Academic	Single
Peggy Walters	Mid 30s	White	Project Manager	Married (Black)
Emma Russell	Early 40s	Black	Homemaker	Married (White)
Jade Wolkoff	Late Teens	Black/White (Jewish)	Student	Single
Robin Peters	Mid 20s	Asian (Japanese, I)/White	Social Worker	Single
Mandy Rodriguez	Mid 40s	Asian (Japanese, I)/White	Writer	Marrried (Puerto Rican)
Majeeda Kibri	Early 20s	Latino (Mexican, I)/Persian, I	Student	Single
Rick Young	Late 20s	Asian (Japanese, I)/Black	Lawyer	Married
Carrie Kashtan	Mid 50s	White (Polish and English)/Armenian, I	Teacher	Divorced (Black)
Kanji Uyematsu	Early 20s	Black/Asian (Japanese)	Student	Single
Greg Douglas	Early 50s	Black (African, American Indian, English, Irish)	Talent Manager/Writer	Married (Jewish/German)

Name*	Age Category	Race/Ethnicity**	Occupation	Marital Status***
Pat Simpson	Early 40s	Black	College Instructor	Married (White)
Eileen Sullivan	Mid 40s	White (German)/White (Irish)	LAN Manager	Married (Black)
Vanessa Moore	Late 60s	White (German)	Retired	Widowed (Black)
Rachel Jefferson	Late 30s	Asian (Japanese, I)/Black	Domestic Engineer	Married (Jewish, Lithuanian)
Ashley Jankowski	Mid 30s	White	Medical Administrator	Divorced (Black)
Hank Gustafson	Late 40s	White (Polish)	Teacher	Married (Black)
Rose Gustafson	Late 40s	Black	Teacher	Married (White)
Brandon Gustafson	Mid 20s	Black/White (Polish)	Student	Single
Casey Wen	Mid 20s	White (Polish)/Asian (Chinese)	Graduate Student	Single
Mark Tachihara	Late 20s	White/Asian (Japanese)	Student	Single
Peter Kent	Late 20s	Asian (Japanese)/White (German)	Computer Consultant	Single
Ann Fox	Mid 40s	White (Jewish)	Clinical Nurse	Married (Black)
Sam Martinez	Mid 20s	White (German/Polish)/Mexican American	Electrical Engineer	Single
Ailis Arnaudy	Late 30s	Black/White	Writer	Single
Angela Chang	Early 20s	Argentinean, I/Asian (Korean)	Student	Single
Leif Hogan	Mid 20s	Asian (Chinese, I)/White (Finnish)	Teacher	Married (White)
Risa Ben-Tofer	Early 40s	White (Jewish)	Community Organizer	Married (Jewish)
Susan Lessing	Late 20s	White (French)/Black (West Indian)	Human Resources	Single
Annmarie Becker	Mid 30s	White (Scottish, Irish, German)	Student	Married (Black, West Indian)
Larry Overstreet	Mid 50s	Black	Realtor	Married (Swedish/Dutch)
Peg Gold	Mid 40s	White (Italian, Polish, French Canadian, Scottish)	Accountant	Married (White, Slovak)
Marcus Fork	Mid 30s	White (Jewish)/Black	Environmental Engineer	Single
Harmony Spencer	Late 20s	Black	Advocacy for Homeless	Married (White, English)

Name*	Age Category	Race/Ethnicity**	Occupation	Marital Status***
Charity Malone	Mid 20s	White (Italian, Scottish, Irish)/Black/Indian (Cherokee)	Student	Single
Geraldine Roberts	Late 30s	White (German)	Teacher	Divorced (Black)
Christine Collins	Mid 40s	White (German, Irish, Czech)	Retail Buyer	Married (Black), Divorced (White)
Bobby Collins	Late 30s	Black	Writer	Married (White)
Beth Flaherty	Early 30s	White (Norwegian,German)/Black	Adoption Lawyer	Single
Karen Britton	Mid 30s	White	Foundation Director	Divorced (Black)
Mariko Frazier	Early 20s	Asian (Japanese)/Black	Student	Single
Estelle Miller	Late 40s	Black	Clinic Administrator	Married (White), Divorced (Black)
Kathleen Wong	Early 50s	White (Irish)	Small Business Owner	Married (Filipino/Chinese)
Mia Guimond	Early 30s	Asian (Chinese)/Black (Haitian, I)	Physical Therapist	Divorced (Japanese/Irish, English)
Lois Jones	Early 60s	Black	Management	Married (White, Czech). Divorced (Black)
Harry Mineta	Early 50s	Asian (Japanese, I)/White (German, English)	Teacher	Married (White, Jewish)
Monique LeBlanc	Early 20s	White (Irish)/ Black	Student	Single
Sandy Giachini	Mid 20s	Asian (Japanese, I)/White (Italian)	Research Assistant	Single
Jamie Thomas	Early 20s	Asian (Chinese)/White	Entrepreneur	Single
Ron Berman	Mid 20s	Asian (Taiwanese, I)/White (Jewish)	Graduate Student	Engaged (White)

* Pseudonyms

** Race of mother/Race of father; Ethnicity in parentheses; I = immigrant

*** Race and ethnicity of partner in parentheses

Appendix B: Methodology

In order to understand how "multiracials" are being made into a recognizable category and social community, I employed several methods. My analysis draws primarily on in-depth interviews with sixty-two participants in groups formed for intermarried couples and their families, as well as those formed by multiracial adults. I also conducted fieldwork in events sponsored by those organizations, public hearings on census classification, fundraisers, college campus classrooms, and mixed race conferences. Most of the interviews were conducted from 1997 to 1999, with a smaller sample conducted from 2003 to 2005. Some interviewees were the leaders and founders of such groups, others were more casual participants.

I focused my search for interviewees on several organizations. Some were originally formed to address concerns of intermarried couples, including Multiracial Americans of Southern California (or MASC, based in Los Angeles), I-Pride (Berkeley, California), Biracial Family Network (Chicago), and Interracial Family Circle (Washington, D.C.). These first four organizations are the longest-lived organizations dealing with multiracial issues. The Association of Multiethnic Americans (AMEA) is an umbrella organization comprised by those and other groups. Hapa Issues Forum (HIF, Berkeley) was formed in the early 1990s. When I conducted my initial interviews in 1997–99, HIF was the only sustained group focused on mixed persons of Asian descent. I also interviewed members of campus organizations as well as Swirl and Mavin, two groups that emerged in the late 1990s and have been most successful in attracting young adult mixed race people on a national basis. (See the end of this appendix for descriptions of organizations and their stated missions.)

Sample Characteristics

My sample is purposively drawn, selected from a pool of people whose actions legitimate and bring to public consciousness the notion of multiracial identity. It is not intended to be representative of "multiracials." A generalizable, randomly drawn sample of mixed race people is not a possibility for a population that is partially hidden and lacks consensus over the criteria for measurement. Random sampling would not be appropriate for this study in any case, because my goal was to talk to those people moved to act, who do the work of group making. Garnering participants from organizations tends to weight a sample toward joiners or professional interviewees and the highly educated. Though a problem for studies that aspire to say something about a general population, for my purposes, whether or not the sample is weighted in a particular way constitutes an important *finding*, since these are the people doing the public work of making "multiracials" recognizable.

And indeed this sample has definite unique characteristics. First, 70 percent of the respondents are women, and 30 percent are men. This is appropriate since women are overrepresented in multiracial organizations. Since the organizations I focus on did not keep systematic membership lists, it is difficult to verify this assertion statistically. According to those involved in the groups, however, women predominate in membership and among those most actively involved.

As a group, this sample is highly educated. All but six respondents had at least a college degree, and of those who did not, five were of college age and still in the process of completing their degrees. Moreover, more than half the sample had graduate degrees. Respondents were mostly middle to upper-middle class, based on their incomes and education. If one uses income as a measure of class, however, this characterization may seem wrong, since almost one-fifth of the sample reports incomes below $20,000. This is because many of the respondents were students whose earned incomes are low. Many of these students, however, receive parental support, so their material circumstances are more secure than the numbers suggest. One respondent, not a student, reported an income of $20,000 to 40,000 but offered that her parents "help out a great deal" and even purchased her home for her.

Clearly this is a "classed" sample, which suggests that this is a classed phenomenon. Fully 20 percent of this sample reported household incomes of $100,000 or more, far above the median incomes for the cities in which they lived. Moreover, most reported coming from middle-class families. If one considers education as a measure of class, the relatively privileged nature of the sample becomes even clearer.

Racial classifications can carry particularly loaded meanings and consequences, and as such it matters to many people what they are racially labeled.

My respondents were no exception. Multiracial respondents were particularly sensitive to the veiled meanings of such categories. They report having their self-identifications questioned by people in authority. They were intimately familiar with experiences like being "eyeballed" by others (stared at) that many felt was objectifying and demeaning. This is in part why many respondents clung to very detailed descriptions of their racial identities, as if to stake a claim to something others could readily dismiss.

So in some ways it is difficult to know how best to convey the ethnoracial variation in the sample. It is ironic to distill ethnoracial affiliations in statistical form even as I am trying to show they are not a fixed characteristic of individuals. Nevertheless, it is central to the phenomenon to show respondents' differing relationship to dominant modes of classification. Respondents sometimes described themselves with reference to the ancestry of their parents, other times with reference to currently recognized ethnoracial categories (Chinese/Haitian or Asian/black). Sometimes those descriptions combined ancestral and ethnoracial categories in a descriptor (Japanese/white or black/Irish). Sometimes their descriptions were meant to convey whom they identified with or what they considered themselves to be, which was not always the same as their ancestry or its ethnoracial proximates (a woman of Japanese/European ancestry who identifies as Latina). At times they "edited" these descriptions, adding or leaving out some aspects of their ancestry. And, of course, sometimes they adopted categories to convey a mixed position, such as "mixed" or "hapa." In other words, respondents described themselves in many different ways with reference to multiple bases (ancestry, race, mixedness), and this varied according to context. Yet all of these descriptors attempt to symbolize a shared substance.

Given this variety, it is difficult to know how to craft a table to represent the ethnoracial distribution of the sample that does not misrepresent the object of study. Each representation necessarily leaves out another way in which respondents think about race. Keeping in mind the multiple and contingent ways respondents describe their ethnoracial identities, below I present some pertinent statistics on the ethnoracial composition of the sample according to dominant modes of racial classification.

Almost two-thirds of the sample are "multiracial" according to common understandings of racial categories, while one-third is "monoracial." Of the multiracial respondents, twenty are of African descent while twenty-four are of Asian descent. Only one respondent (Persian/Mexican) was not "of" either of these two categories. The number of respondents with a white parent totals twenty-nine, while only three respondents have a Latino parent. Ten respondents would be considered "double minorities," eight of whom are black/Asian.

All monoracial respondents are the parents of multiracial children. Of these, ten are black and fifteen are white. There are no Asian parents in the sample. This reflects an interesting difference in the focus of different types of multiracial organizations. The groups from which I drew my respondents have tended to draw black/white families, despite being nominally open to all other kinds of families. In retrospect, I wish I had consciously sought out Asian parents and their spouses to interview, even if relatively few are in these organizations.

There were several differences between multiracial and monoracial respondents. While all monoracials were parents, only one-quarter of the multiracial respondents were parents. This is in part due to age. Monoracial respondents were on average older than multiracial respondents. Average age at the time of interview was forty-five and thirty-one years, respectively.

Respondents varied in the degree, type, and length of involvement in multiracial organizations. While many respondents had been involved in collective multiracial activities for only two years, several had been active for over ten. While some devoted much of their time on a weekly basis to group activities, most participated fairly intermittently. The nature of the group cannot be judged by membership size alone, since most of the membership, although it pays dues, is relatively uninvolved. While most respondents reported enjoying the activities in which they participated, few would describe themselves as activists. Most were *not* involved in the efforts to change state classification. Some suggested they might not be right for the study because they felt they did not do enough to be considered part of this collective effort.

While nearly one-third of the sample reported being raised in the Roman Catholic tradition, nearly half reported no current religious affiliation. Yet even those who reported a religious affiliation attended church only sporadically.

Interviews

The interviews with respondents were conducted between late 1997 and early 1999. A second set of interviews was conducted in 2003 to 2005. All of the interviews with respondents were audio-recorded and most often took place at the respondent's home or office. The interviews lasted an average of one hour and forty-five minutes. My questions centered on several substantive areas, including their involvement in multiracial organizations, family life (relations with immediate and extended family members), attitudes toward racial classification, relations with friends and romantic partners, and concepts of multiracial community. The question format was open-ended so that respondents could identify the experiences and events they deemed salient. I did, however, prompt respondents to tell me more than just what happened and also to convey how they felt about particular events.

I recorded demographic information on each respondent as well in the form of a written survey. I asked many questions, including when and where they were born, ancestry, where they were raised, religious affiliation, marital status, home ownership status, income, and their own and their parents' education and occupation. In the first few interviews I had respondents fill out this information after the interview. I soon decided that I should ask the questions, because I found that some respondents were leaving some information blank, but I could not tell if this was because they did not want to answer the questions or if they had overlooked them. Another reason I began to administer the questionnaire is because I found that the questions prompted respondents to remember stories that we had not covered earlier but which were important for providing context to the interview. Talking about these questions became part of the interview itself.

Analysis

To analyze the interviews, I searched interview transcripts and notes manually, looking for repeated themes and patterns in the data. I also looked for contradictions and exceptions (Strauss and Corbin 1990). I compared responses according to several criteria: by multiracial and monoracial respondents, by ethnoracial distinctions, within and between organizations, by type and extent of involvement in organizations, and by gender. I chose quotes which best illustrate the general trend and/or exceptions to that trend among respondents.

Reflexivity

In any form of social research there are social and epistemological obstacles to gaining understanding the phenomenon at hand—obstacles that have to do with the nature of the phenomenon itself and with the researcher's relationship to it and those she studies. This holds true whether one is studying high-status realms of social life or those of ill-repute. In this case, and with this researcher, there were several challenges with which to deal. Participants in this research were often wary about the gaze and motives of "outsiders" (a term used by more than a few respondents to describe persons not of mixed descent or who did not identify as such or support their activities). One leader of a local organization commented that she was reluctant to grant interviews to other researchers who were not "mixed" because, she believed, they tended not to understand what it was like to be "one of us."

Such caution might be expected of anyone who agrees to talk for two hours, with someone she does not know, about her personal and public life (with a tape recorder going, no less, and after signing a "consent form"). Yet the reluctance of some respondents, far from being paranoia, stems from experience. Multiracials and intermarried persons have often been portrayed by fiction writers, politicians, filmmakers, journalists, and even social scientists as "confused," "tragic," "sellouts," "race traitors," "rice chasers," or possessed by "Jungle Fever." The ostensibly "positive" characterizations that have also developed ("exotic," "beautiful," "naturally unprejudiced")—and which some respondents readily adopted—underscore the fact that persons of mixed descent have been more often seen as social anomalies than as *normal* social beings.

I chose to use pseudonyms for respondents as a means to protect their privacy. I should note, however, that many respondents did not feel the need to hide their identities, and several wanted to be identified for the work they have done. Though the more publicly recognized individuals agreed to sign consents allowing me to use their real names, I opted in the end to use pseudonyms for all interviewees. I feel more comfortable doing this since some readers may find the strategies respondents have employed at various times to deal with stigmatization objectionable. I justify this on theoretical grounds as well. Using real names focuses attention on the individuals themselves and away from the social conditions that make them particularly suited to engage in this process of group making.

In the face of respondents' wariness, being a person who meets the criteria for being multiracial as it is currently conceived (my mother is Irish, my father is African American) greatly facilitated my access to respondents. My interest in the subject, when matched up with my physical appearance, was often taken as prima facie evidence of my solidarity with the "cause," and an assumption that whatever I wrote would be in service to the advancement of the group's agenda. At times the assumption of shared identity and politics felt uncomfortable for me as a researcher, particularly so when it seemed respondents seemed to want to know up front "where I stood" on issues like classification (although no one directly asked me). This assumption created some anxiety for me, as I was ambivalent about the agenda of some individuals, cautious myself about how being characterized as a "member" would mark me outside the black community, and dreading the sense of betrayal I thought some respondents, whom I genuinely liked, would inevitably feel when my final product did not conform to their expectations. Some activist respondents conveyed a hint of antagonism toward academics, expressing the sense that academics came to study them but did not contribute much to the groups. As one man said to me "You guys (academics) just watch while we (activists) do all the work." Veiled within this comment is the expectation that "we" academics, especially those of mixed descent like myself, *are* members and *should* be doing something on behalf of the group.

The assumption that I was in support of their activities is perhaps understandable. The truth is, I was already a "part" of this broader phenomenon before I began to study it. As an undergraduate at Harvard in 1988, my friend Cathy Hinton and I began a discussion group for "mixed race" people called Prism, provoked by our realization that most of our friends who considered themselves to be black, had white mothers, yet never discussed that fact. When I moved to the San Francisco Bay Area in 1990, I first became aware of I-Pride, and intrigued that what my friend and I had been doing in relative isolation, others had also been doing, for over a decade.

Observation

While the analysis is primarily based on the interviews I conducted with respondents, that analysis is also informed by my participation in "the field." My participation in group activities, events around multiracial identity (conferences, community group outings), and informal conversations (at parties, over dinner, out for ice cream, and so forth) with persons in this milieu greatly informed my analysis. Such participation helped me gauge how others create a sense of group identity: what issues are deemed important ones to debate, how people talk about such issues, and who attends such meetings all gave me added perspective on the interviews.

While I do not think that analysis of the multiracial movement is impossible if one is not a "member," I am certain that my credentials as such (if only ostensibly, and by proxy) enabled me to circumvent some of the barriers to entry in this milieu. Based on what interviewees told me, I think it is fair to say that being ostensibly "of the group" allows for a different type of exchange than would be possible were I not intimately familiar with the kinds of experiences of which my respondents spoke. It is not that "monoracial" interviewers would not be told stories of how respondents came to an identity as multiracial, for clearly they have. Rather, it is the tone of the stories, the degree of familiarity assumed, the emotional unguardedness that comes when people feel they are talking to "one of their own" that is different.

The assumption of "membership" gave me access to information I otherwise might not have gotten, perhaps most often from white and multiracial women. With white women, who were all mothers of children of partial African descent, I felt they assumed and at times projected identification with me in the role of "daughter." Many times respondents commented on my appearance, one woman wondering aloud if her black/white daughter might look like me one day. With multiracial women, the connection existed at the level of friend/sister—one who implicitly understands how to manage the conflicted racial, gender, and sexual politics of a "mixed" position (for example, exoticization and the veiled meanings of hair). This sense of commonality was evinced in what one woman said after only a few conversations, "we're practically like family." And certainly I also felt a sense of closeness with my respondents. Almost all of my interviews with mixed women ended, quite spontaneously, with a hug. Many times respondents asked me to tell my family story. In those moments, my role as researcher seemed to meld with that of "fellow mixed person."

While being "mixed" facilitated trust and rapport, my "variety" of mix (black/white) took on variable meanings in relation to respondents. With black/white respondents it seemed to provide them a sense of commonality and comfort with me as an interviewer. For other respondents it was a site of difference. Some mixed race Asians told me they were surprised to realize they shared common experiences with someone not of their "mix," or emphasized the particular aspects of hapas' experience as rationale for creating Asian-focused groups instead of "pan-multiracial." Several respondents talked of a kind of comfort continuum mediated by race, having less comfort around monoracials, more with multiracials of any stripe, and most with those of their specific mix.

Sharing with my respondents a common frame of reference (as opposed to a common identity) as someone situated as multiracial had its difficulties. Relaying that which is familiar is often difficult. The potential is always there to take the familiar for granted and forget or not see that it must be explained.

At times, I confess, my enthusiasm for the project would flag, as I wondered why I should bother doing this anyway, since what I was talking about seemed perfectly obvious to me, and thus, it seemed, to everyone else. In the time that has passed since the active phase of the research project ended, I have been reminded numerous times of the strangeness that interracial kinship can still elicit and the significance people attach to how we define ourselves (or not) in racial terms. Explaining why that it is so is, to me, a useful endeavor.

The Association of Multiethnic Americans (AMEA)

Year Formed: 1988

Location: Los Angeles, CA

Mission: The Association of MultiEthnic Americans (AMEA), a nonprofit organization, is an international association of organizations dedicated to advocacy, education, and collaboration on behalf of the multiethnic, multiracial, and transracial adoption community.

Demographic: Multiethnic, Multiracial, and Transracial Adoption Community

Affiliates:

1. Chicago—Biracial Family Network
2. Edmonton, Canada—(MOXHCA)
3. Eugene, Oregon—Honor Our New Ethnic Youth (HONEY)
4. Los Angeles—Multiracial Americans of Southern California (MASC)
5. Montclair, New Jersey—Getting Interracial Families Together (GIFT)
6. Portland—Oregon Council on Multiracial Affairs (OCMA)
7. San Francisco—Interracial Intercultural Pride (I-Pride)
8. Tucson—Multiethnics of Southern Arizona In Celebration (MOSAIC)
9. Washington D.C.—Interracial Family Circle (IFC)

Biracial Family Network

Year Formed: 1980

Location: Chicago, IL

Mission: To establish spaces of comfort and connection among members of multiracial families. To take action against racist and discriminatory practices. To educate people and communities about multiracial experiences.

Demographic: Multiracial Families

Affiliates: AMEA

Hapa Issues Forum (HIF)

Year Formed: 1993

Location: San Francisco, CA

Mission: Hapa Issues Forum (HIF) is dedicated to enriching the lives of Asian Pacific Islanders of mixed heritage and developing communities that value diversity.

I-Pride

Year Formed: 1979

Location: San Francisco Bay Area, CA

Mission: I-Pride is a nonprofit organization interested in the well-being and development of children and adults who are of more than one racial or ethnic heritage. We uphold the principle that racism of any kind has no legitimate place in this nation of nations, nor can it be tolerated in this world of nations in need of peace.

Demographic: Multiracial and Multiethnic Children and Adults

Recent Activities: Dinner Meeting; Family Night at Fusion Summer Camp for Multiracial Youth

Interracial Family Circle (IFC)

Year Formed: 1984

Location: Washington, D.C.

Mission: Since 1984, the Interracial Family Circle has provided opportunities for the education, support, and socialization of multiracial individuals, families, people involved in interracial relationships, and transracial adoptive families in the Washington, D.C., metropolitan area.

Demographic: Multiracial Individuals and Families, Interracial Couples, and Transracial Adoptive Families

Multiracial Americans of Southern California (MASC)

Year Formed: 1986

Location: Los Angeles, CA

Demographic: Interracial Couples (with or without children), Transracial Adoptive Families, and Multiracial Adults

Affiliates: Affiliate of AMEA

Recent Activity: Present at the Generation MIX Tour stop in Los Angeles; Participating on the One Box Isn't Enough (OBIE) project with MAVIN; Working on board development to obtain new volunteers.

Members: 20

Mavin Foundation

Year Formed: Magazine: 1999; Foundation: 2000

Location: Seattle, WA

Mission: Mavin Foundation creates innovative projects that celebrate and advocate for mixed race people and families to create a cohesive, multicultural society. Our projects explore the experiences of mixed heritage people, transracial adoptees, interracial relationships and multiracial families.

Demographic: Mixed Race People and Families.

Projects: Generation MIX National Awareness Tour; Community MAP (Mixed race Action Plan); MatchMaker Bone Marrow Project; Campus Awareness+Compliance Initiative (CACI)

Circulation: 5,500

Project RACE

Year Formed: 1991

Location: Atlanta, GA

Mission: Project RACE advocates for multiracial children and adults through education, community awareness, and legislation. Our main goal is for a multiracial classification on all school, employment, state, federal, local, census, and medical forms requiring racial data.

Demographic: Multiracial Children and Adults

Swirl, Inc.

Year Formed: 2000

Location: New York, NY

Mission: Swirl, Inc. is an antiracist, grassroots organization that serves the mixed heritage community and aims to develop a national consciousness around mixed heritage issues to empower members to organize and take action toward progressive social change.

Demographic: Mixed Race Individuals and Families, Interracial Couples, and Transracial Adoptive Families

Chapters: San Francisco Bay Area, CA; Boston, MA; New York City, NY

Events: Dinners, Book Clubs, Film Screenings, Panel Discussions

Projects: Everything You Always Wanted to Know About the Census: Gearing up for 2010

Members: Organization: 414; Listserv: 1, 025

Appendix C: Situating Multiracial Group Making in the Literature on Social Movements, Race, and the Work of Pierre Bourdieu

In trying to explain the making of multiracials, two literatures are of most obvious relevance: that which seeks to explain the origins and development of social movements, and that which seeks to account for ethnoracial group formation. Below I describe in what ways each informs my project, highlighting the strengths and limitations of dominant approaches in each field. In addressing some of those limitations for explaining the making of multiracials, I have found the work of Pierre Bourdieu especially useful. The multiple strands of action that my respondents engaged in to make the category "multiracial" a socially recognizable one are part of a broader "classification struggle" (to use Bourdieu's terminology) in which multiracial activists strive to revalue upward the notion of multiraciality in American life. Their attempts to do so comprise a work of *group making*.

Approaches to Movement Origins and Development

In the last three decades, social movement scholars have developed two major approaches to the study of movement origins and development: political process theory and new social movements theory. Political process theory developed out of resource mobilization theory, which posits that the emergence, decline, and degree of success of movements can be understood by studying how resources are mobilized by social movement organizations (McCarthy and Zald 1973, 1977; Oberschall 1973). Resource mobilization theory has been critiqued for equating social movements with formal organizations, for assuming rather than explaining which grievances and which groups are involved in social movement struggles, and because it lacks consistent criteria for defining just what constitutes a "resource" (Cohen 1985; McAdam 1982; McAdam, McCarthy, and Zald 1995). The political process model is built upon the insights of resource mobilization theory and is guided by the assumption that social movements are shaped by the broader environmental context in which they emerge and places heavy emphasis on the role of institutionalized politics and the conditions that make it vulnerable or receptive to challenge (McAdam 1992). This approach is quite useful for explaining activists' success in getting the U.S. Census Bureau to enumerate multiracialism in the form of the MOOM option (see Chapter 2).

Yet the political process model has difficulty explaining the underpinnings of multiracial mobilization, or other movements focused on identity, because it cannot explain (nor attempts to) why some aspects of experience come to be defined as politically salient, as unmet "needs," while others remain unpoliticized or never become defined as "needs" in the first place. To wit: through much of the twentieth century, ethnoracial organizations and activists have managed to politicize issues of exclusion, invisibility, poverty, and discrimination, yet the issue of racial classification criteria, and most especially the one-drop rule, remained unpoliticized. Similarly, neither approach can explain why what was once considered a "settled" issue (in that the one-drop rule has been generally accepted by African Americans since the 1920s, conflicts around phenotypical differences have remained within the community, and such differences have not served as the basis of collective action) is being politicized now.

The structuralist bias of the political process model limits its ability to explain how actors develop an understanding of their needs and grievances. In response to such shortcomings, several scholars have begun to focus on the cognitive and cultural dimensions of collective action, broadly defined as the shared meanings and definitions that motivate movement actors to mobilize. Snow et al. (1986) first described the social psychological dynamics of movements as "frames," borrowing from Goffman's concept. Doug McAdam (1982) described the importance of "cognitive liberation," a new way of understanding one's circumstances as both unjust and subject to change, to movement emergence. McAdam et al. (1995) argue that two aspects of framing are critical to movement emergence—people must feel "aggrieved about some aspect of their lives" and "optimistic that, acting collectively, they can redress the problem." McAdam et al. define framing as the "conscious strategic efforts by groups of people to fashion shared understandings of the world and of themselves that legitimate and motivate collective action" (1995, 7).

In an attempt to develop an operational concept of framing, McAdam et al. limit the concept of framing to explicitly stated ideas and discourse. The cognitive bias of this definition is problematic for two reasons. First, it attempts to understand culture via a study of ideas and discourse extracted from the context in which such discourse develops. As such, it presumes that the meaning people attribute to the action in which they engage is reducible to the conscious, explicitly stated frames they develop to advance their cause (Goodwin and Jasper 2004; Johnston and Klandermans 1995; Polletta 2004). While the strategic and conscious framings of politicized multiracial organizations stress the legal reasons why racial hybridity should be recognized, the motivation for these activists cannot be said to emerge wholly or even most importantly from a sense of the legal injustice of not having a category. Rather, their activism stems in large part from their experience of family and the emotionally charged, deeply held beliefs about what families are supposed to be like.

By limiting the study of meaning in movements to its cognitive dimension, we prematurely foreclose the possibility that noncognitive, emotional bonds are equally important for the construction of meaning in movements and in encouraging mobilization. Moreover, their focus on "strategic and conscious" framings limits the context in which frames develop to social movement organizations, which cuts off the broader social context in which other frames (complementary or competing) may develop that may potentially have consequences within a movement (Benford and Snow 2000; Hunt, Benford, and Snow (1994). The meaning of multiracialism is, of course, also shaped outside of such organizations—in schools, media, and popular culture.

Other attempts to deal with the cultural dimension of social movements have focused on "new social movements," a moniker said to describe those movements predicated on the right to identity, in which identity is the goal, rather than a by-product, of the movement (Cohen 1985). New social movement theorists have argued that identity-based movements are emerging because in postindustrial society, power resides less in relations of production that in the ability to produce *knowledge*, normative guidelines, and sociocultural forms (Giddens 1991; Melucci 1980, 1988; Touraine 1985).[1] While the opposition of economy to culture (rather than arguing for their mutual constitution) has been challenged, the emphasis on culture is well taken. Grievances develop in a broader cultural context, so finding out why movements emerge requires looking at more than just the visible aspects of collective action, such as organizations, protests, and conscious framings. It also requires that we look to the not-yet-politicized networks in which new social identities incubate—what Melucci terms the "invisible pole" of social movements (see also Mueller 1994). Collective multiracial activity did not emerge from groups like the NAACP, which are already organized to address issues of racial inequality. Rather, it came from social support organizations, formed for interracial families, *through* which more conventionally political and formally organized groups that targeted the state for official classification were formed.

Contributions and Limits of Scholarship on Race and Ethnicity

What then of the scholarship on race that deals with the origins and development of ethnoracial groups? Whereas social movements scholars once assumed grievances to be relatively stable features of social life, and thus less interesting for studying movement emergence than shifts in structural factors, most early scholars of race presumed the existence of races and then attempted to explain relations between racial groups in the context of changing structural conditions (Dollard 1957 [1937]; Frazier 1957; Park 1939). In the last thirty years, however, social scientists have largely discarded the idea that race is a biological property of individuals and a natural social grouping, and have sought to explain the idea of race and ethnoracial groups as emergent, contingent, and malleable products of history.

In the endeavor, scholars have disagreed at to whether race should be understood as a fundamental basis of social inequality or a *sign* of yet more fundamental social cleavages like ethnicity, nation, or class. Class-based approaches, for example, link the formation of racial boundaries and identities to the class structure, class formation, or class struggle (in varying degrees) (Bonacich 1980; Cox 1970 [1948]; Hall 1991). What matters in explaining racial division is one's position in a division of labor and the social organization of work. In these formulations, racial distinctions are illusory and ideological, distractions from purportedly more fundamental bases of social inequality.[2]

The structuralist bias of class approaches to race limits their usefulness for explaining why some actors organize to have recognized and to affirm racial identities because they do not address how, if the belief in race represents a false consciousness, such an illusion has been made real. They reduce the question of the real efficacy of racial thinking to whether or not races exist as real, substantial entities. If they do not, this logic suggests, then analysis of racial thinking is superfluous, or at least, not as important as the economic dimension of inequality. But, as many critics have argued, the process by which race becomes reified as a substantial, durable entity must be central in an analysis of the fabrication of race (Brubaker 2004; Comaroff 1987; Omi and Winant 1994). "Race" is not simply class by another name. While ethnoracial distinctions emerge out of structural relations of inequality, they are also produced through the ways that such inequality is symbolized and represented in culture.

In reaction against theories of race that reduce race to other presumably more fundamental bases of social life, Omi and Winant argue that in the United States at least, race is an "autonomous field of social conflict, political organization, and cultural/ideological meaning" rather than an epiphenomenon or an aberration (Omi and Winant, 1994, 53). As such, race should be treated as a constitutive element of social structure, and the object of our analyses ought to be the "unstable and 'decentered' complex of social meanings constantly being transformed by political struggle" (Omi and Winant, 1994, 55) that defines race.

In their necessary attempt to account for the centrality of race in American political and social life, however, Omi and Winant end up naturalizing what they argue is a socially constructed phenomenon. They go so far as to say that "Race will *always* be at the center of the American experience" (1994, 5). Race, a product of history is then treated as a transhistorical element of social structure, thus undermining the indeterminacy that a constructivist framework presupposes. This approach tends to reinforce the analytical opposition between scholarship on race and ethnicity in the United States in a way that makes it difficult to account for why some distinctions thought of in racial terms (for example, Irish and Jewish immigrants in nineteenth and early twentieth century America) come to be imagined as ethnic groups. Despite these shortcomings, Omi and Winant's emphasis on the role of the state and insitutionalized politics in the creation of racial projects is well taken. They, like many other students of race, argue that in states that recognize ethnicity as a legitimate basis of political organizing, ethnic mobilization is most likely to occur and to persist (Barth 1969; Comaroff 1987; Dominguez 1986; Espiritu 1992; Leonard 1992; Nagel 1986, 1994, 1995; Sanchez 1993; Steinberg 1981).

Understanding that the state is quite important in encouraging multiracial mobilization, however, does not go very far toward explaining why my respondents felt so invested in racial identity and classification. Much like in the literature on social movements, in the literature on ethnoracial group formation the relationship between structural conditions and subjective experience has been insufficiently specified. Instead, scholars tend to emphasize either objective or subjective aspects of racial formation rather than their interrelatedness. Cornell (1996) points out that since the publication of Barth's seminal essay in 1969, students of race have increasingly focused on the structural, strategic, and situational conditions that give rise to the construction of boundaries between groups, and have almost totally abandoned study of the contents of ethnic identities, the "stuff" inside the boundaries, that once comprised the bulk of the field.[3] Cornell critiques race scholarship for ignoring the efficacy of agents' subjective ideas about groups and their relationship to the objective conditions in which groups form. He argues that "Positional interests may indeed shape collective identities, but surely the reverse is true as well: our self-concepts shape our perceptions of the world around us and, therefore, our perception of our interests" (1996, 267).[4]

Bourdieu and the Notion of Classification Struggle

Pierre Bourdieu's work is especially helpful in addressing the shortcomings in the race and social movements literatures. The conceptual core of his work—habitus, capital and field—as well as the notion of classification struggle, provide a generative framework for explaining multiracial mobilization. Bourdieu stresses that the tendency to perceive groups in everyday life (as durable, real, substantial entities) masks the reality that groups, "whose numbers, limits, members one claims to be able to define" do not exist as such, but rather are the products of a complex work of *group making* (1991, 228).[5] Social scientists of race should begin by asking "how is the group constituted?" Rather than begin with the presumption that a multiracial community exists, I attempt to show *how* it is being made, in part through the efforts of those involved in collective organizing.

The multiple strands of action that my respondents engaged in to make the category "multiracial" a socially recognizable one are part of a broader "classification struggle" in which multiracial activists strive to revalue upward the notion of multiraciality in American life. Bourdieu's notion of classification struggle provides a framework for thinking about race as but one type of a broader social phenomenon. Struggles over racial categories are attempts to fashion the world according to the ideas and interests of particular groups—to impose the definition of the world that comes to be understood as common sense. "Race" is but one form of social classification (in which humans categorize other humans), setting up arbitrary boundaries that result from and are the objects of struggle within and between groups.

Framing struggles over race as one form of classification struggle allows us to put racial formation in conversation with other forms of social exclusion. This breaks us out of the misleading analytical opposition between ethnicity and race in U.S. scholarship, which insists that because they are thought of and experienced differently in everyday life that we should treat them as fundamentally different social formations in our analytical work. In this I agree with Wacquant (1997) who argues that rather than employing a group-oriented approach to studying race (that studies the history of particular groups), we ought to adopt a problem-oriented approach, exploring what he dubs the "elementary forms of racial domination" (including racial classification, prejudice, discrimination, segregation, ghettoization, and violence), the mechanisms through which racial domination is (re)produced. Doing so allows us to understand how variations in racial classification affect the structure of race relations and processes of group formation and struggle. When we use these analytical categories to understand the processes by which human groups get delineated, the sharp distinction between the two concepts becomes unnecessary.

The advantage of Wacquant's approach, itself an application of Bourdieu's ideas to the field of race, allows us to understand racial formation as a social phenomenon (not a peculiar American aberration) without being reductionist. While this approach insists that the processes that produce ethnic groups are the same as those that produce "racial" groups, it requires us to account for why it is that people *act and think as if* ethnicity is about culture, while race is rooted in nature. In this formulation, race is not reducible to ethnicity, nor can we dismiss it as a kind of false consciousness since the way a social system is symbolized is an irreducible part of its reality.

The concepts at the core of Bourdieu's work—habitus, capital, and field—and their relationship to each other, provide a generative model for understanding the group-making problem among multiracials. This model offers a set of conceptual tools to begin to parse how it is that our collective racial fiction is made real. *Habitus* refers to the taken-for-granted assumptions individuals have about the world that are the product of their socialization, which varies by social location. How we are socialized shapes the categories we use to make sense of the world and our perceptions of what is normal and natural, as well as the very desires that we experience as "personal" and generated from within. Our experiences growing up shape the kinds and amount of resources (capital) we are endowed with and which we may or may not use in various contexts. What counts as capital is whatever can be translated into profit in a given context (field) in which one is trying to "spend" it. *Field* is often described with the metaphor of a game, which requires players who know the rules of the game, have the skills to play, and the desire to do so. There is often a convergence between habitus and field:

our social location predisposes us to desire and pursue the stakes and profits offered by participation in a field.

In this book, I try to make sense of *who* is involved in such collective work without presuming from the outset, as so many commentators do, that such work is the inevitable outcome of the growth in births of mixed descent persons. Instead, I pay attention to the economic, cultural, and symbolic capital of these actors relative to others that made it likely, though certainly not inevitable, that multiracials would organize collectively.[6]

The most involved actors in multiracial mobilization combine a critical set of social properties that allowed them to take advantage of the broader political and social opportunities present during the 1990s. These respondents' recognition of their racial dilemmas *as* dilemmas, and their desire and ability to do something about them, are linked to their educational experience. Their dilemmas, however, are shaped not merely by their own personal situations and are about more than "race." Questions of racial identity and belonging encompass a variety of conflicts over class, sexuality, education, and family history that are understood and expressed through race, precisely because we live in an age where race is central to how Americans organize themselves socially and personally.

The struggle over multiracial classification was an attempt to bring a multiracial identity into existence through public naming. To say that identity is a goal of collective action, however, begs the question whence the desire for such an identity springs. Whereas some critics of multiracial activists consider it an attempt to escape a stigmatized racial category, others consider it a naïve attempt to assert an identity in an inappropriate arena, still others cannot understand why the issue is compelling enough for some that they sacrifice any time and energy on it at all.

Bourdieu (1996) argues that those who act in any field (be it artistic, intellectual, political, and so forth) do so because they are socially predisposed to pursue the stakes and profits offered by participation in the field. It is only when one is *not* predisposed to recognize the stakes in a particular struggle and as such, to have a belief in the game ("the stranger's point of view"), that such an investment in the game appears to be an illusion.[7]

The notion of habitus gives us some purchase on explaining why people raised in interracial families come to see the social rules regarding interracial intimacy and racial identification as problematic and why they are so invested in changing them. While raised within families in which intimacy across racial boundaries is for the most part the norm, they also confront institutional arrangements in which this is decidedly not the case. This mismatch between "habitus" and the "fields" they encounter, generates their grievances.

Bringing emotions back in.   Among my respondents, racial classifications were not simply understood as neutral descriptors of themselves, but were often interpreted as symbols of their relationships to parents, families, and ancestors, and invested with intense feelings of attachment, loss, and longing. Conveying the emotional meaning behind the actions and understandings people have of their situation is important. It adds warm flesh to the often-brittle bones of analytical reasoning. But more than that, they are part of the full truth of the phenomenon, interrelated with objective conditions.

While Bourdieu did not extensively develop analyses of emotion in his work, he stresses that it is "artificial or quite simply beside the point to ask questions concerning the relationship between structures and sentiments" ([1980] 1990, 159). For him, agents' representations of the world, even those experienced as intimate and most uniquely one's own (the emotions), are shaped by and shape structure. It is beside the point to ask what the relationship between structure and feeling is, since this implies they are separate entities that encounter and potentially alter one another.[8]

In talking to the people involved in multiracial mobilization, my respondent told stories about their struggles for acceptance and recognition within their families and communities that were deeply felt, often poignant, and sometimes painful. I use the stories my respondents offered—of the white parent who reacts with "horror" to the news that her child was marrying a black person, a child raised without not knowing his grandparents because he is of a "different race," and the kinds of emotion work people engage in to cope with ruptured expectations about supposedly unconditional love—as both invitations and clues to deciphering the social and cultural logic that produces such behavior and feelings.

For Bourdieu, classification struggles are at bottom struggles for "symbolic life and death," to be recognized as existing in the world. If we use this lens to focus on the multiracial movement, we are left with questions particular to this movement, but which can be applied to any other arena of social action. First, while the ultimate motivation behind this or any other social action may be to be known and recognized, why is the form of recognition sought in this struggle centered around race? To understand this, we need to know about the individuals, groups, and interactions that comprise the movement proper, but we also need to understand the various ways that racial classifications have been and continue to be used in institutional settings like the family, school, and state as mechanisms for distinguishing people, organizing daily life, and distributing rewards. Multiracial actors sought to change the way these classifications were used. Their movement provides a perfect opportunity to understand how such struggles over race proceed—struggles through which the illusion of race is made real. Through an analysis of it we see how a new social category is being made and the color line redrawn.

Notes

Chapter 1

1. In 1974, the Federal Interagency Committee on Education created an Ad Hoc Committee on Racial and Ethnic Definitions that by 1977 resulted in the adoption of Statistical Policy Directive 15 by the Office of Management and Budget (OMB). This classification schema is commonly referred to simply as Directive 15.

2. Two influential works on the topic during this period are Paul Spickard's *Mixed Blood* (1989) and Maria Root's *Racially Mixed People in America* (1992). The emergence of writing on contemporary mixed race people and identity gathered momentum in the 1990s and is largely the work of scholars who identify as mixed.

3. Beginning with the Census 2000, instructions for the race question read "What is Person 1's race? Mark one or more races to indicate what this person considers himself/herself to be." The categories "White," "Black, African Am., or Negro," and "American Indian or Alaska Native" appear as discrete categories, while several Asian national categories are listed separately, as are "Native Hawaiian," "Other Pacific Islander," and "Some other race."

4. The "mulatto" category first appears in the 1850 census, and by 1880 categories indicating Indian mixtures with whites, blacks, and mulattoes appear. By the 1930 census, the racial categories used included white, Negro, Indian, Mexican, Chinese, and Japanese. Mulatto had disappeared, as had other categories denoting racial mixedness (Renn 2004).

5. Newsweek's cover story on Obama in December 2004 was titled, "He'll make the red and blue states see purple"—a reference to his widespread popularity as well as his biraciality.

6. I calculate this figure based on my assessment of organization records or assessments told to me by group leaders.

7. Such multiracial groups are not without precedent. The Manasseh Society in Chicago existed from 1898–1932, while the Penguin Club in New York and the Society for the Amalmagation of the Races in San Francisco, formed for individuals in interracial marriages in the 1920s. Also, during the 1960s, local community groups for interracial couples existed, such as the Rainbow Club in Minneapolis.

8. Brubaker 2004, p. 11.

9. Early social scientists believed that in order for immigrant groups to advance economically, acculturation—the adoption of the values, beliefs, and practices of Protestant whites—was not only desirable, but also necessary (Park 1950; Gordon 1964). Explaining the trajectories of African Americans and other groups required delinking structural incorporation from issues of acculturation. Despite high degrees of acculturation, African Americans were not advancing economically (Blauner 1972; Metzger 1971; Wilson 1978). Despite being assimilated in social and economic terms, in the 1970s whites began elaborating their ethnicity (Alba 1990; Waters 1990). At the same time, post-1965 immigrants such as Asians, Latinos, and West Indians were experiencing social and economic mobility while retaining their cultural distinctiveness (Portes and Zhou 1993; Waters 1999).

10. The most recent research on assimilation processes is instructive here. In it analysts delink aspects of structural incorporation and socioeconomic parity from issues of acculturation and social acceptance (Alba and Nee 2003; Portes and Zhou 1993; Tuan 1998). While interracial marriage may be the result of greater economic parity and acculturation between certain groups, I argue that high outmarriage rates are not commensurate with social acceptance for the offspring of those unions.

11. In her study of American Indian ethnic renewal, Joane Nagel writes, "[I]ndividual ethnic renewal does not automatically produce collective renewal unless personal interest in one's ethnic heritage is translated into some form of collective action . . . Collective ethnic renewals do occur, however, and so do large numbers of individual ethnic renewals. When they occur simultaneously, they are quite likely interrelated and share a set of common causes" (1996, p. 11).

Chapter 2

1. Bourdieu 1991, p. 221.

2. Racial hybrids—the offspring of persons from different racialized categories—have been classified and treated in a variety of ways in different societies. Davis (1991) discusses several of them. They may be given a status lower than (e.g. Amerasians in Vietnam), higher than (e.g., mestizos in Mexico), or in-between (South Africa) both parent groups; a variable status that depends on other criteria in addition to mixed ancestry (Brazil), a status in which ancestry and color are inconsequential (Hawaii), and the status of an assimilating minority (Indian/white in the United States).

3. "Mixedness" or parentage by white slave owners did not necessarily translate into privilege. Rural kin groups of African, European, and Indian descent (sometimes referred to as "triracial isolates") and who trace their "mixedness" to slave times have been largely poor and uneducated, and in no way tied to the black bourgeoisie of which Frazier writes.

4. "Proportionately fewer Negroes of high social status, except intellectuals and 'Bohemians,' marry white persons. Both the social controls of the Negro community, which make it difficult for a person occupying a responsible position to make such a break, and the satisfactions that come with being at the apex of a social group (even though it is a subordinate one) deter such persons" (Drake and Cayton 1993 [1945], 138). Frazier (1957) makes a similar argument.

5. In the preface to the 1962 edition; p. xlv in the 1993 edition.

6. "Both Negroes and whites in such situations are constantly exposed to expressions of disapproval by both races, and it seems much simpler for each to stay on his own side of the color-line" (Drake and Cayton 1993 [1945], 123).

7. From 1994 hearings as quoted in Omi and Espiritu (2000).

8. Instructions for the race question in Census 2000 read, "What is Person 1's race? Mark one or more races to indicate what this person considers himself/herself to be." The categories "White," "Black, African Am., or Negro," and "American Indian or Alaska Native" appear as discrete categories, while several Asian national categories are listed separately, as are "Native Hawaiian," "Other Pacific Islander," and "Some other race."

9. Graham says of Project RACE's beginnings, "It's a grass roots movement and literally, overnight we became a national organization."

10. Root writes, "We have the right to identify differently in different situations—and know we are not mixed up, disloyal, or weak; We have the right to change our identity over our lifetime—and more than once if need be; We have the right to create a vocabulary to communicate about multiraciality because our language is not currently adequate." Root's Bill of Rights is a manifesto of sorts. It details some of the shared grievances of multiracial people, no matter their ancestry, as it creates a common sense of struggle. Root's use of the pronoun "we" along with the language of "rights" reflects a sense that multiracial people are a community, heretofore invisible, that is asserting its unacknowledged but nevertheless inherent right to identity. The language of rights emerges also in AMEA's official testimony at the federal hearings for multiracial classification. Since its presentation at the MASC conference, it continues to receive wide circulation.

11. Carlos Fernandez, keynote speech presented at the annual Kaleidoscope conference sponsored by MASC, October 22, 1994.

12. It must be said that the resources multiracial activists brought to bear on the OMB did not include money. As far as I was able to discern, AMEA and its chapter organizations operated on shoestring budgets largely culled from member dues.

13. The Civil Rights Act of 1964 outlawed discrimination in public accommodations and employment. The Voting Rights Act of 1965 was aimed at reducing barriers to political participation on the basis of race. Racial discrimination in housing was banned through the Housing Act of 1968, while Federal Executive order 11246 put in place procedures to make sure federal contractors complied with fair employment practices (Morris 1984; McAdam 1982).

14. "Generationally mixed" is a term some multiracials have begun using to refer to people with ancestors from multiple ethnoracial categories but whose parents primarily identified with one (and the same) racial group. Their "mixture," in this formulation, originates in generations before the parental generation.

15. Of course, while raising the level of race consciousness and pride of peoples of African descent were central goals of Black Power advocates of the 1960s and 1970s, so too was the attainment of black political and economic advancement. See Asante (1980) and Karenga (1982).

16. Renee Romano summarizes the underlying logic: "If a black person grew up in a predominantly white neighborhood, went to a predominantly white school, and ended up working at a predominatly white corporation, how could his allegiance to the race be determined? . . . How, in a post segregation world, should blacks maintain their distinctive racial identity? And how should the actions of other black people be judged?" (Romano 2003, 221).

17. Espiritu (1992) writes that panethnic coalitions between Asian American ethnic groups began to form to combat anti-Asian prejudice, discrimination, and violence and in so doing to consolidate sense of a shared identity across ethnicities. Partly in response to increased ethnic cohesion and vociferousness of nonwhite groups, whites also experienced a resurgence in ethnic identification, manifest in increased efforts by third generation descendants of immigrants to revive or invent traditions of their immigrant ancestors (Alba 1990; M. Waters 1990).

18. This sense of inauthenticity is revealed in many respondents' likening of publicly declaring their multiracial identity as "coming out" ("It felt like we were coming out of the closet." "You would have thought we were gay."), suggesting that previously their "true" self was hidden behind a façade. Many multiracials involved in organizations say that what they considered their racial identity to be was often at odds with what they thought they were supposed to declare publicly. This fostered in many of them a sense that they had a "personal" private identity and a different public one.

19. See Yanagisako (1995) for an analysis of the use of working-class histories in Asian American studies classes as a means through which academics foster (intentionally and unintentionally) a pan-Asian ethnic identity.

20. While Black Power was most influential from the mid 1960s to mid 1970s forms of black nationalism have a long history within black political thought and continue to be salient today (Dawson 2001; Shelby 2005). During the 1980s when many

of my respondents were in college, commercialized expressions of black nationalist themes appeared with the release of Spike Lee's film Malcolm X and the ubiquitous merchandise (X baseball caps) associated with the movie. On college campuses, T-shirts with the slogan, "It's a black thang. You wouldn't understand" expressed a self-confident and separatist notion of community.

Chapter 3

1. On the unrepresentativeness of spokespeople for the stigmatized ("professionals of stigma") Goffman writes, "Here again representatives are not representative, for representatives can hardly come from those who give no attention to their stigma, or who are relatively unlettered" (1963, 27).

2. In fact, even prior to the 1997 decision by OMB to allow individuals to choose more than one racial category, the state did have a procedure for enumerating multiracials, just not the one some wanted (they were either counted as "other" or assigned to one of the categories they may have checked).

3. See Association of Multiethnic Americans, testimony before the Committee on Census, Statistics and Postal Personnel, 1993.

4. For a discussion of "socioanalysis," see Pierre Bourdieu and Loïc J. D. Wacquant 1992.

5. Most of the names of people and places used in this article are pseudonyms. I have also altered some aspects of informants' biographies in cases where a particular description would make that person readily identifiable. For example, if a person attended Harvard, I may say he attended Yale—both elite, predominantly white universities in the Northeast.

6. For discussion of the importance of kin networks as sources of social support see Stack (1974).

7. On the psychological and social underpinnings of conflicts over phenotype among African Americans, see Russell et al. (1992). On the relationship between skin color and stratification, see Keith and Herring (1991).

8. Lareina was raised Catholic, in the tradition of her mother, which may have been one means through which she connected to some of her West Indian classmates. It is yet another social characteristic distinguishing her from black Americans, who are predominantly Protestant. Most of the relatively few American black Catholics attained their religious affiliation not through their white mothers, but because they are descendants of blacks from areas colonized by the French and Spanish or as a result of their contact with the Catholic Church's educational system.

9. U.S. Bureau of the Census, U.S. Census of Population: 1960, Marital Status, DC (2)-4E.

10. In the United States, only thirteen states and the District of Columbia never had antimiscegenation laws. For a summary of states' laws on intermarriage see Spickard 1989 and Sollors 1997.

11. "What is a prophet from the perspective of sociology? . . . We shall understand the prophet to mean a purely individual bearer of charisma, who by virtue of his mission proclaims a religious doctrine of divine commandment . . . [T]he personal call is the decisive element distinguishing the prophet from the priest . . . [T]he prophet's claim is based on personal revelation and charisma." Max Weber, Economy and Society ([1918–20] 1978), 439-440.

12. By 1960 only 10 percent of blacks were middle class as measured by income and occupation (Landry 1987).

13. The relationship between lighter skin color and material and social privilege has varied by historical period and geographic location. The perception that light skin color is a material and social advantage seems to have held sway for much of U.S. history. For a discussion of the relationship between light skin color and higher social privilege in the mid-twentieth-century United States, see Drake and Cayton (1993 [1945]), Frazier (1957), and Keith and Herring (1991). For a discussion of how African Americans perceive of and the meaning attributed to skin color among themselves, see L. O. Graham (1999) and Russell et al. (1992).

14. In the mid 1990s African Americans held only 3.1 percent of doctoral degrees. U.S. Census Bureau, Statistical Abstract of the United States, 1995, 189.

15. Jack and Jill is a national organization comprised of local affiliates, formed in the 1950s by middle- and upper-class black families for their children to network with each other.

16. Xavier's understanding of his change in identity is aptly captured in Jack Katz's descriptions of the emotional and embodied dimensions of furtive property crimes.

[T]he essence of the sneaky thrill is an attempt to transcend an existential dilemma, but in this case, the dilemma is to relate the inner to outer identity. The shoplifter goes about her sneaky efforts to see if she can get away with it—"it" being a freely drawn, playfully artificial projection of the self into the world. Must I appear to be who I am? Need I struggle to shape what I know about myself into an acceptable appearance to others, or can I play with it? Can I dispense, not with moral appearances but with the struggle to produce moral appearances? Thus, the thrill embodies an awareness that the experience is essentially a play about dilemmas of moral authenticity arranged on a public staging of the self (Katz 1988, 75).

17. Much like Lareina described the experience of first organizing with other multiracials ("It was like coming out of the closet"), Xavier describes his coming out to a public multiracial identity with suspense and intrigue. When Xavier first joined a multiracial organization he was incredulous and reticent, not fully allowing himself to believe that what they were doing (organizing with other multiracials) was okay. He describes his feelings during those initial meetings with adjectives "bad" and "naughty" and expresses a sense of fear that they could get in trouble for doing this. Yet, as when he altered his identity, there was a delicious, attractive quality to per-

forming an illicit act and getting away with it. In much the same way that Katz (1988) describes the "sneaky thrills" promised by vandalism and theft, meeting in a public place to talk with another "black" person who identified as "multiracial," and not getting "caught," is objective proof that he can shield a morally unacceptable self from those who are motivated and inclined to detect it (in this case, other blacks).

18. Struggles over definitions of the most "authentic" mixed experience, and the "right" ways to identify if one is of multiple heritage came up many times in the course of research. While some monoracials may tag multiracials who do not act sufficiently "ethnic" with the label "whitewashed," several multiracials I spoke with reversed the signifier of authenticity, dubbing others who do not claim a multiracial identity "blackwashed." Jamoo, a columnist for the now-defunct *Interrace* magazine, regularly "outed" celebrities of multiple heritage whom he described as "passing for black," turning on its head the more common use of "passing" to refer to those presenting a white identity.

19. "Hapa" is a term borrowed from the Hawaiian term "hapa haole" meaning half-white. It has been taken up by mainland persons of partial Asian descent to designate a mixed identity.

20. Certainly, understanding the ways multiracials have been labeled deviant is a historical and contextual question. Compared to earlier periods in the twentieth century, when "mulattoes" were likened to mules, thought to be unable to reproduce, and to be physically and morally weaker than members of "pure" races (Nakashima 1992; Somerville 2000), it is clear that types and forms of stigmatization change. Such beliefs are largely discredited, and the formal legal means (such as racial classifications, antimiscegenation and segregation laws) employed to prevent the crossing of racial boundaries have been largely abandoned. It is interesting to note, however, that the South Carolina antimiscegenation laws were not removed from their statutes until 1998. Some Japanese American civic organizations, like basketball leagues and beauty pageants, have rules, formal and informal, specifying ancestry and name (a proxy for ancestry) requirements for their participants (King 2002). The value attached to certain types of behavior, who imposes and enforces such rules, and the rules themselves change, and accordingly so does the definition of what constitutes stigma. Moreover, competing representations of stigmatized categories of people can coexist. In popular culture, for example, multiracials are often portrayed in an ostensibly positive light (e.g., as naturally unprejudiced, beautiful, cool).

21. For extended discussions of this phenomenon see Drake and Cayton (1993 1945]), L. O. Graham (1999), and Russell et al. (1992).

22. "[T]he stigmatized person can come to feel that he should be above passing, that if he accepts himself and respects himself he will feel no need to conceal his failing. After laboriously learning to conceal, then, the individual may go on to unlearn his concealment . . . [T]his phase in the moral career is typically described as the final, mature, well-adjusted one—a state of grace" (Goffman 1963, 102).

23. Weber describes ethnic honor as part of a belief in common ethnicity in which members of a group believe they share a specific honor that outsiders do not. This sense of ethnic honor is manifest in rituals and customs that mark a group as distinct and sustained by "the conviction of the excellence of one's own customs and the inferiority of alien ones" ([1918–20] 1978, 390–91).

24. On the turn toward the self, see Beck and Beck-Gernsheim 1995 and Giddens 1991.

25. On the experience of students in integrated institutions, see Mabry (1995) and Zweigenhaft and Domhoff (1991).

26. See Yanagisako (1995) for an analysis of the use of working class histories in Asian American studies classes as a means through which academics foster (intentionally and unintentionally) a pan-Asian ethnic identity.

27. Lareina, Pedro, and Xavier entered college at a time when nonwhite students had unprecedented access to America's colleges and universities (Wilson 1978).

28. Scholars define "middle class" in a variety of ways. While some stress socioeconomic factors such as occupation, income, and education, others add cultural and behavioral dispositions such as tastes, hobbies, and church attendance to their conceptions of class. My use of the category "middle class" employs this broader conception of class. These respondents report household incomes in the range of $20–80,000 (for three respondents, each of whom lives alone). Three respondents rent their housing while one owns three properties. Two of these four informants report having parents who worked in professional occupations, and three report having close friends who are professionals.

Chapter 4

1. Multiracial activists framed their push for state classification as a family issue. Representatives from the Association of Multiethnic Americans testified to the House Subcommittee on Census, Statistics and Postal Personnel in 1993 that "[w]hen government compels a multiracial/multiethnic family to signify a factually false identity for their child, it invades a fundamental right of privacy. Every multiracial family is entitled to safeguard its integrity against unwarranted intrusions by the government. No child should be forced to favor one parent over the other by any governmental agency."

2. In Pace and Cox v. State (1881), the Alabama Supreme Court extended the Greer decision, allowing harsher penalties for interracial fornication and adultery than for similar intraracial actions. This decision was upheld by the U.S. Supreme Court in Pace v. Alabama (1882). Restricting interracial marriage was deemed acceptable as long as both parties involved in the offense were given the same punishment (Moran 2001).

3. By the 1960s, in a context where racial equality and greater sexual and marital freedom was being pursued in popular protests and validated by the courts, antimis-

cegenation laws were vulnerable to challenge. They were finally overturned in the *Loving v. Virginia* case. Childhood friends Richard Loving, a white man, and Mildred Jeter, a black woman, were married in Washington, D.C., in 1958. When they returned to their home state of Virginia, authorities issued warrants for their arrests for violating the state's antimiscegenation law. In lieu of a prison sentence, the Lovings were offered the option of moving out of state and not returning for twenty-five years, an option they exercised. Four years later in 1963, they would seek to vacate the judgment against them through Virginia state courts, but to no avail. In rejecting their claims, judges asserted the same kinds of arguments they had made in establishing the constitutionality of these laws eighty years earlier. Antimiscegenation laws did not violate equal protection or due process and the state had a vital interest in preventing interracial marriage because of the inherent differences between the races (Moran 2001). When the U.S. Supreme Court agreed to hear the case, Virginia's attorneys again invoked eugenicist arguments about the hazards of race mixing, but offered additional rationale that purported to have the best interests of those who would intermarry and their offspring at heart. Those who intermarried were, according to the state's lawyer R. D. McIlwaine "subjected to much greater pressures" than those who did not, and their children faced "almost insuperable difficulties in identification" that would leave them damaged. The Court rejected such arguments, determined that antimiscegenation laws violated due process, and affirmed that the choice of marriage partner was fundamentally up to the individual, regardless of the race of the partners involved (Moran 2001; Romano 2003).

4. In justifying his decision in *Green v. State* (1877), for example, one justice wrote, "Who can estimate the evil of introducing into their most intimate relations, elements so heterogeneous that they must naturally cause discord, shame, disruption of family circles and estrangement of kindred?" (Moran 2001, 78).

5. Based on 1996 Current Population Survey data. I thank Bradley Herring for generating the statistics supporting this claim.

6. According to Schuman et al. (1997), in 1972, less than 30 percent of whites approved of racial intermarriage. By 1996, that percentage had grown to approximately 70 percent. For blacks, approval of intermarriage has hovered around 80 percent since 1972, showing slight increases since 1994. Yet there is a marked difference between attitude and behavior when it comes to intermarriage, as evidenced by very low intermarriage rates.

7. This rationale (of the presumed difficult consequences of one's decision on the life of the child) is similar to the one offered by R. D. McIlwaine in his defense of the state of Virginia's antimiscegenation law in the *Loving* case. It is one often offered to justify the selective abortion of disabled fetuses (Rapp 1995).

8. That some intermarried couples and persons of mixed descent feel they face particular challenges in choosing a place to live because of their interracial status is clear. In 1995, *Interrace* magazine conducted a poll asking respondents to rate how

"interracial-friendly" their cities were and received 543 responses. "Forewarned is forearmed!" read the copy announcing both the best *and* worst cities.

9. Interracial Family Circle, *Collage*, vol. 13, no. 6/7.

Chapter 5

1. Xavier Upton (see Chapter 3) was a notable exception, but an exception nonetheless. Part of his struggle in having his multiracial identity recognized was getting other *multiracials* to authenticate his belonging in the category "multiracial."

2. The term *mixed heritage* was seldom used by my respondents, although in recent years it has grown in usage on mixed race Web sites and in the literature. It is used as a general term for mixed ancestry, applied most often to people with parents of different ethnic group identifications that are deemed significantly different from each other but which according to dominant U.S. notions of race are considered to be of the same race (e.g., Thai and Chinese).

3. Sometimes scuffles over membership did surface between these "categories." At one meeting of AMEA affiliates in 1997, an argument broke out between a monoracial parent of multiracial kids who had been active in political issues and a multiracial adult over who had the right to speak for "multiracials." Arguing for her right to speak for multiracials, the parent insisted, "I am a member of this community. This is my community." Marking a difference between multiracials and this monoracial woman, the multiracial adult explained how she understood the situation: "it doesn't mean you can't work with us and support us, but this is something we have to do ourselves."

4. An interesting indication of the character of the difference between monoracial parents' and multiracial adults' relationship to mixed identity is the language they used to refer to multiraciality. Parents almost universally preferred the term *multiracial* over *mixed*. "Multiracial" was considered more polite. Respondents of mixed descent, however, had no problem with using "mixed" and often did so to refer to themselves and others. Parents' concern for politeness is a concern not to offend that stems from an experiential distance, an unfamiliarity with mixed subjectivity. In relation to parents' almost universal use of the somewhat stilted "multiracial," mixed respondents use of "mixed" took on the power to signal an insider's status.

5. This was also a useful weapon in authenticity struggles among mixed Asians. While those with Asian fathers may have an identifiably Asian last name that potentially granted them recognition as Asian more readily, those with Asian mothers could claim more familiarity with what were considered more authentic cultural markers like food, manners, holidays, and so forth.

6. Noticeably absent have been discussions around sexuality as an axis of difference, which suggests the implicit and unseen heterosexual emphasis of organizations and their goals, especially the recognition of families and the construction of multiracial identity around ancestry drawn from parents. Likewise, discussions of class

among participants were almost nonexistent, reflecting perhaps the largely middle-class origins of respondents.

7. "Mavin: The Mixed Race Experience," 2004, Issue no. 8, p. 9.

8. Jonathan Tilove, Newhouse News Service, April 2000.

Chapter 6

1. Danzy Senna, 1998, p. 12.

2. A notable exception to this rule was a 1996 Ikea catalogue ad featuring a black mother, white father, and their children browsing the various home furnishings departments.

3. Multiracial buying power is expected to grow 32.7 percent between 2002 and 2007. This compares to a projected increase in African American buying power of 30 percent and 26.5 percent in white buying power (Humphreys 2002).

4. I use the term *multiracial* to refer to a broad range of people, including those who identify or are identified by others as being of "racially mixed" ancestry, as well as to intermarried couples.

5. Market segmentation was first theorized in the late 1950s. It arose as a solution to marketers' concerns that in the aftermath of Americans' postwar purchasing frenzy markets for various consumer goods were becoming saturated, and profits could no longer be ensured. By identifying differences in the tastes and habits of consumers, marketers could appeal to those differences and stimulate demand. See Cohen (2003) for a history of market segmentation.

6. Another company, Reneille's, sells interracially matched figurines. In 2005, their "Asian bride" figure was their best seller. Co-owner Ellie Genuardi says, "We can hardly keep it in stock." MixedMediaWatch.com. Accessed June 29, 2005.

7. http://www.meltingpotgifts.com

8. http://www.curls.biz

9. In her analysis of marketing to children, Susan Linn (2004) describes how marketers use the rationale of need to justify the creation and marketing of television programs to infants. The creators of *Teletubbies*, for example, argued that their show would reach an "underserved" market. The term "underserved," Linn points out, is "usually associated with people needing and not getting adequate health care and social services" (p. 56). Infants' putative "need" to have programming directed at them is said to come out of their specific developmental stage of life. That almost all infants go through these developmental stages constitutes them as a class and, therefore, a market.

10. http:// www.curls.biz. Accessed June 28, 2004.

11. Ibid.

12. Ibid.

13. All hair is made up of the same substance. What distinguishes hair textures among people (not just women) is the shape of the hair follicle.

14. Rudy Guevarra, www.multiracialapparel.com. Accessed June 29, 2005.

15. In American literature, themes of interracialism have been explored for over two centuries (Sollors 2004; see also Hall, in Sollors 2004). A recent spate of popular films like *Far From Heaven* (2002), *Die Another Day* (2002), and *Save the Last Dance* (2001) have featured interracial couples (Jones 2002). In contrast, before the late 1990s, multiracials as such had been almost totally absent from advertising.

16. Based on 2000 census figures.

17. Esprit and Cherokee are two other clothing companies that began featuring interracial casts, but unlike Benetton, their ads focused on interracial friendship rather than interracial intimacy.

18. For photos of Colored Francie and a collector's assessment of her value today, see http:/kattisdolls.crosswinds.net/faces/cousins.htm.

19. Jerry Saviola, head of casting at Grey Worldwide in New York City, quoted in Whelan 2001.

20. Paula Sindlinger, a partner in Godlove & Sindlinger Casting in New York City quoted in Whelan 2001.

21. Holt (2000) states that the child workers in Indonesia who make Nike shoes earn roughly two dollars for an eleven-hour work day.

22. Nike paid Jordan $20 million *annually*—"more than the total annual wages earned by Indonesian workers who made the shoe" (Holt 2000, 110).

23. Gatorade's campaign with Jordan popularized a jingle with the refrain, "If I could be like Mike."

24. For a discussion of the market model of governance and its effects on citizens, see Klinenberg 2002. For a discussion of the political ramifications of the "consumerization of the republic," see Cohen 2003.

25. "Best Gifts for Eurasian Kids," June 2002, http://www.eurasianation.com. Accessed June 17, 2003.

26. Advertisement for Children's Tylenol, 2002.

27. Advertisement for Motrin IB, 2001.

28. Personal communication with Manhattan-based casting agent.

29. Arlene Davila (2001) contends that the image of the Hispanic consumer invoked by U.S. advertising firms draws from dominant ideas constructed by Latin American intellectuals about the distinctive nature of Latin American culture—one constructed in contrast to the United States. In this formulation Latin American is to family, religion, and tradition as the United States is to technological innovation, materialism, and a lack of culture.

30. For analysis of residential segregation see Massey and Denton (1992), "American Apartheid"; see also "Racial and Ethnic Segregation in the United States: 1980–2000" (U.S. Census Bureau 2002).

31. MixedMediaWatch liked the ad so much it awarded it it's 2004 Image award for Ousatnding Advertising Campaign, noting "We commend Verizon for featuring

a mixed heritage family so prominently in their advertising, and for showing people that interracial families are as much a part of the American social fabric as any other kind of family."

32. According to a Barbie spokesperson, Kayla, Madison, and Chelsea (Barbie's new friends) are designed to look ambiguous so as to appeal to little girls of a broad range of ethnicities (Walker, 2003).

33. Says one marketing analyst, "By the time the next Census comes around, multiracials may not look like such strange creatures anymore and marketers may by then have found the appropriate visual language to address them directly" (author not listed, Marketing Trendz newsletter, June 6, 2003).

Chapter 7

1. "A Methodological Note" in Drake and Cayton (1993) [1945].

2. *Black Metropolis*, p. 127.

3. The strength and consequences of the tendency to racialize those of African descent in the United States is underscored by the persistent attempts of immigrants of African descent from the Caribbean and African continent to *emphasize* their cultural and linguistic differences from African Americans so as to escape the consequences of such racialization (Waters 1999).

4. OMB Directive 15 guidelines mandated federal agency compliance by 2003. As of 2006, the Education Department had not yet implemented the MOOM option. In August 2006, however, Education Department officials released a proposal for a plan to allow students to mark multiple racial categories that, if adopted, would comply with the federal guidelines.

5. The American College Personnel Association has an estimated 8,000 members.

6. Mavin Foundation has been quite involved in expanding the tracking and donation of bone marrow by mixed race people. They assert that mixed race people in need of bone marrow have difficulty finding matches because they are of mixed race.

7. Winant (1994) contrasts hegemony with domination. Rather than being silenced or repressed, hegemony incorporates opposition and difference (with modi fication) into the social order, as it robs opposition of its critical content.

Appendix C

1. Melucci argues that new social movements are responses to the intrusion of the state into private life. He argues that the key to understanding them is to understand that they involve the appropriation of identity from the private into the public sphere in which "areas formerly zones of private exchange and rewards (sexual relations, interpersonal relationships, biological identity) have become stakes in various conflict situations and are now the scene of collective action" (Melucci 1980, 219).

2. Class reductionists (Bonacich 1980; Cox 1948) argue that race is an ideology that serves to divide the working class and facilitates their exploitation, although they

differ in where they locate the responsibility for the creation of racial antagonisms. Some class theorists grant race a degree of "relative autonomy," i.e., once created, race takes on a life of its own and reacts back upon the economic base (The Birmingham School; Hall 1991). Their positions differ from that of Cox, who did not believe that "beliefs" played a significant role in social processes.

3. Barth (1969) argues that to understand the logic of group formation, of crucial importance is how people define the boundaries between groups, how that boundary is maintained, and how personnel pass through. While some studies emphasize the political, economic, and social circumstances under which boundaries get created (e.g., Espiritu 1992; Nagel 1986; Steinberg 1981), others include more emphasis on the agentic component of group formation (how groups respond to circumstantial factors, shaping and reshaping their identities and the boundaries themselves; see Leonard 1992; Nagel 1994, 1996; Sanchez 1993).

4. The *contents* of ethnic identities, says Cornell (1996), vary according to the relative salience of institutions, interests, and culture. The particular profile of a group along these dimensions is partly the product of the conditions under which the boundary separating the group was constructed, but also has an influence on the trajectory of the group, the kinds of relations engendered within and between groups, individual movement in or out of the group, and collective movement along the various dimensions of identity given certain circumstances.

5. See also Comaroff (1987) and Brubaker 2005.

6. Bourdieu calls for the social scientist to construct a "class on paper" in which "the probability of bringing together, really or nominally, a set of agents . . . is greater when they are closer together in the social space and belong to a more restricted and thus more homogeneous constructed class, nevertheless the alliance of the closest agents is never *necessary* or inevitable . . . and the alliance of the agents that are most separated from one another is never *impossible*" (1991, 233). The constructed class represents a "probable class," *not* a group mobilized for struggle.

7. Bourdieu writes, "Against the initial tendency to take all the passions whose manifestations it observes for granted because they are in the order of things, science must assert their arbitrary, unjustifiable, and if you will, pathological character . . . But it must also account for the passions, founded upon *illusio*, the investment in the game, that are engendered in the relationship between a habitus and the field to which it is adjusted; it must restore to these passions their *raison d'etre*, their necessity" (1996, 3).

8. For recent literature on the role of emotions in social movements, see Goodwin and Jasper, 2004; Goodwin, Jasper, and Polletta, 2001; Aminzade and Goldstone et al. 2001.

Bibliography

Alba, R. (1990). *Ethnic Identity: The Transformation of White America*. New Haven, CT, Yale University Press.

Alba, R. and V. Nee. (2003). *Remaking the American Mainstream: Assimilation and Contemporary Immigration*. Cambridge, MA, Harvard University Press.

Allen, T. (1994). *The Invention of the White Race*. New York, Verso.

Aminzade, R., J., A. Goldstone, et al., Eds. (2001). *Silence and Voice in the Study of Contentious Politics*. Cambridge, UK, Cambridge University Press.

Anderson, M. (1988). *American Census: A Social History*. New Haven, CT, Yale University Press.

Anderson, M. and S. Fienberg. (1999). *Who Counts? The Politics of Census-Taking in Contemporary America*. New York, Russell Sage.

Appiah, K. A. (1992). *In My Father's House: Africa in the Philosophy of Culture*. New York, Oxford University Press.

Asante, M. K. (1980). *Afrocentricity: The Theory of Social Change*. Buffalo, NY, Amulefi.

Bakalian, A. (1993). *Armenian-Americans: From Being to Feeling Armenian*. New Brunswick, NJ, Transaction Publishers.

Ballis-Bal, B. (1986). *The "Chicago School" of American Sociology, Symbolic Interactionism, and Race Relations Theory. Theories of Race and Ethnic Relations*. J. Rex and D. Mason. Cambridge, UK, Cambridge University Press: 280–298.

Banton, M. (1979). "Analytical and Folk Concepts of Race and Ethnicity." *Ethnic and Racial Studies* 2(2): 127–138.

Banton, M. (1989). *Racial Theories*. Cambridge, UK, Cambridge University Press.

Barrera, M. (1980). *Race and Class in the Southwest*. Notre Dame, IN, Notre Dame University Press.

Barron, M. (1951). "Research on Intermarriage: A Survey of Accomplishments and Prospects." *American Journal of Sociology* 57(3): 249–255.

Barth, F. (1969). Introduction. *Ethnic Groups and Boundaries: The Social Organization of Cultural Difference.* Boston, Little, Brown: 9–38.

Barth, F. (1973). *Descent and Marriage Reconsidered. The Character of Kinship.* J. Goody. London, Cambridge University Press: 3–19.

Baudrillard, J. (2000). *The Ideological Genesis of Needs. The Consumer Society Reader.* J. B. Schor and D. B. Holt. New York, The New Press: 57–80.

Bean, F. D. and G. Stevens. (2003). *America's Newcomers and the Dynamics of Diversity.* New York, Russell Sage Foundation.

Beck, U. and E. Beck-Gernsheim. (1995). *The Normal Chaos of Love.* Cambridge, UK, Polity Press.

Becker, H. S. (1963). *Outsiders: Studies in the Sociology of Deviance.* New York, The Free Press.

Bell, D. (1992). *Faces at the Bottom of the Well.* New York, Basic Books.

Benford, R. D. and D. A. Snow. (2000). "Framing Processes and Social Movements: An Overview and Assessment." *Annual Review of Sociology* 26: 611–639.

Benjamin, J. (1988). *The Bonds of Love: Psychoanalysis, Feminism, and the Problem of Domination.* New York, Pantheon Books.

Bennett, C. E., N. R. McKenney, and R. J. Harrison. (1995). Racial Classification Issues Concerning Children in Mixed-Race Households. Annual Meeting of the Population Association of America, San Francisco.

Berreman, G. D. (1972). "Race, Caste and Other Invidious Distinctions in Social Stratification." *Race* 24(3): 385–414.

Blauner, R. (1972). *Racial Oppression in America.* New York, Harper and Row.

Blu, K. (1980). *The Lumbee Problem: The Making of an American Indian People.* Cambridge, UK, Cambridge University Press.

Blum, L. M. (2000). *At the Breast: Ideologies of Breastfeeding and Motherhood in the Contemporary United States.* Boston, Beacon Press.

Blumer, H. (1958). "Race Prejudice as a Sense of Group Position." *Pacific Sociological Review* 1(1): 3–7.

Bobo, L. and V. Hutchings (1996). "Perceptions of Racial Group Competition: Extending Blumer's Theory of Group Position to a Multiracial Social Context." *American Sociological Review* 61(6): 951–972.

Bonacich, E. (1980). "Class Approaches to Ethnicity and Race." *The Insurgent Sociologist* 10(2): 9–23.

Bonilla-Silva, E. 2003. *Racism without Racists: Color-Blind Racism and the Persistence of Racial Inequality in the United States.* Lanham, MD, Rowman and Littlefield.

Bonilla-Silva, E. and T. A. Forman (2000). "'I'm Not a Racist but . . .': Mapping White College Students' Racial Ideology in the USA." *Discourse & Society* 11(1): 50–86.

Bourdieu, P. (1994). "Rethinking the State: On the Genesis and Structure of the Bureaucratic Field." *Sociological Theory* 12: 1–19.

Bourdieu, P. (1996). "On the Family as a Realized Category." *Theory, Culture, and Society* 13(3): 19–26.

Bourdieu, P. ([1979] 1984). *Distinction: A Social Critique of the Judgment of Taste.* Cambridge, MA, Harvard University Press.

Bourdieu, P. ([1980] 1990). *The Logic of Practice.* Palo Alto, CA, Stanford University Press.

Bourdieu, P. ([1982] 1991). *Language and Symbolic Power.* J. B. Thompson. Cambridge, MA, Harvard University Press.

Bourdieu, P. ([1984] 1988). *Homo Academicus.* Palo Alto, CA, Stanford University Press.

Bourdieu, P. ([1986] 1994). *In Other Words: Essays Toward a Reflexive Sociology.* Palo Alto, CA, Stanford University Press.

Bourdieu, P. ([1989] 1996). *The State Nobility: Elite Schools in the Field of Power.* Palo Alto, CA, Stanford University Press.

Bourdieu, P. and L. J. D. Wacquant (1992). *An Invitation to Reflexive Sociology.* Chicago, University of Chicago Press.

Bourdieu, P. with. J.-C. Chamboredon. and J.-C. Passeron. ([1968/73] 1991). *The Craft of Sociology: Epistemological Preliminaries.* New York and Berlin, Aldine de Gruyter.

Brubaker, R. (1994). "Rethinking Nationhood; Nation as Institutionalized Form, Practical Category. Contingent Event." *Contention* 4(1): 3–14.

Brubaker, R. (2004). *Ethnicity without Groups.* Cambridge, MA, Harvard University Press.

Butler, J. (1990). *Gender Trouble, Feminist Theory, and Psychoanalytic Discourse. Feminism/Postmodernism.* K. Nicholson. New York, Routledge.

Calhoun, C. (1993). "Nationalism and Ethnicity." *Annual Review of Sociology* 19:211–239.

Calhoun, C. (1994). *Social Theory and the Politics of Identity. Social Theory and the Politics of Identity.* C. Calhoun. Oxford, UK, Blackwell: 9–36.

Carmichael, S. and C. V. Hamilton. (1967). *Black Power: The Politics of Liberation in America.* New York, Vintage.

Carp, E. W. (1998). *Family Matters: Secrecy and Disclosure in the History of Adoption.* Cambridge, MA, Harvard University Press.

Carson, C. (1995 [1981]). *In Struggle: SNCC and the Black Awakening of the 1960s.* Cambridge, MA, Harvard University Press.

Chau, J. (2005). MixedMediaWatch.

Christopher, A. J. (1994). *The Atlas of Apartheid.* London, Routledge.

Cleaver, E. (1992 [1968]). *Soul on Ice.* New York, Laurel, Stoke, and Dell.

Clifford, J. (1998). *The Predicament of Culture: Twentieth Century Ethnography, Literature and Art.* Cambridge, MA, Harvard University Press.

Cohen, J.L. (1985). 'Strategy or Identity: New Theoretical Paradigms and Contemporary Social Movements.' *Social Research,* vol. 52, no. 4 (Winter).

Cohen, L. (2003). *A Consumer's Republic: The Politics of Mass Consumption in Postwar America*. New York, Alfred A. Knopf.

Colker, R. (1996). *Hybrid: Bisexuals, Multiracials, and Other Misfits under American Law*. New York, New York University Press.

Collier, J., M. Rosaldo, et al. (1992). *Is There a Family? New Anthropological Views*. *Rethinking the Family: Some Feminist Questions*. B. Thorne and M. Yalom. Boston, Northeastern University Press: 31–48.

Collier, J. F. (1997). *From Duty to Desire: Remaking Families in a Spanish Village*. Princeton, NJ, Princeton University Press.

Collins, P. H. (1991). *Black Feminist Thought: Knowledge, Consciousness and the Politics of Empowerment*. New York, Routledge.

Comaroff, J. L. (1987). "Of Totemism and Ethnicity: Consciousness, Practice and the Signs of Inequality." *Ethnos* 52: 301–323.

Cornell, S. (1996). "The Variable Ties That Bind: Content and Circumstances in Ethnic Processes." *Ethnic and Racial Studies* 19(2): 265–289.

Cose, E. (1992). *Rage of a Privileged Class: Why Do Prosperous Blacks Still Have the Blues?* New York, Harper Perennial.

Costello, C. G. (1992). "Legitimate Bonds and Unnatural Unions: Race, Sexual Orientation, and Control of the American Family." *Harvard Women's Law Journal* 15: 79–171.

Cox, Oliver C. 1970 [1948]. *Caste, Class & Race : A Study in Social Dynamics*. Introduction by Joseph S. Roucek. New York : Monthly Review Press.

DaCosta, K. (2003). *Multiracial Identity: From Personal Problem to Public Issue. New Faces in a Changing America: Multiracial Identity in the Twenty-first Century*. L. Winters and H. DeBose. Thousand Oaks, CA, Sage Publications.

Daniel, G. R. (1992). *Beyond Black and White: The New Multiracial Consciousness. Racially Mixed People in America*. M. Root. Newbury Park, CA, Sage Publications.

Daniel, G. R. (2002). *More Than Black? Multiracial Identity and the New Racial Order*. Philadelphia, Temple University Press.

Davila, A. (2001). *Latinos, Inc.: The Marketing and the Making of a People*. Berkeley, University of California Press.

Davis, F. J. (1991). *Who Is Black: One Nation's Rule*. University Park, Pennsylvania State Press.

Dawson, M. C. (2001). *Black Visions: The Roots of Contemporary African-American Political Ideologies*. Chicago, University of Chicago Press.

Degler, C. (1970). *Neither Black nor White: Slavery and Race Relations in Brazil and the States*. Madison, University of Wisconsin Press.

Delaney, C. (1995). *Father State, Motherland, and the Birth of Modern Turkey. Naturalizing Power: Essays in Feminist Cultural Analysis*. S. Yanagisako and C. Delaney. New York, Routledge.

D'Emilio, J. and E. Freedman. (1997 [1988]). *Intimate Matters: A History of Sexuality in America* (2nd ed.). Chicago, University of Chicago Press.

DeMott, B. (1998 [1995]). *The Trouble with Friendship: Why Americans Can't Think Straight about Race.* New Haven, Yale University Press.

Dericotte, T. (1997). *The Black Notebooks: An Interior Journey.* New York, W. W. Norton.

DeVos, G. and H. Wagatsuma. (1967). *Japan's Invisible Race: Caste in Culture and Personality.* Berkeley, University of California Press.

Dikotter, F. (1992). *The Discourse of Race in Modern China.* Palo Alto, CA, Stanford University Press.

DiLeonardo, M. (1988). *The Female World of Cards, Gifts and Letters. Families in the U.S.: Kinship and Domestic Politics.* K. V. Hansen and A. Garey. Philadelphia, Temple University Press.

DiMaggio, P. (1994). *Culture and Economy. The Handbook of Economic Sociology.* N. Smelser and R. Swedberg. Princeton, NJ, Princeton University Press and New York: Russell Sage Foundation: 27–57.

Dollard, J. (1957 [1937]). *Caste and Class in a Southern Town.* Garden City, NY, Doubleday.

Dominguez, V. (1986). *White by Definition: Social Classification in Creole Louisiana.* New Brunswick, NJ, Rutgers Univerity Press.

Dorman, L. (1996). "On Golf: We'll be Right Back, After this Hip and Distorted Commercial Break." *The New York Times.* Retrieved October 26, 2004, from Lexis-Nexis Academic database.

Drake, S. C. and H. Cayton. (1993 [1945]). *Black Metropolis: A Study of Negro Life in a Northern City.* Chicago, University of Chicago Press.

DuBois, W. E. B. ([1903] 1996). *The Souls of Black Folk. The Oxford W. E. B. DuBois Reader.* E. J. Sundquist. New York and Oxford, MI, Oxford University Press.

DuCille, A. (1996). "Toy Theory: Black Barbie and the Deep Play of Difference." *The Consumer Society Reader.* J. B. Schor and D. B. Holt. New York, The New Press: 259–280.

Durkheim, E. and M. Mauss. (1963 [1903]). *Primitive Classification.* Chicago, University of Chicago Press.

Durkheim, E. and M. Mauss. (1982). *The Rules of Sociological Method and Selected Texts on Sociology and Its Method.* S. Lukes. New York, The Free Press.

Espiritu, Y. L. (1992). *Asian American Panethnicity: Bridging Institutions and Identities.* Philadelphia, Temple University Press.

Farley, R. (2002). "Racial Identities in 2000: The Response to the Multiple Race Option." *The New Race Question: How the Census Counts Multiracial Individuals.* J. Perlmann and M. C. Waters. New York, Russell Sage Foundation and The Levy Economics Institute of Bard College.

Fears, D. and C. Deane. (July 5, 2001). "Biracial Couples Report Tolerance; Survey Finds Most Are Accepted by Families." *Washington Post.*

Fernandez, C. (1994). AMEA Networking News.

Fields, B. J. (1990). "Slavery, Race and Ideology in the United States of America." *New Left Review:* 95–118.

Files, J. (June 10, 2005). Report Describes Immigrants as Younger and More Diverse. *The New York Times:* 12.

Fischer, C. (1975). Toward a Subcultural Theory of Urbanism. *American Journal of Sociology,* 80: 1319-41.

Fischer, C. (1984 [1976]). *The Urban Experience.* San Diego, Harcourt, Brace, Jovanovich.

Fischer, C. (1992). *America Calling: A Social History of the Telephone.* Berkeley, University of California Press.

Fischer, C. *et. al* (1996). *Inequality by Design: Cracking the Bell Curve Myth.* Princeton, NJ, Princeton University Press.

Fordham, S. (1997). *Blacked Out.* Chicago, University of Chicago Press.

Frank, T. (1997). *The Conquest of Cool: Business Culture, Counterculture, and the Rise of Hip Consumerism.* Chicago, University of Chicago Press.

Frank, T. (2000). *One Market under God: Extreme Capitalism, Market Populism, and the End of Economic Democracy.* New York, Doubleday.

Frazier, E. F. (1947). "Sociological Theory and Race Relations." *American Sociological Review* 12(3): 265–271.

Frazier, E. F. (1957). *Black Bourgeoisie.* New York, Free Press.

Fredrickson, G. (1982). *White Supremacy: A Comparative Study in American and South African History.* New York, Oxford University Press.

Fuss, D. (1989). *Essentially Speaking: Feminism, Nature and Difference.* New York, Routledge.

Gallup Organization. 2004. *Civil Rights and Race Relations.* Report prepared for the American Association of Retired Persons.

Gans, H. (1962). *The Urban Villagers: Group and Class in the Life of Italian-Americans.* Glencoe, IL, Free Press.

Gans, H. (1992). "Second Generation Decline: Scenarios for the Economic and Ethnic Futures of the Post-1965 American Immigrants." *Ethnic and Racial Studies* 15: 173–192.

Gans, H. J. (1979). "Symbolic Ethnicity: The Future of Ethnic Groups and Cultures in America." *Ethnic and Racial Studies* 2: 1–20.

Gans, H. J. (1999). "The Possibility of a New Racial Hierarchy in the Twenty-first Century United States." *The Cultural Territories of Race: Black and White Boundaries.* M. Lamont. Chicago, University of Chicago Press: 371–390.

Garcia, G. (2004). *The New Mainstream: How the Multicultural Consumer Is Transforming American Business.* New York, Harper Collins.

Gaskins, P. F. (1999). *What Are You? Voices of Mixed-Race Young People.* New York, Henry Holt and Company.

Geertz, C. (1963). "The Integrative Revolution: Primordial Sentiments and Civil Politics in the New States." *Old Societies and New States.* C. Geertz. New York, The Free Press: 105–157.

Gibel-Azoulay, K. (1997). *Black, Jewish and Interracial: It's Not the Color of Your Skin, but the Race of Your Kin.* Durham, NC, Duke University.

Giddens, A. (1991). *Modernity and Self-Identity: Self and Society in the Late Modern Age.* Palo Alto, CA, Stanford University Press.

Goffman, E. (1963). *Stigma: Notes on the Management of Spoiled Identity.* New York, Simon and Schuster.

Goodwin, J., and J. Jasper, Eds. (2004). *Rethinking Social Movements: Structure, Meaning, Emotion.* New York, Rowman & Littlefield Publishers, Inc.

Goodwin, J., J. Jasper, and F. Polletta , Eds. (2001). *Passionate Politics: Emotions and Social Movements.* Chicago, University of Chicago Press.

Goody, J., Ed. (1973). *The Character of Kinship.* London, Cambridge University Press.

Gordon, M. (1964). *Assimilation in American Life.* New York, Oxford University Press.

Gould, S. J. (1981). *The Mismeasure of Man.* New York and London, W. W. Norton and Company.

Gould, S. J. (1990). "Taxonomy as Politics: The Harm of False Classification." *Dissent* Winter: 73–78.

Graham, H. D. (1990). *The Civil Rights Era: Origin and Development of National Policy, 1960–1972.* New York, Oxford University Press.

Graham, L. O. (1999). *Our Kind of People: Inside America's Black Upper Class.* New York, Harper Collins.

Graham, R. (1990). "Racial Ideas and Social Policy in Brazil, 1870–1940." *The Idea of Race in Latin America, 1870–1940.* R. Graham. Austin, University of Texas Press: 7–36.

Graham, S. R. (1996). The Real World. *The Multiracial Experience: Racial Borders as the New Frontier.* M. Root. Thousand Oaks, Sage Publications.

Haizlip, S. T. (1994). *The Sweeter the Juice: A Family Memoir in Black and White.* New York, Simon and Schuster.

Hall, S. (1991). "Ethnicity, Identity and Difference." *Radical America* 23(4).

Halter, M. (2000). *Shopping for Identity.* New York, Schocken Books.

Hanchard, M. (1994). *Orpheus and Power: The Movimento Negro of Rio de Janeiro and Sao Paolo, Brazil.* Princeton, NJ, Princeton University Press.

Hansen, K. V. and A. Garey, Eds. (1998). *Families in the U.S.: Kinship and Domestic Politics.* Philadelphia, Temple University Press.

Harris, A. (1990). "Race and Essentialism in Feminist Legal Theory." *Stanford Law Review* (February): 581–616.

Harris, C. I. (1995). *Whiteness as Property. Critical Race Theory: The Key Writings That Formed the Movement.* K. Crenshaw. New York, The New Press.

Harris, D. (2002). Does it Matter How We Measure? Racial Classification and the Characteristics of Multiracial Youth. *The New Race Question: How the Census Counts Multiracial Individuals.* J. Perlmann and M. C. Waters. New York, Russell Sage Foundation and The Levy Economics Institute of Bard College: 62–101.

Harris, D. and H. Ono (2001). "Cohabitation, Marriage, and Markets: A New Look at Intimate Relationships" (unpublished draft).

Harris, D. and J. Sim (2002). "Who is Multiracial? Assessing the Complexity of Lived Race." *American Sociological Review* 67(4): 614–627.

Harrison, R. J. (2002). Inadequacies of Multiple-Response Race Data in the Federal Statistical System. *The New Race Question: How the Census Counts Multiracial Individuals.* J. Perlmann and M. Waters. New York, Russell Sage Foundation Press, The Levy Economics Institute of Bard College.

Helg, A. (1980). Race in Argentina and Cuba, 1880–1930: Theory, Policies and Popular Reaction. *The Idea of Race in Latin America, 1870–1940.* R. Graham. Austin, University of Texas Press: 37–69.

Herskovits, M. (1928). *The American Negro: A Study in Racial Crossing.* New York, A. A. Knopf.

Herskovits, M. (1992 [1925]). The Negro's Americanism. *The New Negro: Voices of the Harlem Renaissance.* A. Locke. [1992 edition introduction by Arnold Rampersad] New York, Atheneum: 353–360.

Hirschfeld, L. A. (1996). *Race in the Making: Cognition, Culture, and the Child's Construction of Human Kinds.* Cambridge, MA, MIT Press.

Hobsbawm, E. (1983). *The Invention of Tradition.* Cambridge, UK, Cambridge University Press.

Hodes, M. (1993). "The Sexualization of Reconstruction Politics: White Women and Black Men in the South after the Civil War." *Journal of the History of Sexuality* 3(3): 402–417.

Hodes, M. (1997). *White Women and Black Men: Illicit Sex in the Nineteenth Century South.* New Haven, CT, Yale University Press.

Hodes, M. (1999). *Sex, Love, Race: Crossing Boundaries in North American History.* New York, New York University Press.

Holmes Norton, E. (1997). Testimony. Hearings Before the Subcommittee on Government Management, Information, and Technology of the Committee on Government Reform and Oversight, House of Representatives, 105th Congress.

Holt, T. C. (2000). *The Problem of Race in the Twenty-First Century.* Cambridge, MA, Harvard University Press.

Huggins, N. I. (1990 [1977]). *Black Odyssey: The African-American Ordeal in Slavery and Freedom.* New York, Vintage Books.

Hughes, A. (2003). "United Colors of Global Hue." *Black Enterprise:* 186–194.

Hughes, E. C. (1962). "Race Relations and the Sociological Imagination." *American Journal of Sociology* 28(6): 879–890.

Hughes, H. (1854). *Treatise on Sociology.* Philadelphia, Lippincott, Grambo.

Humphreys, J. M. (2002). "The Multicultural Economy 2002: Minority Buying Power in the New Century." *Georgia Business and Economic Conditions* 62(2).

Hunt, S., R. Benford, and D. Snow. (1994). Identity Fields: Framing Processes and the Social Construction of Movement Identities. *New Social Movements: From Ideology to Identity.* E. Larana, H. Johnston, and J. Gusfield. Philadelphia, Temple University Press, 185–208.

Ignatiev, N. (1995). *How the Irish Became White.* New York, Routledge.

Illouz, E. (1997). *Consuming the Romantic Utopia: Love and the Cultural Contradictions of Capitalism.* Berkeley, University of California Press.

Jewell, K. S. (1985). "Will the Real Black, Afro-American, Mixed, Colored, Negro Please Stand Up?: Impact of the Black Social Movement, Twenty Years Later." *Journal of Black Studies* (1): 57–75.

Jacobson, M. F. (1999). *Whiteness of a Different Color: European Immigrants and the Alchemy of Race.* Cambridge, MA, Harvard University Press.

Johnston, H. and B. Klandermans. (1995). *Social Movements and Culture.* Minneapolis, University of Minnesota Press.

Jones, L. (1997). *Bulletproof Diva.* New York, Anchor Press.

Jones, V. E. (November 12, 2002). Mixing and Matching: Interracial Romances, Once Hollywood Taboo, are Creating Sparks on the Big Screen. *The Boston Globe,* E8.

Jordan, W. (1968). *American Attitudes toward the Negro, 1550–1812.* Baltimore, MD, Penguin.

Kane, C. (1998a, May 5). Levi Strauss is Trying to Regain Market Share for Its Jeans, Especially among Young Consumers. *The New York Times,* Retrieved October 26, 2004, from LexisNexis Academic database.

Kane, C. (1998b, August 14). TBWA/Chiat Day Brings "Street Culture" to a Campaign for Levi Strauss Silver Tab Clothing. *The New York Times,* Retrieved October 26, 2004, from LexisNexis Academic database.

Karenga, M. (1982). *Introduction to Black Studies.* Englewood, CA, Kawaida.

Katz, J. (1988). *Seductions of Crime: Moral and Sensual Attractions in Doing Evil.* New York, Basic Books.

Keith, V. M. and C. Herring (1991). "Skin Tone and Stratification in the Black Community." *American Journal of Sociology* 97: 760–778.

Kennedy, R. (2003). *Interracial Intimacies: Sex, Love, Marriage, and Adoption.* New York, Pantheon.

Kich, G. K. (1992). The Developmental Process of Asserting a Biracial, Bicultural Identity. *Racially Mixed People in America.* M. P. P. Root. Newbury Park, CA, Sage: 304–317.

King, R. C., and K. M. DaCosta. (1996). Changing Face, Changing Race: The Remaking of Race in the Japanese American and African American Communities. *The Multi-*

racial Experience: Racial Borders as the New Frontier. M. P. P. Root. Thousand Oaks, CA, Sage.

King, R. C. (2002). Eligible to be Japanese American: Counting on Multiraciality in Japanese American Basketball Leagues and Beauty Pageants. *Contemporary Asian American Communities: Intersections and Divergences.* Linda Trinh Vo and Rick Bonus. Philadelphia: Temple University Press.

Klinenberg, E. (2002). *Heatwave: A Social Autopsy of Disaster in Chicago.* Chicago, University of Chicago Press.

Knight, A. (1980). Racism, Revolution and Indigenismo: Mexico, 1910–1940. *The Idea of Race in Latin America, 1870–1940.* R. Graham. Austin, Austin University of Texas Press: 71–113.

Kornblum, W. (1974). *Blue Collar Community.* Chicago, University of Chicago Press.

Kovel, J. (1970). *White Racism: A Psychohistory.* New York, Pantheon.

Kuran, T. (1995). *Private Truths, Public Lies: The Social Consequences of Preference Falsification.* Cambridge, MA, Harvard University Press.

La Ferla, R. (2003, December 28). "Generation E. A.: Ethnically Ambiguous." *The New York Times:* Retrieved October 26, 2004, from LexisNexis Academic database.

Lancaster, R. (1992). *Life Is Hard: Machismo, Danger, and the Intimacy of Power in Nicaragua.* Berkeley, University of California Press.

Landry, B. (1987). *The New Black Middle Class.* Berkeley, University of California Press.

Lazarre, J. (1996). *Beyond the Whiteness of Whiteness: Memoir of a White Mother of Black Sons.* Durham, Duke University Press.

Lee, C. (1981). *Koreans in Japan: Ethnic Conflict and Accommodation.* Berkeley, University of California Press.

Lee, J. and F. Bean. (2004). "American's Changing Color Lines: Immigration, Race/Ethnicity, and Multiracial Identification." *Annual Review of Sociology* 30: 221–242.

Leland, J. (1997). In Living Colors. *Newsweek:* Retrieved October 26, 2004, from LexisNexis Academic Database.

Leonard, K. I. (1992). *Making Ethnic Choices: California's Punjabi Mexican Americans.* Philadelphia, Temple University Press.

Lieberson, S. (1985). Unhyphenated Whites in the United States. *Ethnicity and Race in the U.S.A.: Toward the Twenty-first Century.* R. D. Alba. New York, Routledge: 159–180.

Linn, S. E. (2004). *Consuming Kids: The Hostile Takeover of Childhood.* New York, New Press.

Lopez, I. and F. Haney (1996). *White by Law: The Legal Construction of Race.* New York, New York University Press.

Luke, C. and A. Luke. (1998). "Interracial Families: Difference within Difference." *Ethnic and Racial Studies* 21(4): 728–753.

Luker, K. (1984). *Abortion and the Politics of Motherhood.* Berkeley, University of California Press.

Luker, K. (1996). *Dubious Conceptions: The Politics of Teenage Pregnancy.* Cambridge, MA, Harvard University Press.

Mabry, M. (1995). *White Bucks and Black-Eyed Peas: Coming of Age Black in White America.* New York, Simon and Schuster.

Maquet, J. (1961). *The Premise of Inequality in Ruanda: A Study of Political Relations in a Central African Kingdom.* London, Oxford University Press.

Marx, A. (1998). *Making Race and Nation: A Comparison of South Africa, the United States, and Brazil.* New York, Cambridge University Press.

Massey, D. and N. Denton (1992). *American Apartheid.* Cambridge, MA, Harvard University Press.

Massey, D., and N. Denton (1998). *American Apartheid: Segregation and the Making of the Underclass.* Cambridge, MA, Harvard University Press.

Mavin. (2004). *Mavin: The Mixed Race Experience:* 9.

McAdam, D. (1982). *Political Process and the Development of Black Insurgency, 1930–1970.* Chicago, University of Chicago Press.

McAdam, D. (1988). *Freedom Summer.* New York, Oxford University Press.

McAdam, D. (1994). Culture and Social Movements. *New Social Movements: From Ideology to Identity.* E. Larana, H. Johnston, and J. Gusfield. Philadelphia, Temple University Press: 36–57.

McAdam, D., J. D. McCarthy, and M. N. Zald (1995). Opportunities, Mobilizing Structures, and Framing Processes: Toward a Synthetic, Comparative Perspective on Social Movements. *Opportunities, Mobilizing Structures, and Framing: Comparative Applications of Contemporary Movement Theory.* McAdam, McCarthy, and Zald. New York, Cambridge University Press.

McBride, J. (1997). *The Color of Water: A Black Man's Tribute to His White Mother.* New York, Riverhead Books.

McCarthy, J. D., and M. N. Zald (1973). *The Trend of Social Movements in America: Professionalization and Resource Mobilization.* Morristown, NJ, General Learning Press.

McCarthy, J. D. and M. N. Zald (1977). "Resource Mobilization and Social Movements: A Partial Theory." *American Journal of Sociology* 82: 1212–1240.

McKee, J. B. (1993). *Sociology and the Race Problem: The Failure of a Perspective.* Urbana, University of Illinois Press.

McReynolds, P. J. (1997). *Almost Americans: A Quest for Dignity.* Santa Fe, NM, Red Crane Books.

Melucci, A. (1980). "The New Social Movements: A Theoretical Approach." *Social Science Information* 19(2): 196–226.

Melucci, A. (1988). "Getting Involved: Identity and Mobilization in Social Movements." *International Social Movements Research* 1: 329–348.

Metzger, L. P. (1971). "American Sociology and Black Assimilation: Conflicting Perspectives." *American Journal of Sociology* 76(4): 627–647.

Miles, R. (1984). "Marxism vs. the Sociology of 'Race Relations'." *Ethnic and Racial Studies* 7: 217–237.

Miles, R. (1993). *Racism after "Race Relations."* London, Routledge.

Miles, R. (1994). Explaining Racism in Contemporary Europe. *Racism, Modernity and Identity on the Western Front.* A. Rattansi and S. Westwood. Cambridge, UK, Polity Press: 189–221.

Mills, C. W. (1959). *The Sociological Imagination.* London, Oxford University Press.

Moran, R. F. (2001). *Interracial Intimacy.* Chicago, The University of Chicago Press.

Morris, A. (1984). *The Origins of the Civil Rights Movement.* New York, Free Press.

Mueller, C. M. (1994). Conflict Networks and the Origins of Women's Liberation. *New Social Movements: From Ideology to Identity.* E. Larana, H. Johnston, and J. Gusfield. Philadelphia, Temple University Press: 234–266.

Nagel, J. (1986). The Political Construction of Ethnicity. *Competitive Ethnic Relations.* S. Olzak and J. Nagel. Orlando, FL, Academic Press: 93–108.

Nagel, J. (1995). "American Indian Ethnic Renewal: Politics and the Resurgence of Identity." *American Sociological Review* 60(6): 947–965.

Nagel, J. (1996). *American Indian Ethnic Renewal: Red Power and the Resurgence of Identity and Culture.* New York, Oxford University Press.

Nakashima, C. (1992). An Invisible Monster: The Creation and Denial of Mixed Race People in America. *Racially Mixed People in America.* M. P. P. Root. Newbury Park, Sage: 162–178.

Nelson, S. S. (April 17, 2000). An Ethnic Strategy on the Census; Population: Campaign Urges African Americans to Retain Clout by Defining Themselves as Only Black, Even if Heritage Mixed. *Los Angeles Times.*

Neuhouser, K. (1998). "If I Had Abandoned My Children: Community Mobilization and Commitment to the Identity of Mother in Northeast Brazil." *Social Forces* 77(1): 331–358.

Nobles, M. (2000). *Shades of Citizenship: Race and the Census in Modern Politics.* Palo Alto, CA, Stanford University Press.

Oberschall, A. (1973). *Social Conflict and Social Movements.* Englewood Cliffs, NJ, Prentice Hall.

Oboler, S. (1995). *Ethnic Labels, Latino Lives: Identity and the Politics of (Re)presentation in the United States.* Minneapolis, University of Minnesota Press.

O'Hearn, C. C., Ed. (1998). *Half and Half: Writers on Growing Up Biracial and Bicultural.* New York, Pantheon Books.

Olzak, S. (1982). "Ethnic Mobilization in Quebec." *Ethnic and Racial Studies* (July): 253–275.

Omi, M. and Y. L. Espiritu. (2000). "Who Are You Calling Asian?": Shifting Identity Claims, Racial Classifications, and the Census. *The State of Asian Pacific America: Transforming Race Relations.* P. M. Ong. Los Angeles, LEAP Asian Pacific American Public Policy Institute and UCLA Asian American Studies Center.

Omi, M. and H. Winant. (1994). *Racial Formation in the United States: From the 1960s to the 1990s.* New York, Routledge.

Page, C. (July 28, 1996). Biracial People Feel "Boxed In" by Census Form. *Chicago Tribune.* B3.

Park, R. (1914). "Racial Assimilation in Secondary Groups with Particular Reference to the Negro." *American Journal of Sociology* 19(5): 606–623.

Park, R., Ed. (1939). *The Nature of Race Relations. Race Relations and the Race Problem.* New York, Glenwood Press.

Park, R. E. (1950). *Race and Culture.* Glencoe, IL, Free Press.

Patterson, O. (1998). *Rituals of Blood: Consequences of Slavery in Two American Centuries.* New York, Basic Civitas.

Pattillo-McCoy, M. (1999). *Black Picket Fences: Privilege and Peril among the Black Middle Class.* Chicago, University of Chicago Press.

Patton, S. (2000). *Birthmarks: Transracial Adoption in Contemporary America.* New York, New York University Press.

Perlmann, J. and M. Waters, Eds. (2002). *The New Race Question: How the Census Counts Multiracial Individuals.* New York, Russell Sage Foundation, The Levy Economics Institute of Bard College.

Polletta, F. (2004). Culture Is Not Just in Your Head. In *Rethinking Social Movements: Structure, Meaning, and Emotion.* J. Goodwin and J. M. Jasper. New York, Rowman & Littlefield Publishers, Inc.: 97–110.

Portes, A., and M. Zhou (1993). "The New Second Generation: Segmented Assimilation and its Variants." *Annual American Academy of Political and Social Science* 530: 74–96.

Rapp, R. (1992). Family and Class in Contemporary America. *Rethinking the Family: Some Feminist Questions.* B. Thorne and M. Yalom. Boston, Northeastern University Press: 49–70.

Rapp, R. (1995). Heredity, or: Revising the Facts of Life. *Naturalizing Power: Essays in Feminist Cultural Analysis.* S. Yanagisako and C. Delaney. New York, Routledge: 69–86.

Rattansi, A. (1994). Western Racisms, Ethnicities, and Identities. *Racism, Modernity and Identity on the Western Front.* A. Rattansi and S. Westwood. Cambridge, UK, Polity Press: 15–86.

Reddy, M. T. (1994). *Crossing the Color Line: Race, Parenting and Culture.* New Brunswick, N.J., Rutgers University Press.

Rekdal, P. (2000). *The Night My Mother Met Bruce Lee.* New York, Pantheon Books.

Renn, K. A. (2004). *Mixed Race Students in College: The Ecology of Race, Identity, and Community on Campus.* Albany, SUNY Press.

Reuter, E. (1917). "The Superiority of the Mulatto." *American Journal of Sociology* 23(1): 83–106.

Roberts, D. (1997). *Killing the Black Body: Race, Reproduction, and the Meaning of Liberty.* New York, Pantheon Books.

Rockquemore, K. A. and D. L. Brunsma. (2002). *Beyond Black: Biracial Identity in America.* Thousand Oaks, CA, Sage Publications.

Roediger, D. (1994). *Toward the Abolition of Whiteness.* London, Verso.

Romano, R. (2003). *Race Mixing: Black-White Marriage in Postwar America.* Cambridge, MA, Harvard University Press.

Root, M. (2001). *Love's Revolution: Interracial Marriage.* Philadelphia, Temple University Press.

Root, M. P. P., Ed. (1992). *Racially Mixed People in America.* Newbury Park, Sage.

Root, M. P. P. (1996). *The Multiracial Experience: Racial Borders as the New Frontier.* Thousand Oaks, CA, Sage.

Rossinow, D. (1998). *The Politics of Authenticity: Liberalism, Christianity, and the New Left in America.* New York, Columbia University Press.

Rubin, G. (1985 [1975]). The Traffic in Women: Notes on the Political Economy of Sex. *Toward an Anthropology of Women.* R. Reiter. New York, Monthly Review Press: 157–210.

Russell, K., M. Wilson, and R Hall. (1992). *The Color Complex: The Politics of Skin Color among African Americans.* New York, Doubleday.

Sanchez, G. J. (1993). *Becoming Mexican American.* New York, Oxford University Press.

Sanjek, R. (1994). Intermarriage and the Future of Races in the United States. *Race.* S. Gregory and R. Sanjek. New Brunswick, NJ, Rutgers University Press: 103–130.

Schiebinger, L. (1993). *The Anatomy of Difference. Nature's Body: Gender in the Making of Modern Science.* Boston, Beacon Press: 115–142.

Schmitt, E. (2001). Blacks Split on Disclosing Multiracial Roots. *The New York Times.*

Schneider, D. M. (1968). *American Kinship: A Cultural Account.* Englewood Cliffs, NJ, Prentice-Hall.

Schneider, D. M. (1984). *A Critique of the Study of Kinship.* Ann Arbor, University of Michigan Press.

Schuman, H., et. al. (1997 [1985]). *Racial Attitudes in America: Trends and Interpretations* (Revised edition). Cambridge, MA, Harvard University Press.

Senna, D., Ed. (1998). *The Mulatto Millennium. Half + Half: Writers on Growing up Biracial + Bicultural.* New York, Pantheon Books.

Shelby, T. (2005). *We Who Are Dark: The Philosophical Foundations of Black Solidarity.* Cambridge, MA, Belknap Press of Harvard University Press.

Shong Huang, S., Rogelio Saenz, and Benigno Aguirre (1997, August). "Structural and Assimilationist Explanations of Asian American Intermarriage." *Journal of Marriage and the Family* 59: 758–772.

Singer, L. (1962). "Ethnogenesis and Negro Americans Today." *Social Research* 29: 419–432.

Skrentny, J. P. (1996). *The Ironies of Affirmative Action: Politics, Culture, and Justice in America.* Chicago, University of Chicago Press.

Sloan, S. (1992). *The Slave Children of Thomas Jefferson.* Berkeley, CA, Orsden Press.

Smith, A. D. (1991). *National Identity.* Reno, University of Nevada Press.

Smith, R. T. (1988). *Kinship and Class in the West Indies: A Genealogical Study of Jamaica and Guyana.* Cambridge, UK, Cambridge University Press.

Snow, D., E. B. Rochford, Jr., S. K. Worden, and R. D. Benford (1986). "Frame Alignment Processes, Micromobilization and Movement Participation." *American Sociological Review* 51: 464–481.

Snow, D. and R. Benford (1988). Ideology, Frame Resonance and Participant Mobilization. *From Structure to Action, International Social Movement Research?* B. Klandermans, H. Kriesi, and S. Tarrow. Greenwich, CT, JAI Press. 1: 197–217.

Solinger, R. (1992). *Wake Up Little Susie: Single Pregnancy and Race before Roe v. Wade.* London, Routledge.

Sollors, W. (1986). *Beyond Ethnicity: Consent and Descent in American Culture.* New York, Oxford University Press.

Sollors, W. (1997). *Neither Black nor White Yet Both: Thematic Exploration in Interracial Literature.* New York, Oxford University Press.

Sollors, W., Ed. (2004). *An Anthology of Interracial Literature: Black-White Contacts in the Old World and the New.* New York, New York University Press.

Solomos, J. (1986). *Varieties of Marxist Conceptions of "Race," Class, and the State: A Critical Analysis. Theories of Race and Ethnic Relations.* J. Rex and D. Mason. Cambridge, UK, Cambridge University Press.

Somerville, S. (2000). *Queering the Color Line: Race and the Invention of Homosexuality in American Culture.* Durham, NC, Duke University Press.

Spencer, J. M. (1997). *The New Colored People: The Mixed-Race Movement in America.* New York, New York University Press.

Spencer, R. (1999). *Spurious Issues: Race and Multiracial Identity Politics in the United States.* Boulder, CO, Westview Press.

Spickard, P., and W. J. Burroughs, Eds. (2000). *We Are a People.* Philadelphia, Temple University Press.

Spickard, P. R. (1989). *Mixed Blood: Intermarriage and Ethnic Identity in Twentieth-Century America.* Madison, University of Wisconsin Press.

Stacey, J. (1993). *Brave New Families: Stories of Domestic Upheaval in Late Twentieth Century America.* New York, Basic Books.

Stack, C. B. (1974). *All Our Kin: Strategies for Survival in a Black Community.* New York, Harper and Row.

Steinberg, S. (1981). *The Ethnic Myth: Race, Ethnicity and Class in America.* New York, Atheneum.

Steinberg, S. (1989). *The Ethnic Myth: Race, Ethnicity, and Class in America.* Boston, Beacon Press.

Strauss, A. and J. Corbin. (1990). *Basics of Qualitative Research: Grounded Theory Procedures and Techniques*. Newbury Park, CA, Sage.

Suttles, G. (1968). *The Social Order of the Slum: Ethnicity and Territory in the Inner City*. Chicago, University of Chicago Press.

Takaki, R. (1993). *A Different Mirror: A History of Multicultural America*. Boston, Little, Brown .

Tambiah, S. J. (1973). "From Varna to Caste through Mixed Unions." *The Character of Kinship*. J. Goody. London, Cambridge University Press: 191–229.

Tanabe, K. (2005). Loving Day Celebrates the Legalization of Interracial Couples. 2005.

Taylor Gibbs, J. and A. M. Hines (1992). Negotiation Ethnic Identity: Issues for Black-White Biracial Adolescents. *Racially Mixed People in America*. M. Root. Newbury Park, Sage Publications.

Texeira, E. (2005). *Multiracial Scenes Now Common in TV Ads*, Associated Press.

Thorne, B. and M. Yalom. Ed. (1992). *Rethinking the Family: Some Feminist Questions*. Boston, Northeastern University Press.

Touraine, A. (1985). "An Introduction to the Study of Social Movements." *Social Research* 52: 749–788.

Tuan, M. (1998). *Forever Foreigners or Honorary Whites? The Asian Ethnic Experience Today*. New Brunswick, NJ, Rutgers University Press.

Tucker, C., S. Miller, et al. (2002). Comparing Census Race Data Under the Old and the New Standards. *The New Race Question: How the Census Counts Multiracial Individuals*. J. Perlmann and M. Water, Russell Sage Foundation and The Levy Economics Institute of Bard College.

Turner, V. (1969). *The Ritual Process: Structure and Anti-Structure*. Ithaca, Cornell University Press.

Twine, F. W. (1996). "Brown Skinned White Girls: Class, Culture and the Construction of White Identity in Suburban Communities." In *Gender, Place and Culture: A Journal of Feminist Geography* 3(2).

U.S. Census Bureau. (1995). *Statistical Abstract of the United States*.

U.S. Census Bureau. (2001). *Two or More Races Population Brief*.

U.S. Census Bureau. (2002). *Racial and Ethnic Segregation in the United States: 1980–2000. Census 2000 Special Report*.

Van den Berghe, P. (1967). *Race and Racism: A Comparative Perspective*. New York, Wiley.

Van Kerckhove, C. (2005). Media Exploits Fear of Interracial Relationships, newdemographic.com. 2005.

Wacquant, L. (2001). "Deadly Symbiosis: When Ghetto and Prison Meet and Mesh." *Punishment and Society* 3(1): 95–133.

Wacquant, L. J. D. (1989). "The Puzzle of Race and Class in American Society and Social Science." *Benjamin E. Mays Monograph Series* 11(1).

Wacquant, L. J. D. (1997). "For an Analytic of Racial Domination." *Political Power and Social Theory II*: 221–234.

Wacquant, L. J. D. (1998). "A Fleshpeddler at Work: Power, Pain and Profit in the Prizefighting Economy." *Theory and Society* 27(1).

Wade, P. (1995). "The Cultural Politics of Blackness in Colombia." *American Ethnologist* 22(2): 341–357.

Wagley, C. (1965). On the Concept of Social Race in the Americas. *Contemporary Cultures and Societies in Latin America*. D. B. Heath and R. N. Adams. New York, Random House: 531–545.

Walker, R. (2002). *Black White & Jewish*. New York, The Berkeley Publishing Group.

Walker, R. (2003). Whassup, Barbie? Marketers are Embracing the Idea of a "Post-Racial" America. Goodbye, Niche Marketing. *The Boston Globe*. Retrieved October 26, 2004 from LexisNexis Academic database.

Wallace, K. (2001). *Relative/Outsider: The Art and Politics of Identity Among Mixed Heritage Students (Contemporary Studies in Social and Policy Issues in Education: The David C. Anchin Center Series)*. Westport, Ablex Publishing.

Wallerstein, I. (1988). Social Conflict in Post-Independence Black Africa; The Concepts of Race and Status-Group Reconsidered. *Race, Nation, Class: Ambiguous Identities*. E. Balibar and I. Wallerstein. London, Verso.

Waters, M. (1990). *Ethnic Options: Choosing Ethnic Identities in America*. Berkeley, University of California Press.

Waters, M. C. (1999). *Black Identities: West Indian Immigrant Dreams and American Realities*. Cambridge, MA, Harvard University Press.

Waters, M. C. (2000). Multiple Ethnicities and Identity in the United States. *We Are a People*. P. Spickard and W. Burroughs. Philadelphia, Temple University Press: 23–40.

Weber, M. ([1918–20] 1978). Ethnic Groups. *Economy and Society*, Berkeley. University of California Press: 385–398.

Webster, Y. O. (1992). *The Racialization of America*. New York, St. Martin's Press.

Wellman, B., Ed. (1998). *Networks in the Global Village: Life in Contemporary Communities*. Boulder, Westview.

Wellner, A. S. (2001). "A Niche in Time: Multiracials: The Bellwethers of Tomorrow's Markets." *American Demographic Forecast*.

Wellner, A. S. (2002). The Next Wave of Census Data. *Forecast*.

West, C. with H. L. Gates., Jr. (1996). *Black Strivings in a Twilight Civilization. The Future of the Race*. New York, Random House.

Weston, K. (1991). *Families We Choose: Lesbians, Gays, Kinship*. New York, Columbia University Press.

Weston, K. (1995). Forever is a Long Time: Romancing the Real in Gay Kinship Ideologies. *Naturalizing Power: Essays in Feminist Cultural Analysis*. S. Yanagisako and C. Delaney. New York, Routledge: 87–110.

Whelan, D. (2001). Casting Tiger Woods. *Forecast*.

Williams, B. (1995). Classification Systems Revisited: Kinship, Caste, Race, and Nationality as the Flow of Blood and the Spread of Rights. *Naturalizing Power: Essays in Feminist Cultural Analysis*. S. Yanagisako and C. Delaney. New York, Routledge: 201–236.

Williams, G. H. (1996). *Life on the Color Line: The True Story of a White Boy Who Discovered He Was Black*. New York, Penguin Books.

Williams, K. (2006). *Race Counts: American Multiracialism & Civil Rights Politics*. Ann Arbor, University of Michigan Press.

Williams, P. (1991). *The Alchemy of Race and Rights*. Cambridge, MA, Harvard University Press.

Williams, R. J. (1994). "The Sociology of Ethnic Conflicts: Comparative International Perspectives." *Annual Review of Sociology* 20: 49–79.

Williams, T. K. (1992). Prism Lives: Identity of Binational Amerasians. *Racially Mixed People in America*. M. Root. Newbury Park, CA, Sage Publications.

Williams, T. K. (1996). Race as Process: Reassessing "What Are You?" *Encounters of Biracial Individuals*. M. Root. Thousand Oaks, CA, Sage Publications. 191–210.

Williams-Leon, T., and C. L. Nakashima, Eds. (2001). *The Sum of Our Parts: Mixed Heritage Asian Americans*. Philadelphia, Temple University Press.

Williamson, J. (1995). *New People: Miscegenation and Mulattoes in the United States*. Baton Rouge, Louisiana State University Press.

Wilson, T. (1992). Blood Quantum: Native American Mixed Bloods. *Racially Mixed People in America*. M. P. P. Root. Newbury Park, CA, Sage.

Wilson, W. J. (1978). *The Declining Significance of Race: Blacks and Changing American Institutions*. Chicago, University of Chicago Press.

Winant, H. (1991). "Rethinking Race in Brazil." *Journal of Latin American Studies* 24: 173–192.

Winant, H. (1994). Racial Formation and Hegemony: Global and Local Developments. *Racism, Modernity and Identity on the Western Front*. A. Rattansi and S. Westwood. Cambridge, UK, Polity Press. 266–289.

Wright, L. (1994). One Drop of Blood. *The New Yorker*. 54.

Wright, W. (1990). *Cafe con Leche: Race, Class and National Image in Venezuela*. Austin, University of Texas Press.

Wu, F. H. (2002). *Yellow: Race in America beyond Black and White*. New York, Basic Books.

Wynter, L. E. (2002). *American Skin: Pop Culture, Big Business, and the End of White America* (1st ed.). New York, Crown Publishers.

Xie, Y., and K. Goyette. (1997). "The Racial Identification of Biracial Children with One Asian Parent: Evidence from the 1990 Census." *Social Forces* 76: 547–570.

Yanagisako, S. (1995). Transforming Orientalism: Gender, Nationality, and Class in Asian American Studies. *Naturalizing Power: Essays in Feminist Cultural Analysis*. S. Yanagisako and C. Delaney. New York: Routledge. 275–298.

Yu, H. (1999). Mixing Bodies and Cultures: The Meaning of America's Fascination with Sex between "Orientals" and "Whites." *Sex, Love and Race: Crossing Boundaries in North American History.* M. Hodes. New York, New York University Press: 444–463.

Zack, N., Ed. (1995). *American Mixed Race: The Culture of Microdiversity.* London, Rowman and Littlefield.

Zhou, M. (2004). "Are Asian Americans Becoming 'White'?" *Contexts,* 3(1), 29–37.

Zhou, M. B. C. I. (1998). *Growing Up American: How Vietnamese Children Adapt to Life in the United States.* New York, Russell Sage Foundation.

Zweigenhaft, R. L. and W. G. Domhoff. (1991). *Blacks in the White Establishment?: A Study of Race and Class in America.* New Haven, CT, Yale University Press.

Index